Legalines

Editorial Advisors:
Gloria A. Aluise
  Attorney at Law
Jonathan Neville
  Attorney at Law
Robert A. Wyler
  Attorney at Law

Authors:
Gloria A. Aluise
  Attorney at Law
David H. Barber
  Attorney at Law
Daniel O. Bernstine
  Attorney at Law
D. Steven Brewster
  C.P.A.
Roy L. Brooks
  Professor of Law
Frank L. Bruno
  Attorney at Law
Scott M. Burbank
  C.P.A.
Jonathan C. Carlson
  Professor of Law
Charles N. Carnes
  Professor of Law
Paul S. Dempsey
  Professor of Law
Jerome A. Hoffman
  Professor of Law
Mark R. Lee
  Professor of Law
Jonathan Neville
  Attorney at Law
Laurence C. Nolan
  Professor of Law
Arpiar Saunders
  Attorney at Law
Robert A. Wyler
  Attorney at Law

ANTITRUST

Adaptable to Fifth Edition* of Pitofsky Casebook

By Mark Lee
Professor of Law

and

Christopher C. White
Attorney at Law

*If your casebook is a newer edition, go to www.gilbertlaw.com to see if a supplement is available for this title.

THOMSON
BAR/BRI

EDITORIAL OFFICES: 111 W. Jackson Blvd., 7th Floor, Chicago, IL 60604
REGIONAL OFFICES: Chicago, Dallas, Los Angeles, New York, Washington, D.C.

SERIES EDITOR
Gail O'Gradney, J.D.
Attorney at Law

PRODUCTION MANAGER
Elizabeth G. Duke

FIRST PRINTING—2004

Copyright © 2004 by BarBri, a Thomson business. All rights reserved. No part of this publication may be reproduced or transmitted in any form or by any means, electronic or mechanical, including photocopy, recording, or any information storage and retrieval system, without permission in writing from the publisher. Printed in the United States of America.

Legalines™

**Features Detailed Briefs of Every Major Case,
Plus Summaries of the Black Letter Law**

Titles Available

Administrative Law	Keyed to Breyer
Administrative Law	Keyed to Strauss
Administrative Law	Keyed to Schwartz
Antitrust	Keyed to Areeda
Antitrust	Keyed to Pitofsky
Civil Procedure	Keyed to Cound
Civil Procedure	Keyed to Field
Civil Procedure	Keyed to Hazard
Civil Procecure	Keyed to Rosenberg
Civil Procedure	Keyed to Yeazell
Conflict of Laws	Keyed to Currie
Conflict of Laws	Keyed to Hay
Constitutional Law	Keyed to Brest
Constitutional Law	Keyed to Choper
Constitutional Law	Keyed to Cohen
Constitutional Law	Keyed to Rotunda
Constitutional Law	Keyed to Stone
Constitutional Law	Keyed to Sullivan
Contracts	Keyed to Calamari
Contracts	Keyed to Dawson
Contracts	Keyed to Farnsworth
Contracts	Keyed to Fuller
Contracts	Keyed to Kessler
Contracts	Keyed to Murphy
Corporations	Keyed to Choper
Corporations	Keyed to Eisenberg
Corporations	Keyed to Hamilton
Corporations	Keyed to Vagts
Criminal Law	Keyed to Boyce
Criminal Law	Keyed to Johnson
Criminal Law	Keyed to Kadish
Criminal Law	Keyed to LaFave
Criminal Procedure	Keyed to Kamisar
Decedents' Estates & Trusts	Keyed to Dobris
Domestic Relations	Keyed to Clark
Domestic Relations	Keyed to Wadlington
Evidence	Keyed to Waltz
Evidence	Keyed to Weinstein
Evidence	Keyed to Wellborn
Family Law	Keyed to Areen
Federal Courts	Keyed to Wright
Income Tax	Keyed to Freeland
Income Tax	Keyed to Klein
Labor Law	Keyed to Cox
Labor Law	Keyed to St. Antoine
Property	Keyed to Casner
Property	Keyed to Cribbet
Property	Keyed to Dukeminier
Property	Keyed to Nelson
Property	Keyed to Rabin
Remedies	Keyed to Re
Remedies	Keyed to Rendelman
Sales & Secured Transactions	Keyed to Speidel
Securities Regulation	Keyed to Coffee
Torts	Keyed to Dobbs
Torts	Keyed to Epstein
Torts	Keyed to Franklin
Torts	Keyed to Henderson
Torts	Keyed to Keeton
Torts	Keyed to Prosser
Wills, Trusts & Estates	Keyed to Dukeminier

All Titles Available at Your Law School Bookstore

THOMSON

BAR/BRI™

111 W. Jackson Boulevard, 7th Floor
Chicago, IL 60604

There are two things BAR/BRI will do for you:

1 ## Get you through LAW SCHOOL

2 ## Get you through the BAR EXAM

[O.K. we'll throw in a highlighter*]

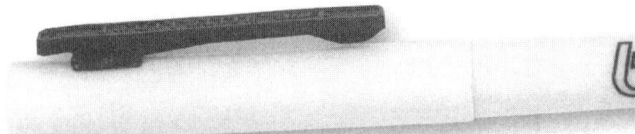

*Available at your local BAR/BRI office

gilbert
LAW SUMMARIES

Over 4 Million Copies Sold!

- Gilbert Law Summaries
- Legalines
- Law School Legends Audio Tapes
- Employment Guides
- Casebriefs Interactive Software

barbri®
BAR REVIEW

Relied On By Over 600,000 Students!

- Lectures, Outlines & Mini Review
- Innovative Computer Software
- Multistate, Essay & Performance Workshops
- Complete MPRE Preparation
- First Year Review Program

THE barbri GROUP

Our Only Mission Is Test Preparation

BAR/BRI Bar Review 1-800-950-7277
GILBERT LAW SUMMARIES 1-800-787-8717

SHORT SUMMARY OF CONTENTS

                                                                                    Page

I.   THE OBJECTIVES AND ORIGINS OF ANTITRUST LAW 1

     A.   The Goals of Antitrust Policy 1
     B.   The Sherman Act and Comparative Legislation 2
     C.   The Historical Sources of Antitrust Legislative History,
          and Early Developments 4

II. THE INSTITUTIONAL FRAMEWORK OF ANTITRUST POLICY 10

     A.   The Department of Justice 10
     B.   The Federal Trade Commission 10
     C.   Private Actions and State Attorneys General 11
     D.   Special Issues Related to Enforcement by the Federal Agencies 11
     E.   Special Issues Related to Private Enforcement 12
     F.   The Limits of Antitrust 13

III. MARKET STRUCTURE AND A FIRST LOOK AT THE PROBLEM OF
     MONOPOLY POWER 15

     A.   Monopolization and the Problem of Market Definition 15

IV. COMPETITOR COLLABORATION IN PRICE FIXING AND
     DIVISION OF MARKETS 22

     A.   Conspiracy—In Theory and Action 22
     B.   Development of the "Per Se" Rule on Price Fixing 22
     C.   Characterization Questions and Other Issues 26
     D.   Division of Territories and Some Other Horizontal Restraints 31

V.   GROUP REFUSALS TO DEAL AND JOINT VENTURES 36

     A.   Refusals to Deal 36
     B.   Joint Ventures Revisited—Issues of Membership and Access 44
     C.   Efforts to Influence Government Action 48
     D.   "State Action" and Tensions with Federalism 56

VI. MARKET CONCENTRATION AND CONSPIRACY 65

     A.   Introduction 65
     B.   Concentration, Price Leadership, and "Conscious Parallelism" 65
     C.   The Role of Trade Associations and Information Dissemination 73

Antitrust - i

VII.	**VERTICAL DISTRIBUTION RESTRICTIONS**		79
	A. The Economics of Vertical Restrictions		79
	B. The Interplay of Common Law and Antitrust Laws		79
VIII.	**ADDITIONAL LIMITATIONS ON A SINGLE FIRM EXERCISING MARKET POWER**		90
	A. Introduction		90
	B. Market Power		90
	C. Attempt to Monopolize		104
	D. Predatory Pricing		106
	E. Tying		111
	F. Partial Vertical Integration by Contract: Exclusive Selling and Exclusive Dealing		118
IX.	**MERGERS**		125
	A. Horizontal Mergers		125
	B. Joint Ventures, Potential Competition, and Conglomerate Mergers		142
	C. Integration Through Vertical Merger		149
X.	**FOREIGN COMMERCE AND THE U.S. ANTITRUST LAWS**		157
	A. Jurisdiction Over Foreign Commerce		157
XI.	**PRICE DISCRIMINATION**		170
	A. Introduction		170
	B. The Robinson-Patman Act		170
	C. The Effects of Price Discrimination		172
	D. Functional Discounts		176
	E. More Remote Effects		178
	F. Defenses to Robinson-Patman Act Actions		179
	G. Brokerage, Ad Allowances, and Services		182
	H. Buyer's Liability for Inducing or Receiving Discriminations in Price		184
TABLE OF CASES			187

TABLE OF CONTENTS AND SHORT REVIEW OUTLINE

		Page
I.	**THE OBJECTIVES AND ORIGINS OF ANTITRUST LAW**	1
A.	**THE GOALS OF ANTITRUST POLICY**	1
1.	*Industrial Market Structure and Economic Performance*	1
2.	*Antitrust Policy*	1
a.	Achieving desirable economic results	1
b.	Promoting competition	1
c.	Fairness	1
d.	Limiting big business	1
e.	Conclusion	2
f.	Comment	2
3.	*What Happened to the Antitrust Movement?*	2
a.	The founding period	2
b.	Period of neglect	2
c.	Period of revival	2
4.	*The Antitrust Paradox*	2
B.	**BASIC PROVISIONS OF THE SHERMAN ACT AND COMPARATIVE LEGISLATION**	2
1.	The Sherman Act	2
a.	Section 1—restraints of trade	2
b.	Section 2—monopolization	2
2.	The Antitrust ("Competition") Law of the European Union	3
a.	Basic provisions	3
b.	Exemptions	3
c.	Enforcement	3
d.	Goals	4
C.	**THE HISTORICAL SOURCES OF ANTITRUST LEGISLATIVE HISTORY, AND EARLY DEVELOPMENTS**	4
1.	The Early Law on Monopoly and Contracts in Restraint of Trade	4
a.	Introduction	4

	b.	Early law on monopolies		4
		1) Grant by the king		4
		2) Guilds		4
	c.	Early cases		4
		1) Covenant not to engage in a trade		4
		2) Starting a competing business		5
		3) Grant of monopoly		5
		4) Sale of a business		5
2.	The Legislative History of the Sherman Act			6
3.	Early Development of Antitrust Law—Two Levels of Law			6
	a.	The first cartel cases		6
		1) Sherman Act makes illegal "all contracts in restraint of trade"		7
		2) Ancillary and indirect restraints		7
		3) Purpose or intent of restraint		7
		4) Expansive definition of trade or commerce		8
		5) Restrictive covenants under state and federal law		8
	b.	Early mergers and the development of the "rule of reason"		9

II. THE INSTITUTIONAL FRAMEWORK OF ANTITRUST POLICY ... 10

A. THE DEPARTMENT OF JUSTICE ... 10

B. THE FEDERAL TRADE COMMISSION ... 10

1. The Clayton Act ... 10

   a. Price discrimination ... 10
   b. Restrictive arrangements ... 10
   c. Mergers and acquisitions ... 10
   d. Interlocking directorates ... 10

2. Concurrent Jurisdiction ... 10
3. Other Responsibilities ... 11

C. PRIVATE ACTIONS AND STATE ATTORNEYS GENERAL ... 11

1. Treble Damages ... 11
2. Parens Patriae Suits ... 11

- D. **SPECIAL ISSUES RELATED TO ENFORCEMENT BY THE FEDERAL AGENCIES** 11
    1. Consent Decrees 11
        a. Court supervision 11
        b. Motivation for consent decrees 11
    2. Intervention 11
    3. Prima Facie Case 11

- E. **SPECIAL ISSUES RELATED TO PRIVATE ENFORCEMENT** 12
    1. Standing, Causation, and "Antitrust Injury" 12
    2. "Unclean Hands" 12
    3. Certainty of Damages 12
    4. The "Passing On" Defense 12

- F. **THE LIMITS OF ANTITRUST** 13
    1. Government Ownership and Regulation 13
    2. Interstate and Foreign Commerce 13
        a. The Sherman Act 13
        b. The Clayton Act 13
        c. The Robinson-Patman Act 14
        d. Foreign commerce 14

III. **MARKET STRUCTURE AND A FIRST LOOK AT THE PROBLEM OF MONOPOLY POWER** 15

- A. **MONOPOLIZATION AND THE PROBLEM OF MARKET DEFINITION** 15
    1. Conceptual Overview 15
    2. Defining the Market: Why and How 15
    3. Expansion As an Offense? 15
    4. What Conduct Is Prohibited? 16
    5. Market Definition: "Reasonable Interchangeability" 17
    6. The Substantial Submarket Test 19

IV. **COMPETITOR COLLABORATION ON PRICE FIXING AND DIVISION OF MARKETS** 22

- A. **CONSPIRACY—IN THEORY AND ACTION** 22

		1.	Introduction	22
		2.	Factors Required for an Effective Cartel—*Cartels: Organization and Functions*	22
		3.	Purpose of Cartels	22

	B.	**DEVELOPMENT OF THE "PER SE" RULE ON PRICE FIXING**	22
		1.	The Rule of Reason and the Rule of Per Se Illegality	22
		2.	The "Price-Fixing" Characterization	23
		3.	Antitrust and the Great Depression	24
		4.	Per Se Illegality	24
		5.	Medical Association Agreements with Group Insurers	25

	C.	**CHARACTERIZATION QUESTIONS AND OTHER ISSUES**	26
		1.	Blanket Copyright License Not a Per Se Violation	26
		2.	Horizontal Restraints Necessary	27
		3.	Spreading Financial Aid: Purported Purposes and Effects that May Trump Considerations of Efficiency	29
		4.	Professional Trade Association's Advertising Restrictions	30

	D.	**DIVISION OF TERRITORIES AND SOME OTHER HORIZONTAL RESTRAINTS**	31
		1.	Generally	31
		2.	Allocating a Scarce Resource	31
		3.	Allocating Territories	32
			a. Applications	32
			1) Timken Roller Bearing Co. v. United States	32
			2) United States v. General Motors Corporation	32
			3) United States v. Sealy Inc.	32
			b. Comment	32
		4.	Allocating Territories in Connection with a Common Trademark	33
		5.	Allocating Territories in Connection with Reciprocal Service Agreement	34
		6.	Allocating Territories by Withdrawing from a Market	35

| V. | **GROUP REFUSALS TO DEAL AND JOINT VENTURES** . . . . | 36 |
| | A. | **REFUSALS TO DEAL** . . . . | 36 |

		1.	Generally	36
		2.	Refusals to Deal and Price Setting	36
		3.	Refusals to Deal and Agreed Non-Price Terms	36
		4.	Group Boycott Per Se Illegal	36
		5.	Public Injury Not Required	37
		6.	Single Buyer Boycott	38
		7.	Use of Standard to Boycott	39
		8.	Exclusion from Cooperative Wholesale Distributor	39
		9.	Concerted Refusal to Provide Information	40
		10.	Restraint Ancillary to Economic Integration	42
		11.	Refusal to Deal Coupled with Expressive Content	42

B. JOINT VENTURES REVISITED—ISSUES OF MEMBERSHIP AND ACCESS **44**

1. Generally 44
2. Mandatory Access 44
3. Where Competing Services Are Available 44
4. Reasonable Exclusion of Competitor from Joint Venture 45
5. Other Examples 46
6. Research Joint Ventures 46

   a. The National Cooperative Research Act of 1984 47
   b. Department of Justice guidelines 47
   c. Patent pool business review letter 47

      1) The proposed patent pool 47
      2) "Essential" patents 47
      3) DOJ's analysis 47

7. Competitor Collaboration Guidelines 48

C. EFFORTS TO INFLUENCE GOVERNMENT ACTION **48**

1. What's at Stake 48
2. Immunity 48
3. The Sham Exception 50
4. Follow-up to *Noerr* 50
5. Law School Accreditation and State Bar Exams 52
6. Sham Exception to *Noerr* Immunity 54

D. "STATE ACTION" AND TENSIONS WITH FEDERALISM **56**

1. Introduction 56
2. The Landmark Case 56
3. State Prompting 56

	4.	What Constitutes "the State Acting as Sovereign"	57
	5.	Need for Active Supervision	57
	6.	Clearly Articulated Policy to Displace Competition with Regulation	58
	7.	Local Government and the *Midcal* Requirements	59
	8.	State Action Antitrust Immunity	60
	9.	Active Supervision and Peer Review	61
	10.	Local Government and Its Response to Citizen Requests	62
	11.	Local Government and Concerted Action	63

VI. MARKET CONCENTRATION AND CONSPIRACY ... 65

A. INTRODUCTION ... 65

B. CONCENTRATION, PRICE LEADERSHIP, AND "CONSCIOUS PARALLELISM" ... 65

1. Inference of Agreement as a Legal Building Block ... 65
    a. Conspiracy established from conduct ... 65
2. Conscious Parallelism ... 66
3. Multiple Vertical Agreements Function as Unlawful Horizontal Agreement ... 67
4. Facilitating Practices ... 68
    a. Delivered pricing ... 68
    b. Practices facilitating consciously parallel pricing ... 69
    c. Salary information exchange as a facilitating practice ... 71
    d. Price information exchanges in oligopoly as facilitating practices ... 72
    e. The European approach to the oligopoly problem ... 73

C. THE ROLE OF TRADE ASSOCIATIONS AND INFORMATION DISSEMINATION ... 73

1. Information Dissemination ... 73
2. Trade Associations ... 74
3. Information Exchange Characterized as Price Fixing ... 74
4. Benign Agreement ... 75
5. Protection Against Fraud ... 75
6. Price Exchange and a Ban on Secret Discounts ... 76
7. Interseller Price Verification ... 76
8. Sharing of Price Data ... 78

VII. VERTICAL DISTRIBUTION RESTRICTIONS ... 79

	A.	THE ECONOMICS OF VERTICAL RESTRICTIONS	79
	B.	THE INTERPLAY OF COMMON LAW AND ANTITRUST LAWS	79

      1. Vertical Price Setting 79
      2. Vertical Maximum Price Setting No Longer Per Se Illegal 80
      3. Consignment and Its Limitations 81
      4. Customer and Territorial Restraints 81

          a. Introduction 81
          b. "Rule of reason" applies 82
          c. Developments after *Sylvania* 83

      5. Refusal to Deal 84

          a. The seminal case 85
          b. Definition of "agreement" or "combination" 85
          c. Complaints by dealers to manufacturer 86
          d. Price vs. non-price restraints 87
          e. Failure to adhere to vertical agreement on minimum price as "antitrust injury" 88

VIII. ADDITIONAL LIMITATIONS ON A SINGLE FIRM EXERCISING MARKET POWER 90

  A. INTRODUCTION 90

  B. MARKET POWER 90

      1. Market Power and the Likely Effect of Challenged Conduct 90
      2. Problems of Market Definition 91
      3. Refusal to Sell at Wholesale Prices 93
      4. Monopolists' Duty to Cooperate With Competitors 93
      5. Monopolist Retains Right to Unilaterally Refuse to Deal 94
      6. *Aspen* Distinguished 95
      7. Duty of Vertically Integrated Monopolist to Deal With Non-vertically Integrated Competitor 95
      8. Business Justifications Versus Exclusionary Conduct in the Technology Sector by a Single Firm 96
      9. Intellectual Property Rights 102
     10. Refusal to License Patented and Copyrighted Information as Antitrust Violation 103

  C. ATTEMPT TO MONOPOLIZE 104

      1. Introduction 104
      2. Refusal to Deal 104

	3.	Right to Institute Changes	105
	4.	Dangerous Probability of Success Required to Show Attempt to Monopolize	105
	5.	Dangerous Probability Element	106

D. PREDATORY PRICING ... 106

1. Generally ... 106
2. Must Show Prospect of Recoupment to Prove Predatory Pricing ... 107
3. The Cost Standard and Areeda & Turner ... 110
4. Alternative Approaches ... 111

   a. Scherer ... 111
   b. Baumol ... 111
   c. Posner ... 111
   d. Jeshow & Keevorick ... 111
   e. Bolton, Brodley, and Riordan

5. "Intent" Standards ... 111

E. TYING ... 111

1. The Clayton Act ... 111
2. Definition ... 112
3. Introduction to the Case Law ... 112
4. Quality Control ... 112
5. Market Power Required ... 113
6. The Market Power Requirement Diluted ... 114
7. Per Se Illegality and Business Justifications ... 114
8. Two Approaches to Tying Arrangements ... 115
9. Tie Between Parts and Repair Service ... 117

F. PARTIAL VERTICAL INTEGRATION BY CONTRACT: EXCLUSIVE SELLING AND EXCLUSIVE DEALING ... 118

1. Exclusive Selling ... 118
2. Exclusive Dealing ... 120

   a. Introduction ... 120
   b. Substantial lessening of competition ... 120
   c. A quantitative test ... 120
   d. Length of time of the contract ... 121
   e. A qualitative test ... 121
   f. Exclusive dealing revisited ... 122
   g. Federal Trade Commission's power ... 123
   h. *Tampa* applied to exclusive dealing contracts ... 124

IX.	MERGERS			125
	A.	HORIZONTAL MERGERS		125

        1. Introduction 125
        2. Clayton Act 125
        3. Presumptive Illegality 125
        4. Product Market 128
        5. Geographical Market 128
        6. The Meaning of Concentration 129
        7. Rebutting the *Philadelphia National Bank* Presumption 130
        8. The Failing Company Doctrine 132

                a. Introduction 132
                b. Narrow defense 132
                c. 1992 DOJ/FTC horizontal merger guidelines 133
                d. Newspaper Preservation Act 133
                e. "Failing" company and the *General Dynamics* defense

        9. Ease of Entry and the *Philadelphia National Bank* Presumption 133
      10. Hospital Acquisitions Under the Clayton Act 133
      11. Antitrust Injury and Mergers 134

                a. Loss due to continued operation of defaulting competitor 134
                b. Lowering of prices by merged firm 135
                c. May a "target" firm invoke section 7 against a
                    hostile takeover? 135

      12. Remedies 136
      13. Department of Justice Horizontal Merger Guidelines 136

                a. Introduction 136
                b. Policy 136
                c. "Market power" defined 136
                d. Product market definition 136

                        1) Provisional market and the profitability test 136
                        2) Example 137
                        3) Predicting how buyers would respond to a price increase 137
                        4) Prospect of price discrimination may narrow product market 137

                e. Geographic market definition 137

                        1) Geographic market—profitability test 137
                        2) Predicting how buyers would respond to a price increase 138
                        3) Prospect of price discrimination may narrow geographic
                           market 138

Antitrust - xi

	f.	Identification of firms that participate in the relevant market	138
	g.	Calculating market shares	138
	h.	Concentration and market share	139
		1) The Herfindahl-Hirshman Index	139
	i.	Enforcement policy	139
		1) Post-merger HHI below 1,000	139
		2) Post-merger HHI between 1,000 and 1,800	139
		3) Post-merger HHI above 1,800	139
		4) Factors affecting the significance of market shares and concentration	139
		5) The prospect of "committed" entry and other nonmarket share/market concentration factors relevant to assessing the threat posed by a merger	140
		6) Merger-generated efficiencies	140
		7) Failing firm defense	141
14.	Horizontal Merger Resulting in Duopoly in Concentrated Market		141

B. JOINT VENTURES, POTENTIAL COMPETITION, AND CONGLOMERATE MERGERS 142

1.	Acquiring a Firm Competing for the Market	142
2.	Joint Ventures	142
3.	Conglomerate Mergers	144
	a. Efficiencies	144
	b. Product line extension merger	144
	c. The perceived potential competition theory	146
	d. The actual potential competitor theory	147
	e. The time horizon of potential competition	148
	f. 1984 Department of Justice merger guidelines: horizontal effect from non-horizontal mergers	148
	1) General approach	149
	2) Factors considered	149

C. INTEGRATION THROUGH VERTICAL MERGER 149

1.	Functions Served	149
2.	Supplier Buys Controlling Stock Interest in Customer	149
3.	The Test for "Substantially Lessen" Competition	151
4.	Backward Integration	153
5.	Realignment, Not Foreclosure	154

		6.	Department of Justice Merger Guidelines for Vertical Mergers 155
			a. How market entry is slowed 155
			b. Criteria used to recognize objectionable barrier 155
			1) Minimal unintegrated capacity 155
			2) High costs 155
			3) Market structure and performance 155
			c. Facilitating collusion in a highly concentrated upstream market through vertical merger 155
			1) Retail level 156
			2) Elimination of a disruptive buyer 156
		7.	Interlocking Directorates 156

X. FOREIGN COMMERCE AND THE U.S. ANTITRUST LAWS 157

A. JURISDICTION OVER FOREIGN COMMERCE 157

1. Foreign Commerce Before 1982 157

   a. Limited reach of Act and immunity of sovereign 157
   b. The Sherman Act and conduct occurring outside the United States 157
   c. Act permitted by government not immune 160
   d. Foreign sovereign permitted to sue 160
   e. International exports 160

2. The Foreign Trade Antitrust Improvements Act ("FTAIA") of 1982 161

   a. The FTAIA and "Comity" 161
   b. Antitrust jurisdiction and the interests of other nations 162
   c. International activity in criminal prosecution 164
   d. Sufficiency of conduct to support jurisdiction under the FTAIA 165

3. Comity and Cooperation 166

   a. Act of state doctrine: comity 166
   b. DOJ/FTC international guidelines 168

       1) Comity 168
       2) Foreign sovereign immunity 168

XI. PRICE DISCRIMINATION 170

A.	**INTRODUCTION**		170
	1. Motivation of Sellers		170
	2. Price Discrimination in Economics		170
	3. Price Discrimination in the Robinson-Patman Act		170
B.	**THE ROBINSON-PATMAN ACT**		170
	1. Basic Provisions of the Act		170
	2. Other Sections of the Act		171
	3. Major Issues		171
		a. Interstate commerce required	171
		b. The requirement of a "commodity."	171
		c. What conduct and which effects are proscribed by the Act?	171
		d. What must the alleged discriminator show to invoke the cost justification or meeting competition defenses?	171
		e. Like grade and quality	171
		f. Proof of damages	172
C.	**THE EFFECTS OF PRICE DISCRIMINATION**		172
	1. Primary-Line Effects of Price Discrimination		172
		a. Introduction	172
		b. Proscribed conduct	172
		c. Competitive responses	174
		d. Meaning of "predatory pricing"	174
		e. Prospect of recoupment	175
		f. Conflict in policy	175
	2. Secondary-Line Effects		175
		a. Introduction	175
		b. Proving substantial injury to competition	175
		c. Factors to consider	176
D.	**FUNCTIONAL DISCOUNTS**		176
	1. Introduction		176
	2. Functional Discounts as Unlawful Price Discrimination		17
E.	**MORE REMOTE EFFECTS**		178
F.	**DEFENSES TO ROBINSON-PATMAN ACT ACTIONS**		179
	1. Cost Justification		179

		a.	Introduction	179
		b.	Inadequate evidence	179
	2.	Good Faith Meeting of Competition		180
		a.	Introduction	181
		b.	Good faith attempt to meet competition	181
		c.	Interseller price verification and reconciling the Sherman Act	181
		d.	No duty of affirmative disclosure by buyer	182
		e.	Meeting competition on area-wide basis	182
G.	**BROKERAGE AD ALLOWANCES, AND SERVICES**			**182**
	1.	Introduction		182
		a.	Section 2(c)	182
		b.	Closed loophole	183
		c.	Per se rule	183
	2.	Reduction in Brokerage Commissions		183
	3.	Advertising Allowances, Services, and Facilities		183
		a.	Introduction	183
		b.	FTC Guidelines	183
		c.	Definition of customers	184
H.	**BUYER'S LIABILITY FOR INDUCING OR RECEIVING DISCRIMINATIONS IN PRICE**			**184**
	1.	Introduction		184
	2.	Inducement by Buyer Where Seller Has Defense		185

TABLE OF CASES **187**

Antitrust - xv

I. THE OBJECTIVES AND ORIGINS OF ANTITRUST LAW

A. THE GOALS OF ANTITRUST POLICY

1. *Industrial Market Structure and Economic Performance* (Scherer and Ross, 1990). Every society faces the "economic problem"; that is, what to produce, how much, by whom, using what resources, for whom, and for what reward. There are three main ways of structuring the economic system in response: tradition, central planning, and the market system. The market system relies on competition and is the superior system. There are strong political reasons for supporting this system:

    a. The atomistic structure of buyers and sellers in a competitive market decentralizes and disperses power.

    b. The forces affecting the market are impersonal, rather than administrative.

    c. In a no-barrier-to-entry market there is freedom of opportunity.

2. *Antitrust Policy* (Kaysen and Turner, 1959). There are four main objectives of antitrust policy:

    a. **Achieving desirable economic results.** These results are of four main kinds:

        (i) Efficiency in the use of resources;

        (ii) Progress, or the growth of total output and output per person;

        (iii) Stability in output and employment; and

        (iv) An equitable distribution of income.

        Results (i) and (ii) may be affected by antitrust policy. Results (iii) and (iv) are affected more in other ways.

    b. **Promoting competition.** The relationship between fostering competition as an end in itself and economic performance is not clear. Market power as discussed here has to do with purely business transactions (market relationships). The arguments for competition involve having decisions made by impersonal market forces and the existence of alternatives. Few markets in the United States are purely competitive in this sense.

    c. **Fairness.** In antitrust, "fairness" means primarily that similarly situated parties are treated similarly and that general notions of fair play are observed.

d. **Limiting big business.** Another objective may be to limit the social and political power of big business and increase that of small business.

   e. **Conclusion.** These policies are not always complementary. However, at the time the Sherman Act was passed they may not have been seen to be conflicting (*i.e.*, the Act was aimed at breaking up the power of large trusts, which were monopolizing and charging the public high prices and driving small businesses out of the market).

   f. **Comment.** Antitrust law is sometimes confusing because these different objectives often mandate different results and there is no consensus on which objective is paramount.

3. *What Happened to the Antitrust Movement?* (Hofstadter, 1965). The United States began as a nation of small farmers and businessmen. There was a distrust of largeness and concentrations of power. And yet by the end of the 1800s the large corporation had come into existence. This transition frightened the populace, and when the common law and the law of the states seemed inadequate to deal with the large aggregation of power, federal laws were enacted. The history of antitrust may be divided into three phases:

   a. **The founding period.** From 1890 to 1914. This was the era of the most vigorous enforcement and the highest public sentiment against big business.

   b. **Period of neglect.** From 1914 to 1937.

   c. **Period of revival.** From 1937 to the present. Antitrust is sustained in this period by the same impulse that began it—a consensus that bigness should be checked. The economic issue is whether antitrust law seriously interferes with the requirements of economic efficiency.

4. *The Antitrust Paradox* (Bork, 1978). Sherman and his colleagues purported to be enacting a statute that merely codified common law, but they considerably overstated the sweep and clarity of the common law in advancing their cause. The legislative history of the Sherman Act supports the view that Senator Sherman's primary purpose was to advance consumer welfare. Many court decisions have been inconsistent with this end.

B. **THE SHERMAN ACT AND COMPARATIVE LEGISLATION**

   1. **The Sherman Act.**

a. **Section 1—restraints of trade.** "Every contract, combination in the form of trust or otherwise, or conspiracy, in restraint of trade or commerce among the several states, or with foreign nations, is hereby declared to be illegal. . . ."

b. **Section 2—monopolization.** "Every person who shall monopolize, or attempt to monopolize, or combine or conspire with any other person or persons, to monopolize any part of the trade or commerce among the several states, or with foreign nations, shall be deemed guilty of a misdemeanor, and, on conviction thereof, shall be punished by fine not exceeding one million dollars, if a corporation, or, if any other person, one hundred thousand dollars, or by imprisonment not exceeding three years, or by both said punishments, in the discretion of the court."

2. **The Antitrust ("Competition") Law of the European Union.**

    a. **Basic provisions.** From its inception in the Treaty of Rome, what is now known as the European Union ("EU") has had its own antitrust law. Article 82 (previously Article 86) prohibits "abuse . . . of a dominant position." Article 81 (previously Article 85-a) prohibits agreements and other concerted practices, "which have as their object or effect the prevention, restriction, or distortion of competition within the Common Market."

    b. **Exemptions.** Until May 1, 2004, The European Commission ("the Commission"), the EU's administrative and executive arm, had the power to grant exemptions from Article 81 for agreements or concerted practices that contribute to improving the production or distribution of goods or to promoting technical or economic progress, while allowing consumers a fair share of the resulting benefit, and that do not:

        (i) Impose on the parties concerned restrictions that are not indispensable to the attainment of these objectives; and

        (ii) Afford such parties the possibility of eliminating competition in respect of a substantial part of the products in question.

    After May 1, 2004, the Commission no longer has the power to grant exemptions, but Article 81, subpart (3), provides an exemption without the need for any official decision.

    c. **Enforcement.** The Commission's loss of its power to grant Article 81(3) exemptions will pave the way for decentralized national authorities and courts. In addition, the Commission's Competition Directorate General will have substantially greater responsibility for the enforcement of both Article 81 and Article 82. A rule to be adopted will provide that when an agreement or practice affects trade between member states, the national authorities and courts will be obliged to apply EU law, even if they also apply their national law, which cannot in any event be inconsistent with

EU law. The EU's Court of First Instance, rather than its European Court of Justice ("ECJ"), will continue to have jurisdiction over competition cases.

    d. Goals. A consensus has developed in the United States that the principal, if not only, purpose of the antitrust laws is to promote consumer welfare. The EU's Commission and courts have interpreted the EU's competition laws as serving additional purposes, such as the expansion of opportunities for cross-border trade.

C. THE HISTORICAL SOURCES OF ANTITRUST LEGISLATIVE HISTORY, AND EARLY DEVELOPMENTS

1. The Early Law on Monopoly and Contracts in Restraint of Trade.

    a. Introduction. The common law of trade regulation followed no consistent pattern; it changed back and forth in its emphasis over time. There were several conflicting lines of cases. Furthermore, many of the precedents cited by the founders of modern antitrust policy were in fact statutes and cases against certain restrictive practices that interfered with others who already had protected trade positions.

    b. Early law on monopolies.

        1) Grant by the king. Originally a monopoly was a license or patent granted by the king that gave an individual the exclusive power to buy, sell, trade, or deal in a particular commodity.

        2) Guilds. In addition, many towns in England had guilds set up by the local craftsmen to protect their home markets from outsiders.

    c. Early cases.

Dyer's Case

        1) Covenant not to engage in a trade--Anonymous—Dyer's Case, Y.B., 2 Hen. V, vol. 5, pl. 26 (1415).

            a) Facts. P sued D on a note; D argued that their contract provided that if he refrained from practicing his trade in the town for six months, the debt would be forgiven. He had so refrained.

            b) Issue. Is a contract in which one party agrees not to engage in a lawful trade for some period of time a valid and enforceable contract?

- c) **Held.** No. A contract in which one party agrees not to engage in a lawful trade is void.

2) **Starting a competing business--Anonymous—The Schoolmaster Case,** Y.B., 11 Hen. IV, f. 47, pl. 21 (1410).

    a) **Facts.** P had a grammar school in the town; D started a new school and P could not charge as much as before. P sued.

    b) **Issue.** May a competing business be shut down by a prior existing business that is losing business due to the new competition?

    c) **Held.** No. No cause of action.

3) **Grant of monopoly--Case of Monopolies,** 77 Eng. Rep. 1260 (1602).

    a) **Facts.** P brought an action against D for manufacturing and selling playing cards in violation of a grant from Queen Elizabeth giving P the sole right to this trade. D pleaded in defense that as a haberdasher he traditionally had the right to engage in this trade.

    b) **Issue.** May the grant of a monopoly be at the expense of those already practicing in the field?

    c) **Held.** No.

        (1) Monopolies are against the common law for several reasons. The practicing of trades benefits the commonwealth and reduces idleness, and monopolies tend to hinder the beneficial practicing of trades. Also, monopolies tend to drive up prices and reduce the quality of goods.

        (2) In addition to being against the common law, this monopoly also violates several acts of Parliament pertaining to freedom of trade.

    d) **Comment.** The Statute of Monopolies, which voided all monopolies granted by the King, was passed in 1623. The local guilds and monopolies granted by Parliament remained untouched, however.

4) **Sale of a business--Mitchel v. Reynolds,** 24 Eng. Rep. 347 (1711).

    a) **Facts.** P sued on a bond. D sold a business to P and agreed not to compete in the same business in the town for five years. D breached the agreement and defends on the basis that such covenants are in restraint of trade and illegal.

    b) **Issue.** Is a covenant not to compete for a certain period valid when it is agreed to in connection with the sale of a business?

- c) **Held.** Yes. The restraint here is reasonable; it is limited in time and place and is ancillary to the sale of a business.

- d) **Comment.** The rule of reason was first enunciated in this case.

2. **The Legislative History of the Sherman Act.** It seems clear that the Sherman Act was passed in response to public feeling against the trusts (Standard Oil, etc.). Hatred of monopoly was a long-ingrained attitude of most Americans; there had even been strong support for a provision in the Bill of Rights outlawing monopolies. In the 1880s, the trusts grew quickly and they were blamed for many abuses. Opinion differed on how to deal with the trusts. Economists generally felt that both competition and combination should be part of the economy. Lawyers generally felt that the common law permitted combination in some instances and prevented it in others. It was thus the common point of wanting to eliminate the "excesses" that allowed opposing viewpoints to get together. A federal solution was required since the states did not have the needed power to regulate interstate commerce. As to the exact meaning or intention of the Act, this may be impossible to fully sort out. The following indications seem relevant:

    a. Most of the members of Congress were proponents of a "private enterprise system" based on the principle of "full and free competition."

    b. Most thought that the common law supported such a system.

    c. They had little understanding of the economic theory underlying such a system or of the implications of economic theory or of the conflicts of economic theory with their own common understanding.

    d. They believed that the ultimate beneficiaries of the theory they supported were the consumers. But they also believed that they were protecting the small businessman from the ruthless practices of large, predatory trusts.

    e. The most specific instances they had in mind against which the Act legislated were trusts that possessed market power akin to monopolies and used such power to control prices, divide markets, and drive competitors out of business.

    f. There is evidence that there was expectation that the court would change and enlarge upon the original meaning of the Act as the conditions of the economic environment changed.

3. **Early Development of Antitrust Law—Two Levels of Law.**

    a. **The first cartel cases.**

1) **Sherman Act makes illegal "all contracts in restraint of trade"--United States v. Trans-Missouri Freight Association,** 166 U.S. 290 (1897).

   a) **Facts.** The United States sued in equity to dissolve the Trans-Missouri Freight Association, an association of 18 railroads whose lines ran from the Mississippi River to the west coast, controlling most of the freight in this area. The association set rates, rules, etc., and enacted penalties for violations. The court of appeals dismissed the complaint, and the United States appeals.

   b) **Issue.** Is the Association an unlawful agreement by its members in restraint of trade and thus a violation of the Sherman Act?

   c) **Held.** Yes. Judgment remanded.

      (1) The Act says "*all*" contracts in restraint of trade" are unlawful. Thus, the Act is broader than the common law, which might be said to make illegal only "unreasonable" restraints.

2) **Ancillary and indirect restraints.** After *Trans-Missouri* came *United States v. Joint Traffic Association*, 171 U.S. 505 (1898), in which Justice Peckham (who wrote the majority opinion in *Trans-Missouri*) amended his views and recognized an exception for "ancillary restraints." In *Hopkins v. United States*, 171 U.S. 578 (1898), and *Anderson v. United States*, 171 U.S. 604 (1898), Peckham retreated further, in opinions that focused on whether the restraint was "direct or indirect."

3) **Purpose or intent of restraint--United States v. Addyston Pipe & Steel Co.**, 85 F. 271 (6th Cir. 1898), *aff'd*, 175 U.S. 211 (1899).

   a) **Facts.** This is a suit in equity for an injunction against six companies (Ds) manufacturing iron pipe and selling in the central and southern states. They had entered into a two-year agreement to divide the sales territory and fix prices: certain cities were assigned to members and rates were set; in other areas a secret auction was held and the winner paid the association a bonus amount. In the "free territory" members could sell without restriction since in this territory there was substantial outside competition. Members had 220,000 tons of capacity; nonmembers in the restricted territory had 170,500 tons; and in the free territory nonmembers had 348,000 tons. There was a significant price advantage in the restricted territory over outsiders (due to freight costs to ship to the territory) and this theoretically set the maximum price that could be charged. Ds argued that: (i) the object was to prevent ruinous competition; (ii) only reasonable prices were charged; (iii) there was always competition from nonmembers; and (iv) prices charged in the free territory were always less since sales were made at a loss in order to keep their plants going.

Antitrust - 7

b) **Issue.** Were the restraints to trade here in violation of the Sherman Act?

c) **Held.** Yes. The restraints were unlawful.

(1) Whatever is unlawful at common law is unlawful here; the common law permitted only reasonable "ancillary" restraints.

(2) Here the restraints were for the sole purpose and object of restraining competition. In this situation it makes no difference how reasonable the prices were, how much the competition was, or what the necessity was of preventing financial distress.

(3) In addition, on the facts, members in their reserved territories really had no competition.

d) **Comment.** In affirming, the Supreme Court rejected the trial court's reasoning (and its own earlier reasoning in *United States v. E.C. Knight Co.*, 156 U.S. 1 (1895)) that manufacturing was not covered by the commerce language of the statute.

4) **Expansive definition of trade or commerce.** In *Swift & Co. v. United States*, 196 U.S. 375 (1905), the Court ruled that the Sherman Act reached intrastate activity that was part of a current of commerce among the states.

5) **Restrictive covenants under state and federal law.** After the Sherman Act became law, federal and state courts evaluated restrictive covenants as the courts had in *Mitchel v. Reynolds* and *Addyston, supra*. In these court opinions, the geographic area covered by the covenant, its duration, and the scope of the barred activities loom large. Courts have tended to invalidate or narrowly interpret covenants appearing in employment more readily than those appearing in contracts for the sale of a business or the organization of a small business. Today, litigation about restrictive covenants is almost always resolved under state law—but there are exceptions. For example, a dominant firm might violate the Sherman Act by enforcing a restrictive covenant that prevents an innovative firm from entering a concentrated market if the litigation is part of a pattern of repetitive litigation. The Restatement (Second) of Contracts section 188 reflects these court decisions.

a) **Definition.** It provides that a promise to refrain from competition that imposes a restraint that is ancillary to an otherwise valid transaction or relationship is unreasonably in restraint of trade if:

(1) The restraint is greater than is needed to protect the promisee's legitimate interest, or

(2) The promisee's need is outweighed by the hardship to the promisor and the likely injury to the public.

- b) **Examples.** Promises imposing restraints that are ancillary to a valid transaction or relationship include the following:

    (1) A promise by the seller of a business not to compete with the buyer in such a way as to injure the value of the business sold;

    (2) A promise by an employee or other agent not to compete with his employer or other principal;

    (3) A promise by a partner not to compete with the partnership.

b. **Early mergers and the development of the "rule of reason."** Mergers, acquisitions, and other consolidations (unlike cartels) may advance efficiency and serve a variety of useful business purposes. So, condemning consolidations because they might give the newly fashioned firm more market power might frustrate the purpose of the antitrust laws. Nevertheless, in *Northern Securities Co. v. United States*, 193 U.S. 197 (1904), the Supreme Court said that "every combination or conspiracy which would extinguish competition between otherwise competing railroads . . . is made illegal by the Act." The holding, however, may not be as broad, and the Court subsequently backed away from this position. In *Standard Oil Co. of New Jersey v. United States*, 221 U.S. 1 (1911), the Court said that section 1 of the Sherman Act did not prohibit every contract, combination, or conspiracy in restraint of trade, only the "unreasonable" ones. In *United States v. American Tobacco Co.*, 221 U.S. 106 (1911), the Court amplified its statement concerning the "rule of reason," indicating that the rule of reason meant that freedom of contract (necessary to do business) was preserved; at the same time, giving the Sherman Act a reasonable construction did not mean that all of the acts and practices condemned by sections 1 and 2 of the Act could be permitted simply by finding that they were "reasonable."

Antitrust - 9

II. THE INSTITUTIONAL FRAMEWORK OF ANTITRUST POLICY

A. THE DEPARTMENT OF JUSTICE

The Antitrust Division of the Justice Department may seek criminal penalties, injunctions, and damages.

B. THE FEDERAL TRADE COMMISSION

After the *Standard Oil* decision, sentiment for new antitrust legislation gathered from two sources: Business was unhappy with the uncertainty of the "rule of reason" and antitrust supporters felt that there were many abuses that escaped such a rule. As a result, in 1914, Congress passed the Federal Trade Commission Act, which created the Federal Trade Commission ("FTC"). Section 5 of the Act made unlawful "unfair competition." The FTC has exclusive authority to enforce section 5. Congress also passed the Clayton Act, which outlawed several specific forms of restraint of competition.

1. **The Clayton Act.**

    a. **Price discrimination.** Section 2 of the Clayton Act was amended by, and is often referred to as, the Robinson-Patman Act. As amended, it prohibits price discrimination between different purchasers, where the effect thereof is substantially to lessen competition or to tend to create a monopoly in any line of commerce.

    b. **Restrictive arrangements.** Section 3 prohibits sales on condition that the buyer not deal with competitors of the seller (*i.e.*, tie-in sales, exclusive dealing arrangements, and requirements contracts) where the effect may be substantially to lessen competition or tend to create a monopoly in any line of commerce.

    c. **Mergers and acquisitions.** Section 7 prohibits mergers where the effect may be to substantially lessen competition or tend to create a monopoly in any line of commerce in any section of the country.

    d. **Interlocking directorates.** Section 8 prohibits any person from being a director of two or more competing corporations, any of which has capital in excess of $1 million.

2. **Concurrent Jurisdiction.** The FTC has concurrent powers to enforce the Clayton Act (with the Justice Department and the courts). The FTC is not responsible for enforcing the Sherman Act, but the courts have held that section 5 is broad enough to cover any acts that might be found to be illegal under this Act as well.

3. **Other Responsibilities.** In addition to its antitrust duties, the FTC is charged with enforcement in a number of other important areas: labeling, packaging, deceptive advertising, etc.

C. **PRIVATE ACTIONS AND STATE ATTORNEYS GENERAL**

1. **Treble Damages.** Section 4 of the Clayton Act provides that "any person . . . injured in his business or property by reason of anything forbidden in the antitrust laws (*i.e.*, for violation of either the Sherman Act or Clayton Act) . . . may recover threefold the damages by him sustained, and the cost of suit, including reasonable attorneys' fees."

2. **Parens Patriae Suits.** Under the Hart-Scott-Rodino Act of 1976, state attorneys general may bring suit on behalf of natural persons residing in their states. They may invoke liberal damage calculation techniques.

D. **SPECIAL ISSUES RELATED TO ENFORCEMENT BY THE FEDERAL AGENCIES**

1. **Consent Decrees.** The government will often agree with a private party defendant on a "consent decree," which is a settlement of an antitrust action where the defendant acknowledges the violation and accepts the determined remedy (without court trial).

    a. **Court supervision.** The court must agree to the decree.

    b. **Motivation for consent decrees.** Such consent decrees are very important, since a judgment against a defendant may be used as prima facie evidence against the defendant in private litigation, whereas a consent decree cannot be so used.

2. **Intervention.** Private parties may seek to intervene in government antitrust suits. The Federal Rules of Civil Procedure (Rule 24) speak of intervention on two bases: of right, and with permission. Generally the courts have denied the right to intervene. But in exceptional situations, the Supreme Court has allowed nonparties to intervene. For example, in *Cascade Natural Gas Corp. v. El Paso Natural Gas Co.*, 386 U.S. 129 (1967), the government suit charged that the defendant's acquisition of a pipeline company was an attempt to strangle competition in the sale of natural gas in California. The State of California and the Southern California Edison Co. (the state's largest industrial user) were allowed to intervene "as a matter of right" in the case. In FTC cases intervention is purely discretionary with the FTC.

3. **Prima Facie Case.** Section 5(a) of the Clayton Act provides: "A final judgment or decree heretofore or hereafter rendered in any civil or criminal proceeding brought by or on behalf of the United States under the antitrust laws to the effect that the defendant has violated said laws shall

be prima facie evidence against such defendant in any action or proceeding brought by any other party against such defendant under said laws . . . as to all matters respecting which said judgment or decree shall be estoppel between the parties thereto; provided, that this section shall not apply to consent judgments or decrees entered before any testimony is taken."

   a. Criminal or civil judgments of fine or injunction brought by the government qualify under this section. Actions brought by the government for damages do not.

   b. Nolo contendere pleas do not qualify, and the courts are split over guilty pleas.

   c. FTC decrees do qualify.

E. **SPECIAL ISSUES RELATED TO PRIVATE ENFORCEMENT**

   1. **Standing, Causation, and "Antitrust Injury."** The casebook authors assert that, in connection with issues of standing, causation, and "antitrust injury," the courts ought to analyze "the purposes of the antitrust laws and the probable costs and benefits to the antitrust system of allowing a particular plaintiff to vindicate its claim to protection against antitrust injuries." The casebook authors also assert that the Supreme Court has increasingly adopted this form of analysis.

   2. **"Unclean Hands."** In *Perma Life Mufflers, Inc. v. International Parts Corp.*, 392 U.S. 134 (1968), the Supreme Court declined to dismiss an antitrust suit brought by a plaintiff who participated in the alleged violation, but did not "aggressively support and further the monopolistic scheme"(the plaintiff was a franchisee). The majority argued that its decision would serve deterrence. The Court did not address whether "truly complete involvement" would have barred the suit.

   3. **Certainty of Damages.** The plaintiff must prove that there have been actual damages. Beyond that, the courts have been willing to estimate the amount of damages on a "reasonable basis" even where uncertainty exists as to the exact amount.

   4. **The "Passing On" Defense.** The defense that the plaintiff passed on his increased costs to his customers is theoretically available to the defendant accused of an antitrust violation. However, in practice this defense is not available since the Supreme Court has indicated that the defendant must show that the plaintiff raised his price in response to, and in the amount of, the overcharge and also that the plaintiff's margin of profit and total sales did not decline. [Hanover Shoe, Inc. v. United Shoe Machinery Corp., 392 U.S. 481 (1968)] Consistent with *Hanover Shoe*,

the Court has also held that an indirect purchaser of materials with a "passed through" illegally set price (that is, the recipient of the pass-on) may not maintain a treble damage action for the overcharge. The Court justified its holding on the difficulty of tracing economic damage beyond the immediate purchaser, and also on the notion that "passing on" should not be allowed to be used offensively if it cannot be used defensively, as *Hanover Shoe* provides. [Illinois Brick Co. v. Illinois, 431 U.S. 720 (1977)]

F. THE LIMITS OF ANTITRUST

1. **Government Ownership and Regulation.** These give rise to express and implied limits.

2. **Interstate and Foreign Commerce.**

    a. **The Sherman Act.** Sections 1 and 2 cover restraints of commerce among the several states or with foreign nations, and monopolizing any part of commerce among the several states or with foreign nations. In *United States v. E.C. Knight Co.*, 156 U.S. 1 (1896), the Supreme Court held that the manufacture and production of goods were not "interstate commerce," even though the goods might be destined for shipment in interstate commerce. Subsequent decisions have indicated that where some activity has a "substantial economic effect" on interstate commerce (although it occurs in intrastate commerce), the jurisdictional requirements have been met. There appears, however, to be a de minimis exception. That is, where the effect on interstate commerce is insubstantial, there may be no jurisdiction under the Sherman Act. There is an unresolved issue as to whether the restraint itself must affect interstate commerce, or whether it is sufficient if some of the defendant's activities affect interstate commerce (for example, the local branch office of a national company engages in local antitrust violations).

    b. **The Clayton Act.** The language of the Clayton Act with respect to jurisdiction is narrower. It indicates that the Act applies only to persons engaged in interstate commerce who do specific acts that have the effect of lessening competition in a line of commerce. Thus, it appears that for jurisdiction to exist the persons or activities involved must exist in the flow of interstate commerce. [Gulf Oil Corp. v. Copp Paving Co., 419 U.S. 186 (1974)] For example, it has been held under section 7 that both the acquiring and the acquired companies must be directly engaged in the production, distribution, or acquisition of goods or services in interstate commerce. [United States v. American Building Maintenance Industries, 422 U.S. 271 (1975)]

c. **The Robinson-Patman Act.** There are specific jurisdictional requirements in this Act indicating that the discriminating seller must be engaged in interstate commerce and at least one of the two sales on which the claim of discrimination is based must be across state lines.

d. **Foreign commerce.** International law recognizes that conduct outside a country may be subject to the laws of the country. Thus, it has been held that the Sherman Act applies to extraterritorial activities where (i) the intent of the parties is to affect commerce in the United States and (ii) the conduct actually does cause effects in the United States. Application of United States law to firms doing international business can create conflicts with the policies of foreign governments. Hence, in some situations it is necessary to accommodate these sources of conflict. Thus, if the defendant's foreign activities are required by foreign law, this activity will not be condemned by United States antitrust law; and unless there is a clear congressional direction to the contrary, the antitrust laws will not be applied where they conflict with settled principles of international law.

III. MARKET STRUCTURE AND A FIRST LOOK AT THE PROBLEM OF MONOPOLY POWER

A. MONOPOLIZATION AND THE PROBLEM OF MARKET DEFINITION

1. **Conceptual Overview.** According to the casebook authors, "monopolization" involves three interrelated antitrust questions: (i) how should market shares be measured or what is the "relevant market?"; (ii) what market share in which circumstances gives rise to sufficient market power to trigger antitrust concern?; and (iii) if a firm has sufficient market power, what kinds of business conduct should trigger condemnation?

2. **Defining the Market: Why and How.** The purpose of defining the market is to identify the firms that would constrain an actor's power to raise prices without reducing net revenues. Identifying these firms may require consideration of supply as well as demand. On the demand side, one must consider not only the nature of the product and the ability or willingness of its users to substitute other products for it, but also the location of the firms. On the "supply" side, one must consider the likelihood that firms will begin or step up production. This will depend on the cost and other barriers to entry.

3. **Expansion As An Offense?--United States v. Aluminum Co. of America,** 148 F.2d 416 (2d Cir. 1945).

    a. **Facts.** Aluminum Company of America (D), begun in 1888, controlled all production of ingot aluminum in the United States, first by patents until 1909, then until 1912 by various restrictive agreements with foreign cartels and covenants not to supply electricity to competing firms. Thereafter, it averaged over 90% market share. D also fabricated aluminum. An action was brought under section 2 of the Sherman Act for "monopolizing." The trial court held that there was no violation.

    b. **Issues.**

        1) Does D's market share of 90% constitute monopoly power, where D was subject to foreign competition?

        2) Was D's monopoly thrust upon it without D having an unlawful intent to monopolize?

    c. **Held.** 1) Yes. 2) No. Judgment reversed and remanded.

        1) In determining whether a monopoly exists, a 90% share constitutes a monopoly; 60-65% is doubtful, and 33% is insufficient.

2) In D's case, there was very little domestic competition, giving D power, within certain limitations, to fix prices. There was foreign production, but D could fix prices within the range of the added tariff and transportation costs so as to underprice imports. There was also possible competition from substitute metals. Still, within a certain range, D had monopoly power.

3) That D earned only a reasonable return is irrelevant. Monopolies may deaden initiative, and for social reasons a system of small competitors may be preferred.

4) Contracts to fix prices are per se illegal. Monopolies fix prices. Hence, where there is an intent to create a monopoly, it is illegal.

5) It is possible that a monopoly has been thrust upon a defendant, and in such a case it is not unlawful. For example, the defendant might be the sole survivor in an industry due to its superior skill and efficiency.

6) D's monopoly was not thrust upon it; D was not a passive beneficiary. The facts show a persistent determination to create and maintain monopoly power. D always anticipated increased demand for the product and was ready to supply it, and D embraced every new opportunity as it came along.

d. **Comment.** The case indicates that it is not necessary to show predatory acts to show intent to monopolize. The case can be read as saying that, despite a disclaimer, even normal aggressive business practices can show an intent to monopolize, and that actual exercise of monopoly power need not be shown to sustain a section 2 violation. In effect, the heavy burden is put on the defendant to show that it just could not help gaining monopoly power.

4. **What Conduct Is Prohibited?**

a. In *Berkey Photo, Inc. v. Eastman Kodak Co.*, 603 F.2d 263 (1979), the Second Circuit ruled that Kodak, an admitted monopolist, had no duty to predisclose to competitors information about its new camera and film products to enable the competitors to manufacture compatible equipment before the date of introduction.

b. In *In re E.I. DuPont De Nemours & Co.*, 3 Trade Reg. Rep. (FTC 1980), the FTC concluded that DuPont, intending to capitalize on low costs and advanced technology, did not violate the antitrust laws in an aggressive production expansion strategy even where the effect was a dramatic increase in market share.

c. In *Olympia Equipment Leasing Co. v. Western Union Telegraph*, 797 F.2d 370 (7th Cir. 1986), Judge Posner opined that a firm with a lawful monopoly has no duty to help its competitors, and if it does so and then later withdraws its help, it does not incur antitrust liability.

5. **Market Definition: "Reasonable Interchangeability"--United States v. E.I. DuPont de Nemours & Co.**, 351 U.S. 377 (1956).

   a. **Facts.** The United States brought an action under section 2 of the Sherman Act against DuPont (D) for "monopolizing" the market for cellophane, of which it controlled 75%. D's defense was that it has only 20% of the "flexible packaging market." The lower court held that there was no monopoly since the relevant market was flexible packaging, and 20% was not a monopoly.

   b. **Issue.** Should the relevant product market be confined to cellophane?

   c. **Held.** No. Judgment affirmed.

   1) Monopoly is the ability to set prices and exclude competitors. D has a monopoly of cellophane since no one can manufacture it without access to D's patents.

   2) Every manufacturer of a differentiated product has a monopoly of sorts, limited by competitive products. A product is competitive based on similarities in character and use and the extent to which buyers will be willing to substitute one for the other.

   3) Products need not be fungible to be part of the relevant market. The rule is that commodities that are reasonably interchangeable by consumers for the same purposes make up that part of the trade or commerce, monopolization of which may be illegal.

   4) The beginning point of analysis is the uses to which the product is put. Cellophane has a combination of characteristics that are not matched by others, but in each of these characteristics other flexible packaging materials are equal or superior, and all of these other materials are used by the same type of users as use cellophane. For example, cellophane supplies 7% of bakery good wrapping, 25% for candy, and 75 to 80% for cigarettes. The interchangeability of uses makes the relevant market "flexible packaging materials."

   5) The fact that cellophane's price is two to three times that of its chief and most similar competitors in the flexible packaging market does not establish monopoly power. Some users are sensitive to price and some are not. (Note that this sensitivity could be argued as a basis for distinction.) It is the variable characteristics of the materials and the marketing of them that determines choice.

6) D had an average of 15.9% after-tax return on capital; this does not demonstrate a monopoly without a comparison of the rates of return of other flexible packaging companies.

d. **Dissent** (Warren, C.J., Black, Douglas, JJ.). Cellophane combines certain elements more definitely than any other packaging material. For example, its lower-priced substitutes do not have the qualities of cellophane. Furthermore, sales increased dramatically over the years despite the fact that cellophane was priced substantially higher than its so-called competitors. D also cut prices but lower-priced substitutes did not, and yet the substitutes retained their market position. D itself considered cellophane a separate market and worked to maintain a monopoly in it. D made tremendous profits, yet only one competitor entered the cellophane market. In one year D raised prices to keep its rate of profit at a desired level; thus, D had substantial control over price. The majority holds that because cellophane has competition for many end uses, those users who can use only cellophane are not entitled to protection (*e.g.*, the cigarette industry was monopolized by cellophane).

e. **Comments.**

1) The majority takes one view, that reasonably interchangeable products should not be arbitrarily eliminated in defining the relevant market. This is an economic approach to antitrust, and introduces a very complex factual inquiry into deciding antitrust cases. Under this approach, every differentiated product is unique and thus has a monopoly over price in some price range, and every product has competition after some price level is reached. The issue becomes one of what price range does a company have monopoly power over.

   a) If the company raises its prices and loses customers, does this prove it has substitute competition? Not by itself, since it may have lower costs than the substitute, higher profits, and enjoy a range of price monopoly up to the point where it loses customers by an increase. Costs versus competitors' costs are some indication of this situation; and unusual profits may be an indicator of such a situation.

   b) If price is decreased and the defendant gained customers, does this indicate that it is not a monopolist? No. It might have some customers with whom it can maintain its prices, since there may be no substitutes for these customers.

   c) There is also the issue as to whether there may be no substitutes for some users and whether the interests of these users should be protected, for example, the cigarette manufacturers in this case. For those users where there is not a close substitute, is it possible that the product can be differentiated in some way so that to other users it has characteristics that make it unusable for the user who has no substitutes? If so, then there is a monopoly. If not, then the user who has no substitutes is still protected because he can buy at the same competitive prices as other users (*i.e.*, the competition that the product receives from substitutes in other uses keeps the price of the product from being monopolistic). Presumably this was the situation in the cellophane case.

d) The issue for the majority is what amount of actual market power the defendant has; *i.e.*, over what price range does it exercise control? Defining this, determining it, and deciding how much is too much is very difficult. Thus, the majority (if this is its approach) has chosen a sophisticated, difficult, expensive, and time-consuming standard for the courts to administer. Note, for example, that there was no discussion in the case of comparable costs among the supposed competitors, or profit margins, etc.

2) The dissent may be saying that it will look at a simpler test—are the products exactly alike? There is justification for such a test, theoretically in the Sherman Act and administratively from the administrative problems of the courts. Of course, if this test is adopted, there is always the case where the defendant appears to have a monopoly in its product but is losing sales to other products and really has no market power—and, hence, is not a monopolist. In addition, the dissent argued that the majority was wrong on its facts. Compare the dissent with the *Alcoa* opinion, where secondary, scrap ingot was eliminated in the definition of the market. Even if this test of "exactly alike products" were used, the courts would still have to examine carefully such factors as price behavior, profits, conditions of entry, etc., at least in situations where the defendant has considerably less than 100% of the market.

6. **The Substantial Submarket Test--United States v. Grinnell Corporation,** 384 U.S. 563 (1966).

   a. **Facts.** Grinnell Corporation (D), a manufacturer of plumbing supplies and fire sprinklers, acquired three companies in the insurance accredited central station property protection (burglary and fire) business. These companies made restrictive agreements between them as to territory, prices, etc. They also started businesses in new cities to exclude competition, cut prices where competition from other services existed, raised it where there was no competition, etc. The United States (P) brought a civil suit under the Sherman Act. D argued that the market was for each type of service separately (burglary, fire, etc.), and that there existed many types of competing services (including nonaccredited, noncentral station, etc.). The District Court held for P; both sides appeal.

United States v. Grinnell Corporation

b. **Issue.** Should the market definition be so broad as to include nonaccredited, noncentral station services?

c. **Held.** No. Judgment affirmed in part and remanded for findings on divestiture.

   1) The market is for accredited central station property protection services, and since D has 87% of this market it has monopoly power. Furthermore, D's acts in acquiring a monopoly indicate that this is an unlawful "monopolization."

   2) The test is the "reasonably interchangeable" test. Submarkets, such as the one here, may be separate economic entities. D has not made a case for either breaking up the market into separate services or adding the other types of services. Nearly all companies offering central station service offer all types (burglary, etc.). There are other types of property protection, but none are so interchangeable that they meet the test. Each has characteristics different from central station service. As for unaccredited central station service, it is different since many users want the safety and lower insurance rates of the accredited service.

   3) The geographic market is the entire United States since D's business is planned and operated on a nationwide basis.

d. **Dissent** (Fortas, Stewart, JJ.).

   1) The geographic market is local. The test is the reality of geographic supplier-customer relations. Competition here is between companies within a 25-mile radius.

   2) The product market includes many alternatives excluded by the majority. In some 20 areas D has been forced to operate at a loss due to competition from other types of property protection systems.

   3) In other words, the majority has not looked at economic realities. It has simply accepted that the market is outlined by the very contours of the defendant's business.

e. **Comments.**

   1) Some commentators have argued that *Grinnell* permits the government to select any "market" it wishes, as long as some legal (*i.e.*, noneconomic), practical criteria are used for selection. Certainly the majority opinion lacks economic data and criteria.

   2) A difference in *Grinnell* and the cellophane case, however, is that in all uses of cellophane, there were other materials available that could be substituted, and it would have been difficult for DuPont to differentiate

the product in order to charge one user one price (where there were no close substitutes) and another user another price (where there were close substitutes). But in *Grinnell*, personal services are involved. Each protection contract is individually contracted for and individually priced, and the price to any specific customer for whom there are not good substitutes is not protected against monopolistic prices by the existence of other users for the same service for which there are substitutes. If this is what *Grinnell* is saying, then the antitrust test is whether there are significant classes of users that are unprotected from monopoly power (due either to product differentiation or cost advantages). If so, then the relevant market will be defined in such a way as to extend protection to this submarket.

3) It has been suggested that if the defendant engages in monopolistic practices (as in *Grinnell*) to secure a monopoly over some type of submarket, then the court will not go deeply into the economic questions over whether there is monopoly power—it will simply infer that the business must have thought that power over this submarket carried with it sufficient power to make it worthwhile to acquire and maintain, and thus that there is a violation.

IV. COMPETITOR COLLABORATION ON PRICE FIXING AND DIVISION OF MARKETS

A. CONSPIRACY—IN THEORY AND ACTION

1. **Introduction.** A cartel is an association of companies that cooperate to eliminate competition among them through such methods as fixing prices and allocating production and territories.

2. **Factors Required for an Effective Cartel**—*Cartels: Organization and Functions* (McGee, 1960). It is no simple matter to organize an effective cartel. Consideration must be given to the following factors:

    a. Number of firms to be involved;

    b. Elasticity of demand for the product;

    c. Preventing or restricting entry into the industry by other firms;

    d. Policing the agreement so that there are no defectors;

    e. Determining the appropriate production amounts and prices to be charged; and

    f. Adjusting to market changes, such as changes in demand.

3. **Purpose of Cartels.** Cartels are set up for one purpose—to eliminate competition and thus to make more profit than would otherwise be the case. Arguments that prices charged in a cartelized industry are not unreasonable should be considered with caution.

    a. Cartels distort resource allocation by attempting to reduce the maximum amount of resources that would ordinarily be available to an industry.

    b. Typically, earnings of cartel members are not high, but this is not a good argument for supporting the cartel because:

        1) There may be inefficiencies of management;

        2) Earnings may be higher than with competition; and

        3) Data on return on investment is deceptive.

B. DEVELOPMENT OF THE "PER SE" RULE ON PRICE FIXING

1. **The Rule of Reason and the Rule of Per Se Illegality.** Only "unreasonable restraints" violate the antitrust laws. But that does not mean that every antitrust case requires a complicated and prolonged inquiry into

the economic context and actual effect of a challenged restraint. In *Addyston Pipe & Steel*, *supra*, the court said, and may have held, that where the challenged restraint had the purpose of raising the price of the defendants' products, the restraint was illegal regardless of the defendants' success or market power. Although this case does not use the "per se" language, it apparently adopts the rule that price-fixing agreements are per se unreasonable and thus illegal. Application of this rule can be rather tricky because "price fixing" turns out to be a term of art, signifying that the challenged restraint is illegal. Some express agreements among erstwhile rivals to set price are not "price fixing" (*see* Chicago Board of Trade, *infra*); some agreements that at least on the surface have nothing to do with price are "price fixing." Analysis is required before the challenged restraint can be properly characterized. What is not required under the "rule" of per se illegality is proof of market power or actual effect (although both may be relevant to proper characterization).

2. **The "Price-Fixing" Characterization--Chicago Board of Trade v. United States,** 246 U.S. 231 (1918).

    a. **Facts.** The Chicago Board of Trade (D) adopted a rule that, following the end of the session at which grain in transit to Chicago was traded, members could trade such grain only at the closing bid price. The Department of Justice (P) claimed that this "call rule" violated section 1. D alleged that the purpose of the rule was not to prevent competition or to control prices, but to promote the convenience of members by restricting their hours of business and to break up a monopoly in that branch of the grain trade acquired by four or five Chicago warehousemen. On P's motion, the court struck these allegations. After a trial, the district court enjoined the adoption and enforcement of the call rule. D appealed.

    b. **Issue.** Does the call rule, which for most of each day sets the price at which rival Board members will trade grain in transit to Chicago, violate section 1, regardless of its purpose?

    c. **Held.** No. The injunction is vacated, and the district court is directed to dismiss the complaint.

        1) Because the call rule set prices for only a small volume of the grain shipped to Chicago or traded on the Board, and set them for only a portion of each trading day, it had no appreciable effect on general market prices or the total volume of grain coming to Chicago.

        2) The rule had the effects claimed by D, and it helped promote an organized, efficient market in grain.

    d. **Comment.** The Court apparently concluded that the explicit price setting contemplated by the call rule was per se legal. It is not clear whether the Court reached this conclusion on the ground that the rule would not have the effect of making most Board members better off at the expense of their customers or on the ground that it would have this effect and that having this effect here is good. In other words, it is not clear whether the Court analyzed the rule in terms of consumer welfare or in terms of group welfare. The fact that the Court ordered the complaint dismissed instead of remanding suggests that the Court may have been analyzing the rule in terms of group welfare. In any event, how a restraint is characterized depends in part on an analysis of its likely effects and in part on the Court's understanding of the purpose of the antitrust laws. Note for future reference that the call rule could also be fairly characterized as a boycott.

3. **Antitrust and the Great Depression--Appalachian Coals, Inc. v. United States,** 288 U.S. 344 (1933).

   a. **Facts.** Cost of mining coal exceeded its selling price. One hundred thirty-seven producers in the Appalachian area formed an association (D) to sell their output. They produced 74% of the coal in the Appalachian area. The government (P) sought an injunction.

   b. **Issue.** Is price fixing in a distress situation legal?

   c. **Held.** Yes. No violation involved.

   1) The intent or purpose of the selling organization is not to fix prices; it is to increase sales.

   2) There is substantial competition remaining; the organization does not have a monopolistic position and thus cannot effectively affect price.

   d. **Comment.** The Court indicated that intent or purpose must be determined by reference to conditions in the industry. This case is thus probably a "Depression" case and may no longer be good law.

4. **Per Se Illegality--United States v. Socony-Vacuum Oil Co.,** 310 U.S. 150 (1940).

   a. **Facts.** Major oil companies (Ds) operating in the midwest states formed an organization to determine who would buy gasoline from independent producers (who were selling their gasoline at "distress" prices below production costs). Ds were integrated companies (producing, selling wholesale, and retailing); the price of their gasoline to jobbers depended on the prevailing market price of gasoline. They controlled 83% of the gasoline produced and bought the remaining 17% from the independents. Thus, by controlling the supply they were able to actually raise the price over a period of a couple of years. The price to retailers and consumers was directly dependent on the price to the jobbers. The district court found that Ds had violated the Sherman Act. The court of appeals held the jury charge to be reversible error, since it was based on the theory that such a combination was illegal per se.

b. **Issue.** Is this consent of action and agreement illegal per se?

c. **Held.** Yes. Judgment reversed.

1) By whatever means used to accomplish it, price fixing is illegal per se. It makes no difference that the arrangement is seeking to stabilize prices in a distressed industry. *Appalachian Coals* is distinguished in that the purpose there was not to fix prices (and in any event the association there was not actually operating at the time suit was brought).

2) It is sufficient if it can be shown (which it was) that the price rise would not have happened but for the combination's buying program. Furthermore, it need not be shown that competition was eliminated, only that a substantial part of commerce in the commodity is involved.

d. **Comment.** Note that this case may set up a requirement of actual effect on prices ***and*** that a substantial amount of commerce be involved. These requirements were met on the facts. In a footnote, however, Justice Douglas indicated that an illegal conspiracy could exist where in reality the combination had no actual power to affect prices (*i.e.*, no actual effect on prices need be shown). Furthermore, Douglas indicated that the amount of commerce involved was immaterial. Compare this with *Appalachian Coals*.

5. **Medical Association Agreements with Group Insurers--Arizona v. Maricopa County Medical Society,** 457 U.S. 332 (1982).

    a. **Facts.** Foundations for medical care (Ds), composed of licensed doctors, agreed in advance on the maximum price they would charge for services rendered to patients covered by certain insurers or employers. The doctor would be free to charge any covered patient less, and charge any noncovered patient any amount. The effect of this plan on prices generally was disputed. Ds alleged that the agreements were in fact procompetitive and resulted in lower prices. The court of appeals held that the actual purpose and effect of the agreement had to be evaluated at a full trial. The Supreme Court granted certiorari.

    b. **Issue.** Are Ds' practices illegal per se?

    c. **Held.** Yes. Judgment reversed.

    1) This is horizontal price fixing. The court has a long history of condemning the practice per se.

2) The fact that Ds are professionals is irrelevant. There is no argument that this restraint assures greater quality of service.

3) The fact that the arrangement may have some procompetitive consequences is of no moment where a per se violation is involved.

d. **Dissent** (Powell, J., Burger, C.J., Rehnquist, J.). While every "price fixing" agreement violates the law per se, not every arrangement affecting prices should be labeled as price fixing. The characterization involves looking at the entirety of the record and taking account, in a case like this, of the strongly procompetitive nature of the agreement. The agreement in question here was a medical cost containment device initiated by the patient's insurers. The Court should have permitted the scheme for the reasons articulated in *BMI*.

C. **CHARACTERIZATION QUESTIONS AND OTHER ISSUES**

1. **Blanket Copyright License Not a Per Se Violation--Broadcast Music, Inc. v. Columbia Broadcasting System, Inc.,** 441 U.S. 1 (1979).

    a. **Facts.** Columbia Broadcasting System (P) brought an antitrust action against Broadcast Music, Inc. ("BMI") and the American Society of Composers, Authors, and Publishers ("ASCAP") (Ds) due to Ds' issuance of blanket licenses. Ds are both societies that negotiate for their members nonexclusive licenses to use the members' works. (They have some 52,000 members.) Ds both evolved as performers sought to be paid for the use of their copyrighted materials. Owing to the number of performers involved, it was easier for each D, as an entity, to negotiate licenses of its members' materials than for each individual performer to negotiate a license with each user of his material. Ds issue licenses and distribute royalties to copyright owners in accordance with a schedule reflecting the nature and amount of use of their music (and other factors). Blanket licenses, setting forth a fee schedule, are issued to radio and television broadcasters, including P. P sued, contending that the issuance of blanket licenses at fees negotiated by Ds is price fixing, per se unlawful under antitrust laws. The district court dismissed P's complaint. The court of appeals held that the blanket licenses were price fixing, illegal per se. Ds appeal.

    b. **Issue.** Are Ds' blanket licenses illegal per se?

    c. **Held.** No. Judgment reversed and remanded for further findings.

    1) P and the court of appeals have interpreted "price fixing" to mean that potential competitors have simply "fixed" a "price."

This is incorrect. "Price fixing" describes certain ***illegal business conduct***. It is not always simple to define that type of business conduct.

2) In 1940 and again in 1950 (and as amended from time to time since then) court decrees have outlined the bounds within which ASCAP can function without violating antitrust laws. (BMI is similarly situated.) These decrees ***do not*** preclude P from dealing directly with performers. (P has a real alternative to dealing with Ds.) Taken as a whole, ASCAP is carefully scrutinized and regulated by the federal executive and the judiciary. Thus, this Court should not be hasty in finding a per se violation of the Sherman Act.

3) ASCAP involves thousands of users, thousands of copyright owners, and millions of compositions. A blanket license is a reasonable way to give a licensee the immediate right to any of millions of pieces. Thus the blanket license should not be held illegal without an examination. The case is remanded for further findings.

d. **Dissent** (Stevens, J.). I agree that ASCAP's blanket license is not a species of price fixing illegal per se, but this court now can and should decide if under the rule of reason, illegal price fixing is involved. I would hold that under that rule the blanket license is illegal. It is an all-or-none license whereby the licensee must pay a percentage of its advertising revenues for D's entire collection of compositions. Measures normally affecting price (*e.g.*, quality of product, quantity of product, etc.) are not taken into account by the blanket licenses. This is illegal economic discrimination.

e. **Comment.** The Supreme Court remanded the case for the district court to determine if, under the rule of reason, the blanket license agreement is illegal. On remand the court of appeals affirmed the district court's dismissal of the complaint.

2. **Horizontal Restraints Necessary--National Collegiate Athletic Association v. Board of Regents of University of Oklahoma,** 468 U.S. 85 (1984).

a. **Facts.** The National Collegiate Athletic Association (D) adopted a plan for the televising of football games involving its members. The purported objective of the plan was to minimize the adverse effects of live television upon football game attendance. Under the plan, ABC and CBS were permitted to telecast 14 games each. Each network was permitted to select games they desired to televise; once a first choice for any given date was made, that network had the exclusive right to submit a bid at a fixed price. The schools involved could not sell the TV rights to another network. The plan also created appearance requirements and limitations. The Board of Regents of the University of Oklahoma (P) and other uni-

[margin note: National Collegiate Athletic Association v. Board of Regents of University of Oklahoma]

versities formed the College Football Association ("CFA") to negotiate television appearances for football games outside of D's plan. D announced it would discipline any of its members that participated in the CFA arrangement. In response, P sued. The trial court found that D's plan had significant anticompetitive effects, including restricting the number of games televised and thus raising the price networks paid for rights. The court held D's plan a violation of the Sherman Act. The Supreme Court granted certiorari.

b. **Issue.** Is a plan by an organization of colleges to restrict negotiations between TV networks and member colleges for televising football games a per se violation of the Sherman Act?

c. **Held.** No. Judgment affirmed under the rule of reason.

1) Ordinarily, horizontal price fixing and output limitation are deemed illegal per se. The per se rule does not apply in this case, however, because the industry involved—college football games—requires horizontal restraints on competition in order to exist. The various colleges must agree to certain ground rules, including the rules of the game itself and player eligibility, in order to preserve the character and quality of the product. D is vital in this process as the means for obtaining the necessary mutual agreement. The rule of reason must be used to assess the competitive significance of the challenged restraint.

2) The trial court found that D's plan, by restraining price and output, had a significant anticompetitive effect. But for the plan, many more games would be televised, and at lower prices to the networks. The plan eliminates competitors from the market. D clearly has market power sufficient to cause these effects.

3) D claims that its plan is a joint venture such as BMI and ASCAP in the *Broadcast Music* case. While a joint venture that creates a new product may be permitted, D's plan does not create a new product; it merely provides for the sale of individual games in a noncompetitive market. The plan has no procompetitive efficiencies and is not necessary to enable D to penetrate the TV market. D's product is already unique.

4) D's plan does not protect live attendance because the televised games are shown at the same time as other games are being played. D's protection justification is actually a scheme to protect noncompetitive ticket sales by limiting output of more popular televised games—a typical monopolist tactic.

5) The restraints on TV rights are not similar to the other mutual agreements that make college football possible. The plan does not serve to equalize competition; it merely limits one of many sources of revenue. D's other rules are clearly sufficient to preserve competitive balance and

preserve amateurism. Thus, the plan cannot stand under the rule of reason.

3. **Spreading Financial Aid: Purported Purposes and Effects that May Trump Considerations of Efficiency--United States v. Brown University,** 5 F.3d 658 (3d Cir. 1993).

   a. **Facts.** In 1958, MIT and eight Ivy League schools organized the "Ivy Overlap Group." The group met annually to establish the methodology by which to measure a student's "need" for financial aid. Each school made its own calculation of each admitted student's "need." If, however, a student were admitted to more than one of the schools and the need figures diverged, representatives of the schools eliminated the divergence and agreed to offer the student no more aid than necessary to meet that "need." The United States (P) claimed that these practices constituted price fixing. All of the schools except MIT (D) consented to a judgment ordering them to discontinue these practices. D asserted that the challenged practices did not occur in "trade or commerce" and that they were legal. They were legal, D argued, because, by facilitating a more "effective" allocation of scholarship funds, the challenged practices enabled more "needy" students to attend elite schools and permitted the schools to admit a more "diverse" group of students; rather than reducing competition, the challenged practices simply required students to choose among elite schools on the basis of non-price factors. According to the district court, *Goldfarb v. Virginia State Bar* (in which the Supreme Court condemned lawyers' minimum fee schedules), taught that the challenged practices occurred in "trade or commerce" within the meaning of the Sherman Act, but it also taught that a court should hesitate before condemning the practices of a nonbusiness defendant as illegal per se. Giving the practices a "quick look" under the "rule of reason," the district court, citing *National Society of Professional Engineers v. United States*, held that the purported social purposes and effects of these practices could not trump considerations of economic efficiency. Thus, the district court condemned the challenged practices as unreasonable restraints of trade. D appealed.

   b. **Issue.** Do the purported benefits of the challenged practices—promoting socioeconomic diversity among students and improving "consumer choice" for those students who could not have gone to an Ivy League school without a scholarship—require more than a "quick look" under the "rule of reason?"

   c. **Held.** Yes. Case remanded.

      1) The Sherman Act applies to the exchange of money for services (payment of tuition for educational services), a quintessential commercial transaction, even when a nonprofit organization provides

the services. Regardless of the motive for providing financial aid, providing it permits D to compete for the top applicants.

2) The trial court should have given more weight to not-for-profit D's argument that the challenged practices promoted socioeconomic diversity among students and improved "consumer choice" for those students who could not have gone to an Ivy League school without a scholarship—an argument that could not have saved the practices condemned in *Professional Engineers* and *FTC v. Indiana Federation of Dentists*.

d. **Dissent.** The Sherman Act does not apply to the challenged practices, which are designed to provide high quality education to those with demonstrated academic talent without regard to financial status. The practices do not constitute untoward business dealings.

California Dental Association v. FTC

4. **Professional Trade Association's Advertising Restrictions--California Dental Association v. FTC,** 526 U.S. 756 (1999).

a. **Facts.** The California Dental Association (D), a voluntary nonprofit association of local dental societies to which some 19,000 dentists belong, about three-quarters of those practicing in the state, provides its members with preferential financing arrangements, marketing, lobbying, litigation, and insurance benefits. D promulgated a Code of Ethics that prohibited "misleading advertising." The code defined "misleading advertising" to include (i) statements describing fees as "low" or "reasonable" or providing specific price information, and (ii) claims relating to quality. Members of D obligated themselves to abide by the code. The FTC challenged the advertising restrictions as violations of section 5 of the FTC Act. Employing an abbreviated rule of reason analysis, the ALJ held that the D's advertising restrictions violated section 5. The Ninth Circuit affirmed. The Supreme Court granted certiorari.

b. **Issues.**

1) May the Commission exercise jurisdiction under the FTC Act over a not-for-profit association such as D?

2) Do the challenged advertising restrictions require more than "quick look" antitrust scrutiny?

c. **Held.** 1) Yes. 2) Yes. Judgment vacated and remanded.

1) The FTC Act does cover a membership organization that provides significant economic benefits to its members.

2) The challenged advertising restrictions require more than "quick look" antitrust scrutiny because of the difficulty of ascertaining their

impact on competition and the welfare of patients. A "quick look" or abbreviated rule of reason analysis is only appropriate if even an economically unskilled observer would readily conclude that the challenged actions would have an anticompetitive effect. The possible validity of D's proffered justification for the regulations as having a procompetitive effect by preventing market distortion through misleading advertising merit closer study. Due to the competing theories about the advertising restriction's possible effects, the obvious anticompetitive effects of the regulations necessary for application of the quick look rule of reason have not been established.

    d. **Dissent and concurrence** (Breyer, Stevens, Kennedy, Ginsburg, JJ.). The FTC correctly concluded that D's advertising restrictions constituted unreasonable restraints of trade.

D. DIVISION OF TERRITORIES AND SOME OTHER HORIZONTAL RESTRAINTS

    1. **Generally.** An agreement between rivals (a "horizontal" restraint) need not explicitly deal with price in order to merit antitrust scrutiny and perhaps condemnation. For example, an agreement setting production limits or allocating sales territories or customers could have the same effect. In some situations, rivals will find it far easier to reach and police this kind of agreement than one about price.

    2. **Allocating a Scarce Resource--National Association of Window Glass Manufacturers v. United States,** 263 U.S. 403 (1923).

        a. **Facts.** Hand-blown glass manufacturers faced rivalry from lower cost automated glass manufacturers and a dwindling supply of experienced glass blowers. The hand-blown glass manufacturers who were members of the Association (D) agreed that each would use the available skilled labor only during one-half of the production year (and shut down during the other half). The Department of Justice (P) claimed that this agreement constituted a contract to curtail production in violation of section 1. The district court found for P and enjoined the agreement. D appeals.

        b. **Issue.** Does the production schedule agreement violate section 1?

        c. **Held.** No. The injunction is vacated, and the district court is reversed.

            1) The purpose and most likely effect of this agreement was to secure employment to the available skilled labor for the whole of the production year while making it possible for each manu-

National Association of Window Glass Manufacturers v. United States

facturer of hand-blown glass to operate most cost-effectively when producing.

    2) The domination of the automated manufacturers makes it unlikely that this agreement will unreasonably restrain trade.

3. **Allocating Territories.** In some markets, an agreement between rivals to allocate territories will have the same effect as an agreement on prices. Moreover, such an agreement may serve a variety of purposes, many of which are not obviously inconsistent with the antitrust laws.

    a. **Applications.**

        1) **Timken Roller Bearing Co. v. United States.** In Timken Roller Bearing Co. v. United States, 341 U.S. 593 (1951), the Court condemned an agreement between Timken, British Timken, and French Timken (all controlled by the same owners), reached in connection with a license of the Timken trademark, to allocate sales territories among themselves and fix prices on products sold by one of them in the territory of the other. The companies also "cooperated to protect each other's markets and to eliminate competition, and participated in cartels to restrict imports to and exports from the United States." (It is not clear whether the Court would have reached the same result if the case had arisen today. Note, too, that Justice Jackson, dissenting, argued that the Timken agreement would permit manufacturers of Timken roller bearings to overcome a host of trade barriers worldwide and thereby increase rivalry in the roller bearing market.)

        2) **United States v. General Motors Corporation.** In United States v. General Motors Corporation, 384 U.S. 127 (1966), the Court condemned an agreement between GM and a group of its dealers to monitor and enforce, by termination if necessary, compliance with the location clause in the dealer franchise agreement. This agreement was aimed at dealers who sold cars through discounters.

        3) **United States v. Sealy Inc.** In United States v. Sealy Inc., 388 U.S. 350 (1967), the Court condemned an arrangement between 30 mattress manufacturers whereby they formed Sealy Corporation, and then had Sealy license each of them to use the Sealy trademark in their respective territories on the condition that retail prices on Sealy mattresses be maintained.

    b. **Comment.** Whether the agreements challenged in *General Motors* and *Sealy* should have been characterized as "horizontal" was a matter of considerable controversy. It is not clear whether these decisions completely survive the Court's later decisions in *Monsanto v. Spray-Rite* and *Business Electronics*, briefed *infra* in connection with vertical restraints.

4. **Allocating Territories in Connection with a Common Trademark--United States v. Topco Associates, Inc.,** 405 U.S. 596 (1972).

   a. **Facts.** Twenty-five small-to-medium-size food chains formed a buyer association (D) that had suppliers manufacture private label brands for the members. Sales of the members amounted to $2.3 billion, larger than all but three national grocery chains. Each member had from 1.5% to 6.0% of the market in its area; the private labels amounted to about 10% of the members' sales. D's rules provided that each member had a veto over new members joining (thus protecting each member's competitive geographic position) and that no member could sell the private brands except in the area where it was licensed by D. Also, permission of D had to be granted before a member could sell the private labels wholesale. (Although applied for, permission had never been granted.) The district court found no violation of section 1 of the Sherman Act, and entered judgment for D. The United States (P) appeals.

   b. **Issue.** Does a purchasing co-op with attendant territorial restraints violate the Sherman Act as a per se unlawful horizontal market division?

   c. **Held.** Yes. Judgment reversed.

      1) D argues that the arrangement enables members to compete with the larger chains by offering private brands like the chains do and that the restrictive provisions are necessary to make the private brand system work. However, courts cannot weigh the effects of destruction of competition in one sector of the economy against the benefits of promotion in another sector. Restrictions on territories and customers are per se unlawful.

   d. **Concurrence** (Blackmun, J.). This ruling will enable the big chains to get bigger and thus is at odds with the public interest. However, the per se rule is firmly established and any relief must be by way of legislation.

   e. **Dissent** (Burger, C.J.). The Court has never before held that market sharing agreements are per se illegal. This plan promotes competition. There should be no per se rule in situations where there is no price fixing, where only trademarked products are involved and there is no monopoly or near monopoly in the products involved.

   f. **Remand.** The lower court allowed D to continue granting areas of "primary responsibility" (where a member could be penalized for not adequately advertising and promoting the private brands), and allowing "passovers" (where a member sold in an area other than his primary territory, it had to pay a pro-rata share of the primary territory member's advertising and other promotional expenses).

General Leaseways Inc. v. National Truck Leasing Association

5. **Allocating Territories in Connection with Reciprocal Service Agreement--General Leaseways Inc. v. National Truck Leasing Association,** 744 F.2d 588 (7th Cir. 1984).

   a. **Facts.** When a truck leasing firm leases on a "full service" basis, it obliges itself to maintain and repair trucks at locations throughout the nation. Lacking nationwide service facilities, 130 small firms formed the National Truck Leasing Association (D) to establish a reciprocal service arrangement pursuant to which members promised to provide each other with prompt and efficient repair services at previously negotiated prices. In this manner, the members could better compete with national firms like Avis. As a condition of membership, each member accepted a franchise designating a particular location at which it could conduct its business and forbidding operations as a franchisee of D at any other location. For convenience in picking up trucks and facilitating regular maintenance, a business leasing a truck invariably deals with a firm having an outlet within a few miles of its establishment. D's policy was to space franchises at least 10 miles apart. Members could open up outlets at unauthorized locations, but then had to forgo reciprocal service. When General Leaseways (P) defied the location restriction, D sought to expel it. P claimed that the division of markets among members of D constituted a per se violation of section 1. The district court enjoined P's expulsion and enforcement of the location restriction pending trial on the merits. D appeals.

   b. **Issue.** Is it per se illegal for a league of truck leasing firms to divide the market among themselves in connection with an agreement whereby they provide service for each other's trucks at previously negotiated prices?

   c. **Held.** Yes. Order affirmed.

      1) The argument that D's market division prevents each member from taking a free ride on the services provided by the others in connection with D's nationwide truck leasing system is much weaker than the analogous argument made in *Sealy* and *Topco*. Members of D provide emergency repair service, not information, and they charge one another for it. Even if they charged each other less than market price, it is not at all clear that an expansion-minded member like P would gain anything at the expense of the others. Moreover, D has neither shown that its members do not charge remunerative prices nor explained why they do not.

      2) D's market division does not permit it to create and sell a distinctive product or to economize on transaction costs as the blanket license did for the members of ASCAP and BMI. (*See* Broadcast Music, *supra*.) There is no organic connection between the restraint and the cooperative needs of the enterprise that might render the

market division "ancillary." This practice "facially appears to be one that would always or almost always tend to restrict competition and decrease output."

d. **Comment.** What is perhaps most noteworthy about this opinion is the effort to justify the per se illegal conclusion instead of relying on *Sealy* and *Topco*. This effort suggests that subsequent Supreme Court opinions have undermined their authority.

6. **Allocating Territories by Withdrawing from a Market--Palmer v. BRG of Georgia, Inc.,** 498 U.S. 46 (1990).

   a. **Facts.** From 1976 to 1979, BRG and HBJ (Ds) each offered Georgia bar review courses. In 1980, Ds agreed that HBJ would not compete with BRG in Georgia and that BRG would not compete with HBJ outside of Georgia. HBJ granted BRG an exclusive license to market HBJ's material in Georgia and to use its trade name, "Bar/Bri," in return for $100 per student enrolled by BRG and 40% of all revenues over $350. Immediately thereafter, the price of BRG's bar review course increased from $150 to more than $400. A law student who contracted with BRG for the bar review course (P) claimed that the 1980 agreement constituted a per se offense under section 1 of the Sherman Act. The trial court granted Ds' motion for summary judgment on the grounds that (i) Ds had not agreed on the prices that they would charge or that they would consult about prices and (ii) Ds had not subdivided a relevant market in which they had competed. The Eleventh Circuit affirmed, and P appealed.

   b. **Issues.**

      1) To commit a per se price fixing offense, must erstwhile competitors agree on the prices that they will charge or that they will consult about prices?

      2) To commit a per se territorial allocation offense, must erstwhile competitors agree to divide a relevant market in which they had competed?

   c. **Held.** 1) No. 2) No. Judgment reversed and case remanded.

      1) The 1980 agreement coupling HBJ's withdrawal from the Georgia market and revenue sharing served to permit a dramatic price increase, the kind of harm the antitrust laws are designed to prevent.

      2) *United States v. Topco Associates, Inc.* teaches that agreements between competitors to allocate territories to minimize competition are illegal per se regardless of whether the agreement subdivides an existing territory or merely reserves specified markets.

Palmer v. BRG of Georgia, Inc.

Antitrust - 35

V. GROUP REFUSALS TO DEAL AND JOINT VENTURES

A. REFUSALS TO DEAL

1. **Generally.** Refusals to deal may serve a variety of purposes, both commercial and noncommercial. They may serve the purpose of enforcing a cartel arrangement by driving rivals from the market or deterring them from engaging in much rivalry.

2. **Refusals to Deal and Price Setting.** In *Montague & Co. v. Lowry*, 193 U.S. 38 (1904), a group of tile and fireplace fixture wholesalers in the San Francisco area and manufacturers of such products located in other states formed an association. Association bylaws prohibited buying from nonmember manufacturers and selling to nonmember wholesalers. The bylaws required that wholesaler members refrain from selling to nonmembers at anything less than "list" prices, which were about 50% higher than prices for members. Prior to the formation of the association, a San Francisco dealer had purchased tiles from manufacturers who were now members and now refused to sell at prices below list. The dealer claimed that this concerted refusal to deal violated section 1 of the Sherman Act. The Supreme Court found that when members of a trade association set a minimum price on sales to the public, their refusal to deal with a rival violates the antitrust laws.

3. **Refusals to Deal and Agreed Non-Price Terms.** In *Paramount Famous Lasky Corp. v. United States*, 282 U.S. 30 (1930), the Supreme Court condemned an agreement between 10 film producer/distributors, controlling 60% of the films produced in the United States, to use a standard contract with exhibitors. The contract provided that any dispute would go to arbitration and that, if the exhibitor failed to arbitrate or to obey an award, all 10 firms would (i) demand security for performance of their contracts with the exhibitor, and (ii) if security were not forthcoming, cancel these contracts.

4. **Group Boycott Per Se Illegal--Fashion Originators' Guild of America v. FTC,** 312 U.S. 457 (1941).

   a. **Facts.** Members of a textile manufacturer's association and members of a garment manufacturer's association joined together in the Fashion Originators' Guild of America (D). They agreed that they would not sell to retailers who sold "copies" of original designs of the members of the association. Together the association controlled a significant percentage of the garment business. D enforced the arrangement by patrolling the retail stores, and fined members of the association who violated its rules. In addition, D had other restrictive rules curtailing retail advertising, discounts, and selling of garments to retailers in homes. The FTC brought an action under section 5.

Fashion Originators' Guild of America v. FTC

b. **Issue.** Is the arrangement illegal and is D barred from arguing that its purpose was to prohibit allegedly tortious conduct?

c. **Held.** Yes. Findings by the FTC that the boycott violated section 5 are affirmed.

   1) Group boycotts are per se illegal. Competition is unreasonably restrained by limitations on outlets that manufacturers can sell to and limitation on sources from which retailers can buy.

   2) It makes no difference that the purpose of the boycott is to regulate practices that may be a tort under state law.

5. **Public Injury Not Required--Klor's, Inc. v. Broadway-Hale Stores, Inc.**, 359 U.S. 207 (1959).

   Klor's, Inc. v. Broadway-Hale Stores, Inc.

   a. **Facts.** Klor's (P) operated a small retail store in San Francisco, selling appliances. Broadway-Hale Stores, Inc. operated one of its chain stores next door, selling the same brands of appliances. Broadway-Hale Stores, Inc. and 10 national manufacturers of appliances (Ds) agreed that manufacturers would not sell to P or would sell only for higher prices. There were other competitors in the vicinity, so there was no showing that the public was injured by this group boycott. P brought an action for damages and an injunction. Ds were granted summary judgment by the district court. The court of appeals affirmed, and the Supreme Court granted certiorari.

   b. **Issue.** Is a boycott a violation even when the public is not harmed and the only injury is to the disadvantaged competitor?

   c. **Held.** Yes. Judgment reversed and remanded.

      1) It makes no difference that no public injury can be shown. A group boycott is per se illegal.

   d. **Comment.** Despite the Court's language in *Klor's*, concerted refusals to deal cannot be per se illegal. Without concerted refusals to deal, almost no form of cooperative enterprise would be possible. Recognizing this, the lower courts struggled with and resisted application of the per se rule. For example, in *Worthen Bank & Trust Co. v. National BankAmericard, Inc.*, 485 F.2d 119 (8th Cir. 1973), the court refused to apply it to the defendant's rule that member banks could not also be members of the Master Charge system. The defendant's rule, according to the court, promoted competition between charge card systems. Cases involving league sports pose much the same dilemma. Perhaps the most challenging cases have been those involving arguably noncommercial boycotts.

Antitrust - 37

NYNEX Corp. v. Discon, Inc.

6. **Single Buyer Boycott--NYNEX Corp. v. Discon, Inc.,** 525 U.S. 128 (1998).

   a. **Facts.** To provide long distance carriers with access to the "baby Bells" telephone networks—as required by the 1984 AT&T divestiture decree—the "baby Bells" had to install new switching equipment. Discon (P) removed some old equipment for New York Telephone, a subsidiary of NYNEX (D) and the largest buyer of removal services in New York, until Material Enterprises, another NYNEX subsidiary, switched its purchases of these services to the only competitor then operating in New York. According to P, the competitor charged more than P, but Material Enterprises passed the higher prices on to New York Telephone who passed them on to its telephone customers in the form of higher regulatory-agency-approved rates. At the end of the year, according to P, the competitor provided a rebate that Material Enterprises shared with its parent, D. P claimed that this conduct on the part of D constituted a per se antitrust offense. The district court dismissed P's complaint for failure to state a claim. The court of appeals reversed in part. The Supreme Court granted certiorari.

   b. **Issue.** Does a buyer commit a per se offense by purchasing from one supplier instead of another without a legitimate business justification?

   c. **Held.** No. Judgment vacated and case remanded. To prove an antitrust offense, the disfavored seller would have to allege and prove harm to competition itself.

      1) Unlike the challenged practices in *Fashion Originators' Guild of America v. FTC* (*supra*), which involved an agreement between a group of competitors, and *Klor's Inc. v. Broadway-Hale Stores, Inc.* (*supra*), which involved a number of appliance suppliers, D's contract with P's competitor has no horizontal component. Thus, the contract does not constitute a per se offense unless it includes some agreement on price or price levels.

      2) If D's telephone customers suffered harm, it flowed from the unchecked exercise of D's lawful market power.

      3) The prospect of switching suppliers stimulates competition, and applying per se scrutiny to switching would greatly discourage it.

      4) The law of unfair competition and business torts as well as regulation provide remedies for the kind of behavior to which P objects.

      5) D's alleged bad faith motive does not transform D's actions into an antitrust offense. Even an act of pure malice by one business competitor against another does not, without more, state a claim under the federal antitrust laws.

7. **Use of Standard to Boycott--Radiant Burners, Inc. v. Peoples Gas Light & Coke Co.,** 364 U.S. 656 (1961).

   a. **Facts.** Radiant Burners, Inc. (P) is a manufacturer in Illinois of radiant heaters, using gas. The American Gas Association (D) operated testing labs to determine the safety and utility of gas burners, affixing a seal of approval on those that met its standards. D was made up of gas companies and also companies making such burners. P submitted its burner for approval, but was rejected. P brought suit and argued that the rejection was arbitrary in that the heater was better than its competitors. Since it could not get approval, gas companies would not supply gas to people owning P's heater. The district court granted summary judgment for D, and the court of appeals affirmed. The Supreme Court granted certiorari.

   b. **Issue.** Is the use of quality standards to arbitrarily exclude a competitor a violation of the Sherman Act?

   c. **Held.** Yes. Judgment reversed.

   d. **Comment.** In *Structural Laminates, Inc. v. Douglas Fir Plywood Association*, 261 F. Supp. 154 (D. Or. 1966), the court held that a standard-setting trade association did not violate the antitrust laws when a good faith delay in testing a product and changing a standard allegedly caused the plaintiff in that case to go bankrupt.

8. **Exclusion from Cooperative Wholesale Distributor--Northwest Wholesale Stationers, Inc. v. Pacific Stationery & Printing Co.,** 472 U.S. 284 (1985).

   a. **Facts.** Pacific Stationery & Printing Company (P), which was engaged in both retail and wholesale sales of office supplies, was a member of Northwest Wholesale Stationers, Inc. (D), a cooperative that acted as a wholesaler for its nearly 100 office supply retailer members. D adopted a rule that prohibited members from engaging in both retail and wholesale, but it permitted P to continue as a member. P's owners sold the controlling stock in the company. The new owners, in violation of a cooperative bylaw, did not notify D. Subsequently, D expelled P without notice. P sued, claiming the expulsion was a group boycott. D's wholesale operation sold to all retailers, whether members or not, but it distributed its profits through a rebate to members based on their purchases. P claimed that its expulsion limited its competitive position. The trial court granted summary judgment for D, finding no anticompetitive effect. The court of appeals reversed, holding that the expulsion was an anticompetitive concerted refusal to deal with P. Although section 4 of the Robinson-Patman Act permits price discrimination resulting from an expulsion brought about through self-regulation, the court held that under *Silver v. New York Stock Exchange*, 373 U.S. 341 (1963), D had a duty to provide

Antitrust - 39

procedural safeguards to claim the protection of Robinson-Patman. D appeals.

b. **Issue.** Does the per se rule apply to a cooperative wholesaler's exclusion of one of its members, absent a showing that the wholesaler had market power or unique access to a business element necessary for effective competition?

c. **Held.** No. Judgment reversed.

1) Concerted refusals to deal or group boycotts have long been held to be per se violations of the Sherman Act. The court of appeals, however, held that D could find relief in the Robinson-Patman Act, and then relied on *Silver* to require D to provide adequate procedural safeguards.

2) The Robinson-Patman Act is different from the Securities Exchange Act under which *Silver* was decided. Section 4 of the Robinson-Patman Act is merely an immunity from the price discrimination prohibitions of the Act itself; it is not a broad mandate for industry self-regulation. In addition, procedural protection cannot save a concerted activity that amounts to a per se violation of the Sherman Act.

3) Group boycotts that are per se illegal generally consist of joint efforts by firms to disadvantage competitors by denying, or persuading or coercing others to deny, relationships the competitors need in the competitive struggle. However, not every cooperative activity involving a restraint or exclusion is illegal. It depends on whether the particular form of concerted activity characteristically is likely to result in predominantly anticompetitive effects.

4) D's activity was intended to increase economic efficiency and make the market more competitive by giving the retailers cost savings and inventory; it was not likely to result in anticompetitive effects. P does not challenge D's existence, but only P's exclusion from D. But D has to have some rules to govern its membership. The expulsion was not likely to result in predominantly anticompetitive effects because there was no showing that D possesses market power or exclusive access to an element essential to effective competition; therefore, the per se rule does not apply. On remand, the court of appeals must evaluate the trial court's rule of reason analysis.

FTC v. Indiana Federation of Dentists

9. **Concerted Refusal to Provide Information--FTC v. Indiana Federation of Dentists,** 476 U.S. 447 (1986).

a. **Facts.** As a means of containing the cost of dental treatment, insurers required dentists to submit dental x-rays with insurance claim forms to permit review of the diagnosis and treatment. The Indiana Dental Association succeeded in getting its members to refuse to submit the x-rays, but the Federal Trade Commission (P) ordered it to cease these efforts. In response, the Indiana Federation of Dentists (D) was formed to continue resistance to the x-ray submission requirements of insurers. In certain cities, D persuaded the majority of dentists to refuse to submit x-rays. P found that D's practice violated section 5 of the FTC Act. The court of appeals vacated the order as not being supported by substantial evidence. P appeals.

b. **Issue.** Is it a violation of section 5 of the FTC Act for professionals to agree among themselves not to provide information required by insurers to monitor the quality of care?

c. **Held.** Yes. Judgment reversed.

1) P found that in the absence of concerted behavior, individual dentists would have had incentives to comply with the insurers' request to respond to competition. The effect of D's activity was to deny the information the customers requested in the form they requested it, forcing them to choose between forgoing the information or acquiring it through more expensive means. D restrained competition among dentists with respect to cooperation with insurers.

2) Because D's activity consists of a concerted refusal to deal on particular terms with insured patients, it resembles a group boycott. Group boycotts have been deemed unlawful per se, but that approach has been limited to cases involving the use of market power to discourage suppliers or customers from doing business with a competitor. This is not the case here. Thus, the rule of reason should apply.

3) D's refusal to compete with respect to the services provided to customers has much the same effect as a refusal to compete with respect to price; it impairs the market's ability to ensure that goods and services are provided at a price approximating the marginal cost of providing them. Under the rule of reason, the restraint cannot be upheld unless it has some countervailing procompetitive virtue. D's policy lacks such a virtue.

4) D claims that because P did not make specific findings about the definition of the relevant market, it could not properly conclude that D unreasonably restrained trade. However, P made findings that D's activity actually did have an adverse effect on competition in two specific cities, so there was no need for further proof of market power. Nor was P required to prove that D's activity made dental services more costly; the withholding of information desired to evaluate the cost-effectiveness of a particular purchase of services is likely to disrupt the proper functioning of the price-setting market mechanism.

5) D also claims that the x-rays, by themselves, provide inadequate information to diagnose dental problems, so that if insurers rely on the x-rays, they may decline to pay for needed treatment to the detriment of the patients. This argument is really a claim that customer access to this information will lead them to make unwise or dangerous choices. This same argument has already been rejected.

10. **Restraint Ancillary to Economic Integration--Rothery Storage and Van Co. v. Atlas Van Lines,** 792 F.2d 210 (D.C. Cir. 1986).

    a. **Facts.** Like most nationwide common carriers of household goods, Atlas Van Lines (D) employed independent moving companies throughout the country as its agents to find customers and handle packing, loading, hauling, and storage. D set the rates for shipment, chose routes, arranged back-hauls, collected revenues, and paid agents for their services. It also conducted national advertising, established uniform rules for appearance and quality, maintained insurance, and handled claims. In 1982, D announced that it would terminate agency arrangements with any affiliated company that handled interstate carriage on its own account as well as for D. Agent carriers could compete in the interstate market by setting up separate corporations with new names, but could not use the facilities or services of D. At the time, D's share of the national market for interstate van lines was 5.86%. The top 15 firms accounted for less than 70%. Some carrier agents challenged D's policy as a group boycott illegal per se.

    b. **Issue.** Was the challenged restraint illegal per se?

    c. **Held.** No.

        1) The challenged restraint was ancillary to the economic integration of D's enterprise. It responds to the problem of agent carriers taking a free ride on D's name and investments.

        2) The challenged restraint could not restrict output because D's share of the market was far too small to have any such effect.

    d. **Concurrence.** The challenged restraint appears to enhance the efficiency of the van lines, more than compensating for any Sherman Act evils. Balancing is required, despite D's small market share, because the Sherman Act evils include more than a decrease in output and a rise in price.

11. **Refusal to Deal Coupled with Expressive Content--FTC v. Superior Court Trial Lawyers Association,** 493 U.S. 411 (1990).

    a. **Facts.** A group of private Washington, D.C. lawyers—all members of the Superior Court Trial Lawyers Association (D)—who regularly undertook appointments to represent indigent criminal defendants agreed that they would refuse such appointments unless the D.C. city government increased their pay. D publicized the lawyers' actions and secured the support of the press and the public. Faced with the imminent collapse of the criminal justice system, the government negotiated a modest fee increase. The FTC (P) charged D with conspiring to fix prices and conduct a boycott in violation of section 5. P found a per se violation. The court of appeals remanded, holding that such boycotts intended to convey a political message to the public should not be condemned unless there was a serious risk of competitive harm, which required an assessment of D's market power.

b. **Issue.** Is a concerted refusal to deal while seeking higher pay illegal per se if it includes an expressive component like the one involved in this case?

c. **Held.** Yes. The appeals court judgment is reversed and the FTC's ruling is reinstated.

   1) Because this concerted refusal to deal was designed to increase the price of the services sold by the actors, it is illegal per se. The per se rule economizes on judicial resources. It avoids the necessity of a complicated and prolonged investigation into the history of the industry involved, as well as related industries, in an effort to determine whether a particular restraint has been unreasonable. If small parties were allowed to prove lack of market power as a defense, all parties would have that right, thus introducing the enormous complexities of market definition into every price-fixing case.

   2) Every concerted refusal to do business with someone includes an expressive component analogous to the one included here. There is nothing unique or specially protected about this boycott or its expressive component. Creating an exception for it would create a gaping hole in the fabric of antitrust laws.

   3) Application of the per se rule to boycotts like this, regardless of the actors' market power, reduces the risk that such boycotts will cause antitrust injury.

   4) The impact on D's boycott of the D.C. government shows that D had the power to cause antitrust injury.

d. **Dissent** (Brennan, Blackmun, Marshall, JJ.). An expressive boycott that operates on a political, rather than economic level, should not be condemned under a per se rule. Historically, such boycotts have been essential to the "poorly financed causes of little people" who often cannot use established organizational techniques to advance their political interests.

B. JOINT VENTURES REVISITED—ISSUES OF MEMBERSHIP AND ACCESS

1. **Generally.** Joint venture agreements may result in the exclusion of competitors from access to the jointly created new product, technology, or facility. Such agreements might then be characterized as boycotts or concerted refusals to deal. Whether they should be treated similarly under the antitrust laws is the subject of this section.

2. **Mandatory Access--United States v. Terminal Railroad Association,** 224 U.S. 383 (1912).

    a. **Facts.** Twenty-four railroads terminated at the banks of the Mississippi River near St. Louis. Available space for terminal facilities was limited on the west bank; the Terminal Railroad Association (D) bought up all of the terminals and shared the facilities among its 14 members, refusing to allow other railroads to join. There was no evidence that exorbitant prices were charged.

    b. **Issue.** May the use of facilities be denied to competitors where the facilities are available and competitors have no alternative?

    c. **Held.** No.

      1) It is no defense that prices were reasonable. The association must allow other railroads to join and reasonable prices must be charged.

3. **Where Competing Services Are Available--Associated Press v. United States,** 326 U.S. 1 (1945).

    a. **Facts.** More than 1,200 newspapers subscribed to the Associated Press (D). According to the bylaws, members agreed to be bound by its rules, and violations were enforced by heavy fines. No member could sell news from its own area to nonmembers or make news supplied by D available to nonmembers in advance of publication. New members could not be admitted without a majority vote of the members and meeting other requirements, depending on whether the applicant was in competition with an existing member. The United States (P) brought an action under sections 1 and 2 of the Sherman Act. Ps motion for summary judgment was granted. Both sides appeal.

    b. **Issue.** Is it unlawful to deny access or severely limit it where alternatives are available?

    c. **Held.** Yes. Judgment affirmed.

1) D limited opportunity for any newspaper to enter competition where there was already an Associated Press member.

2) Independent associates have become associates in a common plan to reduce competition. This is an unreasonable combination, which might be used to achieve victory over nonmember firms.

3) It makes no difference that there are other news services; members control 96% of the circulation of morning papers. But even if nonmembers can still compete, this is a violation.

4) It is not required that the product or service be indispensable in order to compete.

5) D may continue; but membership cannot be unreasonably restricted.

4. **Reasonable Exclusion of Competitor from Joint Venture--SCFC ILC, Inc. v. Visa USA, Inc.,** 36 F.3d 958 (10th Cir. 1994).

   a. **Facts.** Visa USA (D) provides credit card payment services to its member banks and other issuers of Visa credit cards. Four other firms compete with D's system: MasterCard, American Express, CitiBank (Diners Club and Carte Blanche), and Sears (Discover Card) (P). CitiBank and P are also credit card issuers. In terms of charge volume, they ranked first and second, although the issuer market is remarkably unconcentrated, with issuers offering a wide range of interest rates and terms. Anyone capable of obtaining FDIC insurance could become a Visa member until 1988 when, faced with an application by a bank owned by P, D adopted a bylaw prohibiting membership by anyone directly or indirectly issuing Discover, American Express, or other competing cards. In 1990, P (doing business as SCFC ILC), acquired a bank that issued Visa cards. D refused to print cards for the bank and caused the bank to lose its membership, citing its bylaw provision. P brought suit claiming that D's conduct constituted an unlawful restraint of trade. A jury returned a verdict for P, the trial judge denied D's motion for JNOV, and D appeals.

   b. **Issue.** Does refusing membership to a current competitor unlawfully restrain trade?

   c. **Held.** No. Judgment reversed.

   1) Joint ventures like this one do not warrant per se condemnation because their integrated operations may well achieve efficiency and result in expanded output.

   2) The parties stipulated that the relevant market was general purpose charge cards in the United States. P was the largest issuer of credit cards next to Citicorp in terms of charge volume. D lacked market

power so its exclusion of P was unlikely to cause consumers to suffer any harm. In fact, P had competed successfully with D, and its exclusion from D did not bar it from the market. No evidence suggested that P could introduce a new card ["Prime Option"] only with D's help or that D's exclusion of P disabled P from developing its new card under the Discover mantle.

3) The exclusionary bylaw was necessary to prevent others from free riding on D's investment.

d. **Comment.** Note the extraordinarily far-reaching last paragraph of this opinion:

> Given Visa USA's justification [of] the bylaw [as] necessary to prevent free-riding in a market in which there was no evidence price was raised or output decreased or Sears needed Visa USA to develop the new card, we are left with a vast sea of commercial policy into which Sears would have us wade. To impose liability on Visa USA for refusing to admit Sears or revise the bylaw to open its membership to intersystem rivals, we think, sucks the judiciary into an economic riptide of contrived market forces. Whatever currents Sears imagines Visa USA has wrongly created, we believe can be better corrected by the marketplace itself. The Sherman Act ultimately must protect competition, not a competitor, and were we tempted to collapse the distinction, we would distort its continuing viability to safeguard consumer welfare. . . .

5. **Other Examples.** In *United States v. Realty Multi-List, Inc.*, 629 F.2d 1351 (5th Cir. 1980), the court declined to condemn as per se illegal bylaws of a real estate multiple listing service that barred members from giving nonmembers access to pooled information and required that prospective members (i) have a favorable credit report and business reputation, (ii) maintain a real estate office open during customary business hours, and (iii) pay an initiation fee unrelated to start up costs and a pro rata contribution toward maintenance and development of the list. After concluding that the service had market power and that membership was a competitive advantage and perhaps a necessity, the court held that the bylaws were not "fair" and thus ran afoul of the rule of reason. In *In re Tysons Corner Regional Shopping Center*, Antitrust & Trade Reg. Rep. No. 722, p. E-1 (FTC 1975), the FTC condemned as illegal per se lease clauses that gave to an anchor tenant of a major shopping center a blanket veto over would-be tenants.

6. **Research Joint Ventures.**

   a. **The National Cooperative Research Act of 1984.** Congress enacted a statute to facilitate joint research and development. [15 U.S.C. §4301]

The Act applies the rule of reason to joint research and development ventures, and provides for only actual, not treble, damages if a venture filed with the FTC and Justice Department proves illegal.

b. **Department of Justice guidelines.** The Justice Department's 1980 guidelines acknowledge that much research may be engaged in without violating the antitrust laws.

c. **Patent pool business review letter.** In connection with a proposed patent pool of manufacturers of DVDs and DVD-ROMs the Department of Justice's (DOJ's) Antitrust Division issued an instructive business review letter in 1999.

   1) **The proposed patent pool.** On behalf of the licensors, Toshiba would assemble and offer a package license of more than 100 patents "essential" to manufacturing products in compliance with the DVD-ROM and DVD-Video formats. The licensors would promise to license each other and third parties to make, use, and sell DVD products under "essential" future patents as well.

   2) **"Essential" patents.** A patent would qualify as "essential" if it is "necessarily infringed," or "there is no realistic alternative" to it, in implementing the DVD standard specifications. At the outset, each licensor would identify its own "essential" patents; afterwards an expert individual or panel, with "full and sufficient knowledge and skill in the relevant technology," would review the patents each licensor had designated to determine whether they satisfied the criteria set forth in the agreement. If a patent were then deemed not "essential," it would be excluded from subsequent DVD patent licenses, although current licensees would have the option to retain it in their existing licenses.

   3) **DOJ's analysis.** The DOJ discussed the benefits of a patent pool, *i.e.*, integrating complementary technologies, reducing transaction costs, clearing blocking positions, and avoiding costly infringement litigation, while at the same time acknowledging that some patent pools can restrict competition. Limiting the pool here to patents essential to compliance with the standard specifications, which by definition have no substitutes, would ensure that the pool would integrate only complementary patent rights patents. As a result, rivalry would not be foreclosed among patents within the pool nor between patents in the pool and patents outside it. The DOJ gave three reasons why the proposed agreement was not likely to impede competition in "downstream" markets, such as the manufacture of DVD discs and players or the creation of content that is incorporated in DVD discs: (i) the relatively small size of the agreed royalty compared to the total costs of manufacture reduced the likelihood that it would enable collusion among sellers of DVD discs, decoders, or players; (ii) the agreement would enhance, not limit, access to the licensors' "essential" patents; and (iii) Toshiba would probably not have access to "com-

petitively sensitive proprietary information, such as cost data." No facet of the proposed program would facilitate collusion or dampen competition among the licensors in the creation of content for software. Finally, that the proposed agreement covered "essential" future patents may yield both procompetitive and anticompetitive effects. On the "pro" side, this not only reduces transaction costs but ensures that "no party to the pool will be able to benefit from the pool while blocking other parties from utilizing the Standard Specifications." On the "anti" side, this might reduce the parties' incentives to innovate.

7. **Competitor Collaboration Guidelines.** The Competitor Collaboration Guidelines purport to set forth the antitrust enforcement agencies' analytical approach to horizontal collaborations. The Guidelines highlight six factors that bear on the ability and incentive of the participants in a competitor collaboration to compete or to collude: (i) the extent to which the relevant agreement is nonexclusive in that participants are likely to continue to compete independently outside the collaboration in the market in which the collaboration operates; (ii) the extent to which the participants retain independent control of the assets necessary to compete; (iii) the nature and extent of the participants' financial interests in the collaboration or in each other; (iv) the control of the collaboration's competitively significant decisionmaking; (v) the likelihood of anticompetitive information sharing; and (vi) the duration of the collaboration. [Competitor Collaboration Guidelines, §3.34] The Guidelines do not expressly take into account the prospect that a competitor collaboration might foreclose or limit competition by rivals not participating in a collaboration; nor do the guidelines address the possible anticompetitive effects of standard setting. The agencies do, however, reserve the right to take appropriate actions if they observe such effects.

C. EFFORTS TO INFLUENCE GOVERNMENT ACTION

1. **What's at Stake.** Firms frequently seek government action that will deter or reduce rivalry. They may seek such action in a variety of ways, including lobbying, public relations campaigns, participating in administrative proceedings, and litigating. These techniques may be quite effective, for they hold out the promise of imposing more costs on rivals and potential rivals than on the firms engaging in them. Condemning all such conduct, however, would create its own severe problems.

Eastern Railroad Presidents Conference v. Noerr Motor Freight Co.

2. **Immunity--Eastern Railroad Presidents Conference v. Noerr Motor Freight Co.,** 365 U.S. 127 (1961).

   a. **Facts.** A group of railroads (Ds) hired a public relations firm (D) to conduct a publicity campaign against truckers designed to foster the adoption and retention of laws and law enforcement practices destructive of the trucking business. The public relations firm conducted the campaign in such a way as to suggest that the sentiments expressed were coming from sources other than Ds. Ds allegedly succeeded in persuading Pennsylvania's governor to veto the "Fair Truck Bill," which would have permitted truckers to carry heavier loads over Pennsylvania roads. In response, the truckers engaged in a similar public relations campaign. A group of truckers (Ps) challenged Ds' campaign as an antitrust offense, and in a cross-claim, Ds similarly challenged Ps' campaign. The district court awarded treble damages to Ps and effectively enjoined Ds from any publicity activities against the truckers.

b. **Issue.** Does a group of firms violate the antitrust laws when it engages in a public relations campaign to influence public opinion and secure government action for the purpose of harming competitors, while deliberately disguising the sponsorship of the campaign?

c. **Held.** No. Judgment reversed.

1) Merely attempting to influence legislation and law enforcement does not violate the antitrust laws. To hold otherwise would substantially impair the power of government to take actions through its legislature and executive to restrain trade because it would deter people from informing and petitioning their representatives. This might run afoul of the Constitution.

2) That Ds' purpose was to destroy the truckers as competitors for the long distance freight business does not transform otherwise lawful conduct into an antitrust offense. Such selfish purposes typically motivate efforts to influence legislation and law enforcement. Thus, making purpose determinative would have much the same undesirable consequences as holding that such efforts themselves violated the antitrust laws.

3) That Ds deliberately disguised the sponsorship of their public relations campaign does not render it an antitrust offense. The Sherman Act does not and should not create a code of ethics for such political activities.

4) Ds' campaign does not constitute an antitrust offense merely because the campaign itself—apart from any legislative or executive action the campaign might have secured—may have hurt Ps' business and Ds may have desired this effect. Such effects could and often do attend any effort to secure government action. If a public relations campaign was a mere sham to cover what was nothing more than an attempt to interfere directly with the business relationships of a competitor, the Sherman Act would apply. But here Ds were making a genuine effort to influence legislation and law enforcement practices.

d. **Comment.** *Noerr* makes it clear that pretextual public relations campaigns fall within the sham exception. What it does not make clear is what other activities, if any, fall within the exception.

3. **The Sham Exception.** In *California Motor Transport Co. v. Trucking Unlimited*, 404 U.S. 508 (1972), one group of truckers claimed that another such group had violated the antitrust laws by instituting agency proceedings and lawsuits to delay and defeat applications for competitive operating rights. The defendants invoked *Noerr*. The Supreme Court observed that while *Noerr* involved attempts to influence legislation and law enforcement, "the same philosophy governs the approach of citizens or groups of them to administrative agencies . . . and to courts." Under the sham exception, however, asserted the Court, immunity does not extend to legal actions designed to "harass and deter the plaintiffs in their use of administrative and judicial proceedings." In this case, according to the Court, the defendants were not seeking to influence public officials but rather "to bar their competitors from meaningful access to adjudicatory tribunals and to usurp the decisionmaking process." The Court observed that in the adjudicatory process unethical conduct is often treated differently than it is in a political campaign. *California Motor Transport* may raise more questions than it answers. Does the application of the sham exception turn on the forum? On the nature of the conduct? In *Woods Exploration and Producing Co. v. Aluminum Co. of America*, 438 F.2d 1286 (5th Cir. 1971), *cert. denied*, 404 U.S. 1047 (1972), the court held that the exception did not apply where competitive injury occurred because of false production forecasts filed by defendants with the Texas Railroad Commission. Could a series of non-pretextual lawsuits run afoul of the antitrust laws? If the lawyers for those filing the suit think that they will probably lose? If those filing the suit would not have done so except for the expected impact on rivals? Could a single lawsuit run afoul of the antitrust laws?

Allied Tube & Conduit Corp. v. Indian Head, Inc.

4. **Follow-up to *Noerr*--Allied Tube & Conduit Corp. v. Indian Head, Inc.,** 486 U.S. 492 (1988).

    a. **Facts.** The National Fire Protection Association ("NFPA"), a private organization, publishes fire protection codes. Its National Electrical Code encompasses standards for the design and installation of electrical wiring systems. A substantial number of state and local governments routinely adopt the code with little or no change. Nonconforming products are normally shunned by private certification labs and many electrical inspectors, contractors, and distributors. Many underwriters refuse to insure nonconforming structures. When Indian Head, Inc. (P) began producing plastic conduit, the code permitted the use of steel electric conduit. P sought code approval for its conduit. Fearing the competitive threat posed by plastic conduit's advantages, Allied Tube & Conduit Corp. (D) organized the nation's other steel conduit producers to block code approval by packing the NFPA annual meeting at which the members would vote on P's product. (D cited plausible but unsubstantiated concerns about toxic fumes in its public statement.) P appealed to the board of directors, but the board denied the appeal on the ground that while D had circumvented NFPA rules, it had not violated them. P sued alleging that D and its allies had violated section 1. Instructed that P bore the burden of showing that the anticompetitive effects of D's conduct outweighed any procompetitive benefits of standard setting, the jury found for P. It specially found that D's conduct was not the least restrictive means of expressing opposition to P's product. The jury awarded damages for lost profits resulting from the effect that excluding P's product from the code had of its own force (as opposed to its adoption by governments). The court granted judgment n.o.v. for D, invoking *Noerr*. The appeals court reversed, and the Supreme Court granted certiorari.

b. **Issue.** Does an economically interested party who exercises decisionmaking authority in formulating a product standard for a private association that comprises market participants enjoy *Noerr* immunity for the effect the standard has of its own force in the market?

c. **Held.** No. The appeals court judgment is affirmed.

1) The applicability of *Noerr* "varies with the context and nature of the activity." NFPA is a private body that should not be treated as "quasi-legislative" simply because legislatures routinely adopt its code. It enjoys no official authority, and its decisionmaking body is composed, at least in part, of persons with economic incentives to restrain trade.

2) In this context, *Noerr* does not protect rounding up economically interested persons to set standards. The context and nature of this conduct make it the type of commercial activity traditionally scrutinized under the antitrust laws. The conduct did not take place in the open political arena where partisanship is the hallmark of decisionmaking. The antitrust laws permit standard setting by groups like D on the understanding that the process will be run in a nonpartisan manner offering procompetitive benefits.

3) D did not confine itself to efforts to persuade an independent decisionmaker, but rather organized and orchestrated the actual exercise of NFPA's decisionmaking authority. This amounts to an exercise of market power; an agreement to exclude P's product from the code is in effect an agreement not to trade in it.

4) Lack of *Noerr* immunity will not deprive the government of input and information from interested individuals or organizations because they can still engage in direct lobbying, publicity campaigns, and other traditional avenues of political expression, and they can still present and vigorously argue accurate scientific evidence before a nonpartisan private standard-setting body.

d. **Dissent** (White, O'Connor, JJ.). Since D's conduct constituted a genuine and successful effort to influence government action through the standard-setting process, *Noerr* protects it, regardless of D's motivation. Permitting D's motivation to count in some "contexts" and with respect to some conduct creates

Massachusetts School of Law at Andover, Inc. v. American Bar Association

substantial uncertainty that will tax judicial resources and tend to deter those with experience and expertise from participating in the process.

5. **Law School Accreditation and State Bar Exams--Massachusetts School of Law at Andover, Inc. v. American Bar Association,** 107 F.3d 1026 (1997).

   a. **Facts.** Beginning in 1921, the American Bar Association ("ABA") developed standards of accreditation for legal education programs and petitioned state supreme courts to rely on its accreditation decisions in connection with bar admission decisions. Now, all 50 states and the District of Columbia consider graduation from an ABA-accredited law school sufficient for the legal education requirement of bar admission. Many states permit an applicant to satisfy this requirement in other ways, such as legal apprenticeship, practice in another state, or graduation from a school approved by a state agency or the American Association of Law Schools ("AALS"), and each state authorizes its bar admission authority to waive its rules.

   Massachusetts School of Law (P) won a waiver of New Hampshire's rules to allow its graduates to take the bar examination in 1995, and has filed petitions seeking similar relief in Connecticut, Maine, New York, and Rhode Island. Maryland and Washington, D.C. have granted petitions of graduates of P to take the bar examination. P graduates can take the bar examination immediately after graduation in California, Massachusetts, New Hampshire, Vermont, and West Virginia, and in 12 other states after practicing in another state first. P applied for provisional ABA accreditation during the fall of 1992, seeking a waiver from the ABA's accreditation standards with which P never intended to comply. The ABA denied the waiver.

   Subsequently, P brought suit under the Sherman Act alleging that the ABA, AALS, Law School Admissions Council ("LSAC")—which refused to allow P to participate in its student recruiting conferences, and 22 other individuals (Ds) combined and conspired to enforce anticompetitive accreditation standards, thereby boycotting P in violation of section 1 and monopolizing legal education, law school accreditation, and the licensing of lawyers in violation of section 2. The standards allegedly (i) fixed faculty salaries; (ii) required reduced teaching hours, paid sabbaticals, and lower student/faculty ratios; (iii) limited the use of adjunct professors; (iv) prohibited the use of required or for-credit bar review courses; (v) required schools to limit the number of hours students could work; (vi) prohibited schools from accepting credit transfers from unaccredited schools and from enrolling graduates of unaccredited schools in graduate programs; (vii) required more expensive and elaborate physical and library facilities; and (viii) required the use of the LSAT. P claimed that the challenged conduct (i) put it at a competitive disadvantage in recruiting students because graduates of unaccredited schools cannot take the bar examination in most states; (ii) gave it a stigma, independent of the bar examination issue; and (iii) caused it to incur higher costs, particularly in connection with faculty salaries. The district court entered summary judgment for Ds, and P appeals.

b. Issues.

1) Does *Noerr* protect the ABA's efforts to persuade legislatures and courts to adopt bar admission rules generally requiring legal education and permitting applicants to satisfy this requirement by graduating from ABA-accredited law schools?

2) Did the ABA's enforcement of its accreditation standards and the related conduct of the other Ds cause any harm remediable under the Sherman Act?

3) Did LSAC's refusal to allow P to participate in its student recruiting conferences violate the Sherman Act?

c. Held. 1) Yes. 2) No. 3) No. Judgment affirmed.

1) Ds cannot bear liability for the rules governing admission to the bar since legislatures and courts adopt the rules.

2) The ABA's lobbying for these rules from the 1920s to approximately the mid 1970s is insulated from antitrust scrutiny by *Noerr* (*supra*). Statements defending the ABA standards constitute indirect petitioning activity. Whatever stigma might have attached from lack of accreditation was incidental to that petitioning. To recognize a claim for stigma injury in this case would severely limit *Noerr* immunity since a petitioner for governmental action is likely to urge that the action is needed to ensure that standards are met, thereby suggesting that some entities do not meet appropriate standards.

3) The ABA's justification of its decision to deny accreditation to P does not qualify as an attempt to persuade anyone directly not to deal with P, which would fall outside the protection of *Noerr*.

4) P's claim that it suffered injuries as a result of the ABA's enforcement of its faculty salary standards failed because evidence in the record showed that P raised salaries for other reasons and because P relied, and planned to rely, exclusively on adjunct faculty. P failed to prove that it suffered any injury as a result of the accreditation standards prohibiting schools from accepting transfers or graduate students from unaccredited schools.

5) LSAC's refusal to allow P to participate in its student recruiting conferences did not violate the Sherman Act because LSAC did not possess a monopoly over access to law students or pre-law advisors or even over recruiting fairs.

Professional Real Estate Investors, Inc. v. Columbia Pictures Industries, Inc.

6. **Sham Exception to *Noerr* Immunity--Professional Real Estate Investors, Inc. v. Columbia Pictures Industries, Inc.,** 508 U.S. 49 (1993).

   a. **Facts.** Professional Real Estate Investors (D) operated a resort hotel, installed videodisc players in the rooms, and rented videodiscs to guests. D also sought to develop a market for the sale of videodisc players to other hotels wishing to offer in-room viewing of prerecorded material. Columbia Pictures Industries, Inc., and seven other major motion picture studios (Ps) owned the copyrights on the motion pictures recorded on D's videodiscs. Ps also licensed the transmission of copyrighted motion pictures to hotel rooms through a wired cable system called Spectradyne. When Ps sued D for infringement of their copyrights, D counterclaimed under the Sherman Act, alleging that Ps had brought their suit, which D characterized as a "sham" within the meaning of *Noerr*, in order to monopolize or restrain trade in the market for in-room entertainment services. The parties filed cross-motions for summary judgment on Ps' copyright claim and postponed further discovery on D's antitrust counterclaims. Since Ps conceded that the Copyright Act's "first sale" doctrine permitted D to rent purchased videodiscs, and since D conceded that the playing of videodiscs constituted "performance" of motion pictures, the only issue was whether rental of videodiscs for in-room viewing infringed Ps' exclusive right to "perform the copyrighted work[s] publicly." On this issue the district court ruled for D. The court of appeals affirmed the grant of summary judgment for D on the grounds that a hotel room was not a "public place" and that D did not "transmit or otherwise communicate" Ps' motion pictures. On remand, the district court opined that "[i]t was clear from the manner in which the [infringement action] was presented that [Ps were] seeking and expecting a favorable judgment. Although I decided against [Ps], the case was far from easy to resolve, and it was evident from the opinion affirming my order that the court of appeals had trouble with it as well. I find that there was probable cause for bringing the action, regardless of whether the issue was considered a question of fact or of law." The district court then denied D's request for further discovery on Ps' intent in bringing the copyright action and granted summary judgment to Ps on D's antitrust counterclaim. The court of appeals affirmed, opining that Ps' infringement suit did not qualify as a "sham" since D neither "allege[d] that the lawsuit involved misrepresentations" nor "challenge[d] the district court's finding that the infringement action was brought with probable cause, *i.e.*, that the suit was not baseless," but simply argued that "the copyright infringement lawsuit [was] a sham because [Ps] did not honestly believe that the infringement claim was meritorious." D appeals.

   b. **Issue.** Does *Noerr* shield Ps' infringement action from antitrust scrutiny?

   c. **Held.** Yes. Judgment affirmed.

54 - Antitrust

1) Litigation cannot be deprived of immunity as a sham unless the litigation is objectively baseless.

2) We decline D's invitation to adopt an approach under which either indifference to outcome, or failure to prove that a petition for redress of grievances would have been brought but for a predatory motive, would expose a defendant to antitrust liability under the sham exception. An objectively reasonable effort to litigate cannot be a sham regardless of subjective intent. To make immunity turn on subjective intent would utterly fail to supply real "intelligible guidance" and undermine, if not vitiate, *Noerr*.

3) To qualify as "sham" litigation, a suit must be objectively baseless in the sense that no reasonable litigant could realistically expect success on the merits. Only if challenged litigation is objectively meritless may a court examine the litigant's subjective motivation. Under this second part of our definition of sham, the court should focus on whether the baseless lawsuit conceals "an attempt to interfere directly with the business relationships of a competitor," through the use of the governmental process—as opposed to the outcome of that process—as an anticompetitive weapon. When a court has found that an antitrust defendant claiming *Noerr* immunity had probable cause to sue, that finding compels the conclusion that a reasonable litigant in the defendant's position could realistically expect success on the merits of the challenged lawsuit.

d. **Concurrence** (Stevens, O'Connor, JJ.). I agree that an objectively reasonable effort to litigate, like this one, cannot be a sham regardless of subjective intent, but I disagree with the broad dicta in the Court's opinion equating objectively baseless with the answer to the question whether any "reasonable litigant could realistically expect success on the merits." It might not be objectively reasonable to bring a lawsuit just because some form of success on the merits, no matter how insignificant, could be expected. A "sham" is the use of the governmental process—as opposed to the outcome of that process—as an anticompetitive weapon. The distinction between abusing the judicial process to restrain competition and prosecuting a lawsuit that, if successful, will restrain competition must guide any court's decision whether a particular filing, or series of filings, is a sham. So a suit should qualify as a "sham": (i) if the plaintiff was indifferent to the outcome of the litigation itself but pursued it to impose a collateral harm on the defendant by, for example, impairing his credit, abusing the discovery process, or interfering with his access to governmental agencies or (ii) if the plaintiff had some reason to expect success on the merits but because of its tremendous cost would not bother to achieve that result without the benefit of collateral injuries imposed on its competitor by the legal process alone.

e. **Comments.**

1) As the concurring opinion observes, the majority may have articulated more than one standard for evaluating the scope of the "sham" exception

to *Noerr* immunity. In that connection, note that limiting its scope by using a rigorous standard is especially appealing in connection with litigation designed to enforce intellectual property rights.

2) In a footnote to this case, the Court identified a tactic that might permit some parties in D's position to pursue antitrust claims somewhat similar to the one dismissed here. The Court noted that the court of appeals held that Ps' alleged refusal to grant copyright licenses was not "separate and distinct" from the prosecution of its infringement suit. The Court also held that D had failed to establish how it could have suffered antitrust injury from Ps' other allegedly anticompetitive acts. Thus, whatever antitrust injury Ps inflicted must have stemmed from the attempted enforcement of copyrights. The Court said it would not consider whether Ps could have made a valid claim of immunity for anticompetitive conduct independent of petitioning activity.

D. "STATE ACTION" AND TENSIONS WITH FEDERALISM

1. **Introduction.** State and local governments often regulate markets with the purpose or effect of creating or maintaining a monopoly or a cartel. Arguably, this regulation conflicts with the antitrust laws. This section takes up the question of the extent to which antitrust displaces such regulation under the Constitution's Supremacy Clause.

2. **The Landmark Case--Parker v. Brown,** 317 U.S. 341 (1943).

   a. **Facts.** The California Agricultural Prorate Act authorized regulations that restricted agricultural output and fixed prices. Plaintiff producer challenged the regulations as contrary to the Sherman Act.

   b. **Issue.** Does a clearly articulated system of state regulation, affirmatively designed to replace private competition, violate the Sherman Act?

   c. **Held.** No.

      1) In a dual system of government where all power resides in the states unless the Constitution expressly delegates authority to Congress, an unexpressed purpose to nullify a state's control over its agents and officers is not lightly to be attributed to Congress.

3. **State Prompting.** *Goldfarb v. Virginia State Bar,* 421 U.S. 773 (1975), dealt with an antitrust challenge to minimum fee schedules. Through its

legislature, Virginia had authorized its highest court to regulate the practice of law. That court adopted ethical codes dealing in part with fees, and explicitly directing lawyers not "to be controlled" by fee schedules. The Supreme Court said that the threshold inquiry in determining if an anticompetitive activity is state action is whether the activity is required by the state acting as sovereign. The Court found that it could not be said that Virginia, through its Supreme Court Rules, required the anticompetitive activities of the State Bar and a county bar association. No statute required them; state law did not refer to fees, leaving regulation of the profession to the Virginia Supreme Court. The Court further found that although the ethical codes mentioned advisory fee schedules, they did not direct the State Bar or County Bar Association to supply them, or require the type of price floor that arose. Although the State Bar apparently had been granted the power to issue ethical opinions, there was no indication in the record that the Virginia Supreme Court approved the opinions. The Supreme Court held that it is not enough that "anticompetitive conduct is prompted by state action; rather, anticompetitive activities must be compelled by direction of the State acting as sovereign."

4. **What Constitutes "the State Acting as Sovereign"?** In *Cantor v. Detroit Edison Co.*, 428 U.S. 579 (1976), a light bulb retailer attacked a utility's light bulb "giveaway" program, which was embodied in a tariff filed with the state regulatory commission. The Supreme Court rejected the utility's state action defense, noting that the state had no independent interest in the light bulb market and that the light bulb program had been initiated by the utility and never considered by the commission. In *Bates v. State Bar of Arizona*, 433 U.S. 350 (1977), two attorneys attacked disciplinary rules forbidding advertising. The Court upheld the State Bar's state action defense. In contrast to the minimum fee schedules involved in *Goldfarb*, the Court argued, these rules are "the affirmative command of the Arizona Supreme Court." In contrast to the regulation of light bulbs purportedly involved in *Cantor*, the Court continued, "the regulation of the bar is at the core of the State's power to protect the public. . . . [T]he light bulb program . . . was instigated by the utility with only the acquiescence of the state regulatory commission. The State's incorporation of the program into the tariff reflected its conclusion that the utility was authorized to employ the practice if it so desired. . . . The disciplinary rules reflect a clear articulation of the State's policy with regard to professional behavior. Moreover, . . . the rules are subject to pointed reexamination by the policymaker—the Arizona Supreme Court—in enforcement proceedings." A similar approach was taken by the Court in *New Motor Vehicle Board of California v. Fox*, 439 U.S. 96 (1978).

5. **Need for Active Supervision--California Retail Liquor Dealers Association v. Midcal Aluminum, Inc.,** 445 U.S. 97 (1980).

   a. **Facts.** The State of California required wholesalers and retailers of wine to sell at prices dictated by the manufacturer. Midcal (D), a distributor, sold below this price and was charged with violating the system. D ad-

California Retail Liquor Dealers Association v. Midcal Aluminum, Inc.

mitted that it had broken the law and filed suit to enjoin the system as violative of the Sherman Act. The state court of appeal ruled that the scheme violated the Act. The Dealers Association (P) intervened and the Supreme Court granted certiorari.

b. **Issue.** Does a clearly articulated and affirmatively expressed policy of state regulation that is not also actively supervised qualify for antitrust immunity under *Parker v. Brown*?

c. **Held.** No. Judgment affirmed.

1) The state authorized and enforced resale price maintenance laws but did not set the prices itself, nor review their reasonableness. This lack of active supervision suggests that the program is not one in which the state intends to supplant competition but is merely a state sanction of private price fixing.

6. **Clearly Articulated Policy to Displace Competition with Regulation-- Southern Motor Carriers Rate Conference v. United States,** 471 U.S. 48 (1985).

a. **Facts.** In North Carolina, Georgia, Tennessee, and Mississippi, public service commissions set motor carriers' rates for intrastate transportation of general commodities. Common carriers must submit proposed rates for approval. A proposed rate becomes effective if the commission takes no action within a specified period of time. If a hearing is held, the proposed rate becomes effective only if, and to the extent that, the commission so orders. Three of the states expressly permit, but do not compel, common carriers to agree on proposed rates and submit them jointly through "rate bureaus" like Southern Motor Carriers Rate Conference and North Carolina Motor Carriers Association (Ds). The relevant Mississippi statute provides that the commission shall set "just and reasonable" rates, but does not expressly deal with rate bureaus. The state commission has actively encouraged collective ratemaking. The United States (P) sought to enjoin Ds' collective ratemaking as an antitrust violation. Ds moved to dismiss on the grounds that their collective ratemaking was immune from antitrust scrutiny under the *Parker* state action doctrine. The district court denied the motion, and the appeals court affirmed. The Supreme Court granted certiorari.

b. **Issue.** Does the *Parker* state action doctrine immunize collective ratemaking when it is permitted but not compelled by a state?

c. **Held.** Yes. Judgment reversed.

1) *Midcal* makes private action regulated by a state immune under the *Parker* state action doctrine if (i) undertaken pursuant to a clearly articulated state policy and (ii) actively supervised by the state. The

first prong does not require "compulsion," although "compulsion" may be the most powerful evidence of the policy. By permitting collective ratemaking, a state enables providers to share the cost of preparing rate proposals, and by facilitating a reduction in the total number of proposals, permits the relevant commission to give more careful consideration to each. At the same time, the state allows for the possibility that competition could check rates that were set too high. A rate bureau member could submit its own rate and thereby capture a greater market share by undercutting the group.

2) The North Carolina, Georgia, and Tennessee statutes expressly permit collective ratemaking by common carriers. The Mississippi statute makes it clear that rates will be set by a regulatory agency rather than by the market. This is sufficient to satisfy the first prong of the *Midcal* test. If more detail than a clear intent to displace competition were required of the legislature, states would find it difficult to implement their anticompetitive policies through regulatory agencies.

7. **Local Government and the *Midcal* Requirements--Town of Hallie v. City of Eau Claire,** 471 U.S. 34 (1985).

    a. **Facts.** The City of Eau Claire (D) obtained federal funds to help build a sewage treatment facility in the city. It was the only one available to the residents of the surrounding towns. D refused to supply sewage treatment services to residents of four adjacent towns unless the residents agreed to annexation by D and to use D's sewage collection and transportation services. The towns (Ps) alleged that these actions violated the Sherman Act. A Wisconsin statute authorized cities to construct sewage systems and to "describe with particularity the district to be [served]." Another statute provides that the state Natural Resources Department may require a city's sewage system to be constructed so that other towns may connect to the system, and it may order connection, but not if the unincorporated area refuses annexation. Invoking the state action doctrine, the district court ruled for D and the appeals court affirmed.

    b. **Issue.** Are a city's anticompetitive activities protected by the *Parker* state action exemption when the activities are authorized, but not compelled by the state, and the state does not actively supervise the conduct?

    c. **Held.** Yes. Judgment affirmed.

        1) Wisconsin statutes authorized D's conduct. Because they allow a city to condition service upon annexation, anticompetitive behavior is foreseeable and thus contemplated by the statutes. The legislature need not specifically state that it intends for the statute to have anticompetitive effects. Such a requirement would be unwork-

Town of Hallie v. City of Eau Claire

able. A legislature cannot be expected to catalog all of the anticipated effects of a statute.

2) D need not show that the state compelled it to act. We may presume, absent a showing to the contrary, that a municipality acts in the public interest. (Compulsion, however, may be the best evidence of state policy.)

3) To invoke the state action defense, a municipality need not show state supervision. There is little or no danger that the municipality is involved in a private price-fixing arrangement. Its interests can be expected to coincide with those of the state. In some rare instances, the municipality may seek to further its own goals, but this is limited by the requirement that the municipality act pursuant to a clearly articulated state policy.

FTC v. Ticor Title Insurance Co.

8. **State Action Antitrust Immunity--FTC v. Ticor Title Insurance Co.,** 504 U.S. 621 (1992).

   a. **Facts.** The FTC's (P's) administrative complaint alleged that Ticor and several other title insurance companies (Ds) had violated section 5 of the FTC Act by fixing the price of title searches. Because the prices had been submitted to state agencies for review, Ds claimed immunity under the state action doctrine. Most of these agencies employed a negative check off: unless the agency notified Ds within a certain period following the submission of the prices, they became effective. The ALJ ruled this defense unavailable and the court of appeals reversed. The Supreme Court granted certiorari.

   b. **Issue.** Are Ds entitled to state action immunity because they had to submit their prices to state agencies for possible review?

   c. **Held.** No. Judgment of court of appeals reversed and remanded.

   1) A state law or regulatory scheme can provide antitrust immunity if the state has articulated a clear and affirmative policy to allow the anticompetitive practices and the state provides active supervision of the anticompetitive conduct undertaken by private actors.

   2) P conceded that the first element was met. Thus the question narrows to whether the negative review system constituted sufficient supervision. The mere existence of a state regulatory program, even if staffed, funded, and empowered by law, does not satisfy the active supervision requirement. An agency's deference to private price fixing agreements does not yield immunity. The proper inquiry is not whether an agency exists but whether it has played a substantial role in determining the specifics of the economic policy. When the veto review method is employed, as in this case, the party claiming

immunity must demonstrate that state officials have undertaken the necessary steps to determine the specifics of the price-fixing or rate-setting scheme. Accordingly, there was no active supervision and the title insurance companies are not entitled to immunity under the state action doctrine.

d. **Concurrence** (Scalia, J.). I agree with the dissent that the Court's standard will lead to uncertainty and litigation and will result in the abandonment of some state programs. However, I am willing to accept these consequences because I see no alternative.

e. **Dissent** (Rehnquist, C.J., O'Connor, Thomas, JJ.). The Court's holding is not supported by precedent and it is not sound as a matter of policy. The Court does not say just how active a state's regulators must be before the "active supervision" requirement will be satisfied. In this case, the conduct was approved by a state agency. This is consistent with our prior statement that the active supervision requirement serves mainly an "evidentiary function."

9. **Active Supervision and Peer Review--Patrick v. Burget,** 486 U.S. 94 (1988).

   a. **Facts.** The partners in a private group medical practice (D) comprised a majority of the staff members of a town's sole hospital. Dr. Patrick (P), a surgeon, claimed that they engaged in a peer review process designed to reduce competition by excluding him. The jury found for P. The appeals court reversed on state action grounds, citing the statutes relating to, and the activities of, the Health Division and the Board of Medical Examiner, and the review of certain peer review decisions by the state's courts. The Supreme Court granted certiorari.

   b. **Issue.** Do the activities of the Health Division, the Board of Medical Examiner, and the state courts constitute "active supervision" within the meaning of the *Midcal* test?

   c. **Held.** No. Judgment reversed.

      1) To ensure that the state action doctrine will shelter only the particular anticompetitive acts of private parties that actually further state regulatory policies, the active supervision requirement mandates that the state exercise ultimate control over the challenged anticompetitive conduct. The mere presence of some state involvement or monitoring does not suffice.

      2) The Health Division (which has general supervisory powers over matters relating to the preservation of health and which enforces the statutory directive that each hospital shall have a peer review system) has no power to review private peer review decisions and

Patrick v. Burget

overturn a decision that fails to accord with state policy. Neither does the Board of Medical Examiner.

3) To the extent that the state courts may review private peer review decisions at all, they would not review the merits of a dismissal.

10. **Local Government and Its Response to Citizen Requests--Columbia v. Omni Outdoor Advertising, Inc.,** 499 U.S. 365 (1991).

   a. **Facts.** Columbia Outdoor Advertising, Inc. ("COA") has engaged in the billboard business in the City of Columbia (D) since the 1940s. By 1981, COA controlled 95% of the relevant market and had deep roots and connections with officials of D. In 1981, Omni Outdoor Advertising, Inc. (P) began erecting billboards in and around the city. COA responded by meeting with D's officials to seek enactment of an ordinance restricting billboard construction. There were also a number of citizens and newspaper editorials concerned with the explosive growth of billboard construction and advocated restrictions. In 1982, D passed an ordinance requiring city council approval for every billboard and imposed a 180-day moratorium on construction. The state court invalidated the ordinance, and then D enacted a second ordinance that restricted the size, location, and spacing of billboards. P brought suit against D alleging antitrust violations. A jury found for P, but the trial court granted j.n.o.v. The Fourth Circuit reversed and reinstated the jury verdict, and the Supreme Court granted certiorari.

   b. **Issue.** Does proof that citizens and government officials "conspired" cause them to forfeit *Parker* or *Noerr* immunity?

   c. **Held.** No. Judgment reversed and remanded.

      1) D correctly invoked *Parker* immunity by showing the city has the authority to regulate billboards under its zoning power and that there is a clear articulation of a state policy that has suppression of competition as a "foreseeable result."

      2) It is inevitable and desirable that public officials side with citizen groups, but a conspiracy exception would render such behavior vulnerable to antitrust claims. An exception limited to instances of "corruption" would be impractical, requiring the court to make a judicial assessment of the "public interest" and to subjectively decide whether officials "thought" that their decision served that interest.

      3) Other laws passed by Congress, including anti-bribery laws, are aimed at preventing corruption, but the Sherman Act is not.

4) The "sham" exception is inapplicable. The *Noerr* doctrine immunizes COA's lobbying activities and a "conspiracy" exception to *Noerr* would create the same problems as a "conspiracy" exception to *Parker*.

d. **Dissent** (Stevens, White, and Marshall, JJ.). The majority decision significantly enlarges the state action exemption. The statute that conferred authority on D to enact zoning laws was not a state policy authorizing displacement of competition, but was instead expressly adopted to promote the health, safety, morals, and general welfare of the community. The decision to embark upon economic regulation is nondelegable, and must be expressly made by a state in the context of a specific industry to qualify for state action immunity.

11. **Local Government and Concerted Action--Fisher v. City of Berkeley,** 475 U.S. 260 (1986).

    a. **Facts.** The City of Berkeley (D) enacted an initiative, pursuant to popular vote, which placed a ceiling on rent charged for most private housing. A landlord could raise rents above the base rate only pursuant to annual general adjustment by a Rent Stabilization Board of appointed commissioners or after the landlord successfully petitions the Board for an individual adjustment. A group of landlords owning rental property in Berkeley (Ps) brought suit claiming that the ordinance violated the Due Process and Equal Protection Clauses of the Fourteenth Amendment. The ordinance was upheld by the trial court, but struck down by a state appellate court. Ps appealed to the California Supreme Court, where it was alleged that federal antitrust law preempted the ordinance. The California Supreme Court held that the ordinance was not preempted because there was no conflict between it and the Sherman Act. The Supreme Court granted certiorari.

    b. **Issue.** Is a rent control ordinance enacted pursuant to popular initiative unconstitutional when it sets a ceiling on rents that would violate the Sherman Act if set by private parties?

    c. **Held.** No. Judgment affirmed.

    1) A section 1 violation requires a "contract, combination . . . or conspiracy" made between separate entities. It is of considerable importance that independent activity be distinguished from concerted efforts. This statute lacks the element of concerted action. A restraint imposed unilaterally by the government does not become concerted action within the meaning of section 1 of the Sherman Act simply because it has a coercive effect upon parties who must obey the law. While the ordinance does give tenants—certainly a group of interested parties—some power to trigger enforcement of

its provisions, it places complete control over maximum rent levels exclusively in the hands of the Rent Stabilization Board.

2) With no indication that corruption has tainted the rent controls enacted under the ordinance, the absolute control of government officials proves that this rent control scheme is not a cloak for private action among the landlords or concerted action between the landlords and the city.

d. **Concurrence** (Powell, J.). Under *Parker v. Brown*, a general grant of authority to the city to regulate rents would have sufficed for exemption purposes. The history of the challenged ordinance shows even more than that. An earlier version of the ordinance was approved by concurrent resolution of both houses of the California legislature, but the California Supreme Court invalidated it on the ground that it lacked procedural safeguards necessary to protect landlords from confiscatory rent ceilings. The city's citizens then adopted the challenged ordinance that contains the required procedural safeguards.

e. **Dissent** (Brennan, J.). There is a functional combination between the city and its officials on the one hand and the landlords on the other to fix prices. This ordinance is more effective than any private agreement could ever be at eliminating price competition in this market. There are serious doubts that the pro forma approval of the earlier ordinance by the California legislature qualifies for the *Parker* exemption, but the ordinance's later invalidation by the California Supreme Court eliminates even that possibility.

VI. MARKET CONCENTRATION AND CONSPIRACY

A. INTRODUCTION

Following the early attacks on the merger to monopoly movement, the United States challenged sizable mergers that did not create a monopoly firm, notably the mergers that led to the formation of the United States Steel Corporation. One of the government's arguments in cases like this one was that such mergers would make it easier for the remaining firms in the market to coordinate their behavior without engaging in a detectable conspiracy. But the courts paid little or no attention to this argument. How important this development was depended, in part, on how easily the government could launch an antitrust attack on such coordination.

B. CONCENTRATION, PRICE LEADERSHIP, AND "CONSCIOUS PARALLELISM"

1. **Inference of Agreement as a Legal Building Block.** A contract, combination, or conspiracy in restraint of trade can be proved by circumstantial evidence. But under what circumstances may a jury (or judge in a bench trial or the FTC) infer one of these? And may coordinated behavior be condemned without finding one of these, despite the language of section 1? The cases and materials in this section speak to these questions.

   a. **Conspiracy established from conduct--Interstate Circuit, Inc. v. United States,** 306 U.S. 208 (1939).

   Interstate Circuit, Inc. v. United States

   1) **Facts.** A company with two subsidiaries in the movie exhibition business (D), owning all first-run theaters in six major Texas cities and many subsequent-run theaters, demanded that eight distribution companies (Ds), controlling 75% of all first-class feature films, require subsequent-run theaters in these cities to charge higher admissions and not run films shown in first-run theaters in double bills when they were later shown in subsequent runs. The letter making the demands was sent to all eight distributors, and with all eight names on it. Meetings were held with the exhibitor and the distributors; all distributors adopted the proposal and acted on it (two incorporated the restrictions in their exhibition contracts). The Government (P) charged a conspiracy in restraint of trade between the distributors and between the distributors and the exhibitors, and sought an injunction. The district court found against Ds.

   2) **Issue.** Absent direct evidence of an agreement, may one be inferred from course of conduct?

   3) **Held.** Yes. Judgment affirmed.

a) Conspiracy may be inferred from the conduct of the distributors under the circumstances: (i) the nature of the proposals (which would raise prices and be more profitable to all parties); (ii) the unanimity of action; (iii) all were aware of the plan and the need for all to cooperate if it was to work; (iv) the plan was a radical departure from past ways of doing business; and (v) Ds did not call as witnesses any of their superior officials who were involved in negotiating the agreement.

b) While the district court's finding of an agreement of the distributors among themselves is supported by the evidence, we think that in the circumstances of this case such agreement for the imposition of the restrictions upon subsequent-run exhibitors was not a prerequisite to an unlawful conspiracy. It was enough that, knowing that concerted action was contemplated and invited, the distributors gave their adherence to the scheme and participated in it.

2. **Conscious Parallelism--Theatre Enterprises v. Paramount Film Distributing Corp.**, 346 U.S. 537 (1954).

   a. **Facts.** Major film producer/distributors (Ds) refused to license first-run films to a suburban Baltimore theater (P). P sued, claiming that Ds had violated section 1 by conspiring to restrict first-run films to downtown theaters. Each D explained that it expected to earn more total revenues if it granted an exclusive license for its first-run films to a downtown Baltimore theater. P introduced no evidence of an express agreement between Ds. P cited *United States v. Paramount Pictures Inc.*, 334 U.S. 131 (1948), in which Ds suffered an adverse judgment for conspiring to impose a uniform system of runs and clearances without adequate explanation to sustain them as reasonable restraints of trade. After P's motion for a directed verdict was denied, the jury found for Ds, and the district court entered judgment accordingly. The court of appeals affirmed. The Supreme Court granted certiorari.

   b. **Issue.** Does consciously parallel behavior require a finding of agreement or conspiracy under the Sherman Act?

   c. **Held**. No. Judgment affirmed.

      1) Consciously parallel behavior does not necessarily indicate an agreement or conspiracy, especially when each defendant has a plausible independent business motivation for its conduct.

      2) That Ds conspired earlier does not require that a different inference be drawn now.

d. **Comment**. The more difficult question remains: under what circumstances may the trier of fact find a contract, combination, or conspiracy without any smoking gun evidence, like clandestine meetings or some other plus factor?

3. **Multiple Vertical Agreements Function as Unlawful Horizontal Agreement--Toys "R" Us, Inc. v. FTC**, 221 F.3d 928 (7th Cir. 2000).

    Toys "R" Us, Inc. v. FTC

    a. **Facts.** Toys "R" Us (D), a major toy retailer with up to 49% of the market in some areas, purchases about 30% of the total output of toy manufacturers. D marks these toys up about 30%. Traditional toy stores use a 40-50% markup, general discounters (like Kmart & Target) use a 22% markup, and warehouse clubs (like Costco) 9%. Warehouse clubs cut significantly into D's profits beginning in 1990. D responded by contacting each toy manufacturer individually to inform them that D would not carry their toys unless they (i) refrained from selling comparable toys to the warehouse clubs, (ii) offered all specials to D first, and (iii) sold new or promoted products to warehouse clubs only if they carried the whole toy line. Toy sales at warehouse clubs declined while sales of other products increased at double digits. The FTC (P) brought suit for alleged antitrust violations and won an injunction prohibiting D from attempting to enter into any agreements with suppliers to limit sales of toys, requesting information from suppliers about sales to discounters, and for a period of five years, refusing to purchase toys from a supplier because they also sold to discounters. D appeals.

    b. **Issues.**

        1) Did the series of vertical agreements constitute an unlawful horizontal agreement in practice?

        2) If they did constitute a horizontal agreement, was it lawful because D lacked market power or because the agreement served as a legitimate response to free riding?

        3) Was P's injunction improperly broad?

    c. **Held.** 1) Yes. 2) No. 3) No. Judgment affirmed.

        1) When circumstantial evidence is used to establish a horizontal agreement, some evidence must demonstrate that the alleged conspirators did not act independently. Here, the evidence demonstrated that the manufacturers wanted to become less dependent on D so each entered into the contract only with the understanding that the other manufacturers would do likewise.

        2) Because the agreement was unlawful per se under *Northwest Wholesale Stationers* (*supra*), an inquiry into D's market power was not

Antitrust - 67

necessary. But if it were, D's market power was established by the anticompetitive effects the boycott had on the warehouse stores.

3) While antitrust law does permit nonprice vertical restraints that are designed to facilitate the provision of extra services, the manufacturers already provided D with additional funds for advertising and for the additional cost for carrying a full line of toys. Thus the warehouse clubs were not free riding.

4) The injunction left D with sufficient latitude to make business decisions about what suppliers to deal with and what particular products to stock.

4. **Facilitating Practices.** A variety of practices may make it easier for oligopolists to coordinate their behavior without engaging in a detectable conspiracy. Some enforcement officials and commentators assert that delivered pricing systems constitute one such practice.

a. **Delivered pricing--Boise Cascade Corp. v. FTC,** 637 F.2d 573 (9th Cir. 1980).

1) **Facts.** Boise Cascade Corp. and other manufacturers of softwood plywood with mills located in the southern United States (Ds) all used delivered pricing, which utilized the computation of rail freight charges from the Pacific Northwest in determining the price of southern plywood. The freight factor is an important element in the price competition for this relatively fungible product. Until 1947, all plywood was produced in Washington and Oregon. Manufacturers there typically quoted a "delivered price," consisting of a "mill price" plus the amount for rail freight from the west coast. When technological advances made it possible to produce plywood from pine grown in the south, manufacturers there also adopted delivered pricing, thereby greatly simplifying price comparison between southern and western plywood. Southern plywood production grew quickly, but remained concentrated. Even after the southern manufacturers began supplying all of the demand in the south, they continued to use west coast freight charges in their price quotes. They also all employed certain methods for estimating shipping weight and relied on particular commercial price reporters as the basis for setting the index price to which west coast freight was added. This reduced uncertainty about pricing. The range of prices narrowed, but none of this conduct resulted in exactly matching price quotes to any customer; customers found it worthwhile to shop for price by phone. The FTC (P) claimed that each D violated section 5 of the Federal Trade Commission Act by continuing to quote delivered prices showing rail freight charges from the Pacific Northwest

as part of the price. According to P, uniform use of this practice in the southern plywood industry tended to inhibit price competition. The ALJ ruled for P, the FTC affirmed, and Ds appeal.

2) **Issue.** Given the structure and conditions of the southern plywood industry, does a manufacturer violate section 5 by independently adopting and maintaining a delivered pricing system used by the other manufacturers?

3) **Held.** No. The FTC's order will not be enforced.

   a) Section 5 requires that the FTC show at least a tacit agreement to use a pricing formula that has the effect of fixing prices. In the absence of evidence of an overt agreement to utilize delivered pricing to avoid price competition, the FTC must show that the challenged practice actually had the effect of fixing or stabilizing prices.

   b) The record reflects no such effect. Evidence that systematic price matching did not occur and that customers found it worthwhile to shop by phone provides a prima facie inference that competition has not been affected by the pricing system. P failed to introduce evidence to overcome this inference. No evidence showed that the pricing system narrowed the range of prices, and even if it had, that would have been no reason to be suspicious of it. Moreover, lack of buyer objection to the pricing system, and in some instances express buyer preference, confirms the inference.

   c) Ds do not have to prove that the practice had no effect on the price level. The burden of proof to show the prohibited effect remains with the FTC. Where the challenged practice was and may still be a competitive response to buyer preferences, the practice constitutes neither a per se offense nor a violation of section 5.

b. **Practices facilitating consciously parallel pricing--Ethyl Corp. v. FTC,** 729 F.2d 128 (2d Cir. 1984).

   Ethyl Corp. v. FTC

   1) **Facts.** From 1974 through 1979, only Ethyl, Du Pont, PPG, and Nalco (Ds) produced lead antiknock compounds (PPG exited this market in 1983). Chemically, these compounds are nearly identical no matter who makes them. Ds sold these compounds to gasoline refiners who used them in certain grades of gasoline. Some of these refiners are aggressive, sophisticated buyers who could have entered this market had they found it economically attractive to do so. In 1975, the EPA made entry into this market extremely unattractive when it required that all new cars be equipped with catalytic converters. Since lead fouls converters, demand for antiknock compounds began a steady decline. Ds experienced excess

capacity, but their accounting profits were much higher than those earned in the rest of the chemical industry. Ds' list prices were highly uniform even though they rose over time. Nalco and PPG, however, engaged in substantial discounting from list prices. Ethyl and Du Pont competed by billing late and permitting customers to buy in advance of price increases. They also offered costly "free" services. Ds quoted prices on a "delivered" basis only (on average the transportation portion was about 2% of prices). The FTC (P) attacked delivered pricing and certain other non-collusive conduct as "unfair methods of competition" violating section 5 of the Federal Trade Commission Act: (i) Ethyl, Du Pont, and to a limited extent, Nalco used a "most favored nation" clause; (ii) all Ds obligated themselves to give the advance notice of price increases to their customers and to the press; and (iii) Ethyl and Du Pont gave more than the 30 days' notice provided by their contracts. According to P, this conduct reduced uncertainty about competitors' prices and thereby facilitated the maintenance of uniform price levels and the reduction of price competition. The ALJ ruled for P, and the FTC affirmed. Ds appeal.

2) **Issue.** Given the characteristics of the antiknock market, do the challenged business practices constitute "unfair methods of competition" simply because they facilitate consciously parallel pricing at identical levels?

3) **Held.** No. The FTC order is vacated.

   a) Heightened scrutiny must be used when the challenged practices do not violate the antitrust or other laws, lest efficient practices be deterred.

   b) Conduct that is not the product of agreement, tacit or express, may be condemned as "unfair" under section 5 only if the actor (i) had an anticompetitive intent or purpose or (ii) lacked an independent legitimate business reason for its conduct.

   c) No substantial evidence supported the FTC's finding that the challenged practices significantly lessened competition or that elimination of these practices would improve competition. The practices did not make price coordination significantly easier than it already was; transaction prices were not, in fact, uniform; and the practices served a number of efficiency-enhancing functions.

4) **Comment.** Because of the alternative reasons invoked by the court in support of its holding and the conclusory language used by the court to describe noncollusive conduct prohibited by section 5, it is not entirely clear how much this decision limits the scope of section 5. In any event, the FTC might have relied on exactly the same economic evidence to support a finding that Ds had colluded tacitly. Although the court would probably have

overturned this finding because the evidence was weak, this approach seems to survive the court's decision.

c. **Salary information exchange as a facilitating practice--Todd v. Exxon Corp.,** 275 F.3d 191 (2d Cir. 2001).

    1) **Facts.** Exxon and 13 other companies (Ds) regularly exchanged detailed reports on job descriptions, starting salaries, bonuses, and other employment-related information. At meetings where the survey data was discussed, they attempted to standardize job descriptions for nonunion managerial, professional, and technical ("MPT") employees. Todd (P), an MPT employee of Exxon, alleged that all this resulted in artificially low salaries and benefits. The district court dismissed for failure to state an antitrust claim. P appeals.

    2) **Issue.** Does P's complaint sufficiently allege a plausible product market, a market structure that is susceptible to collusive activity, a data exchange with anticompetitive potential, and an antitrust injury?

    3) **Held.** Yes. Judgment vacated and remanded.

        a) The exchange of information may constitute an unreasonable restraint of trade, not merely evidence from which to infer a price fixing agreement. The structure of the industry involved and the nature of the information exchanged are the two factors most heavily relied on when determining the competitive effects.

        b) P alleged that the relevant market was the "services of experienced, salaried, non-union MPT employees in the oil and petrochemical industry, in the continental United States." Ds represent 80-90% of this market; moreover P alleged specific anticompetitive effects as evidence of Ds' market power.

        c) Concentration, fungible products, and inelastic demand render a market susceptible to the exercise of market power through coordination. Although 14 companies are involved, the market could still be considered concentrated. The standardization of job descriptions by Ds suggested that the positions were fungible. And the supply of labor has an inherently inelastic quality.

        d) Ds exchanged very detailed current salary, benefit, and job description information, which was individually identifiable rather than aggregated. They met frequently to discuss the salary information. They did not disseminate any of the information to the public. All of this suggests the possibility that the information exchange may have had an anticompetitive effect.

Todd v. Exxon Corp.

Blomkest Fertilizer, Inc. v. Potash Corp. of Saskatchewan, Inc.

d. **Price information exchanges in oligopoly as facilitating practices--Blomkest Fertilizer, Inc. v. Potash Corp. of Saskatchewan, Inc.,** 203 F.3d 1028 (8th Cir. 2000).

1) **Facts.** Blomkest Fertilizer and other fertilizer producers (Ps) brought suit against the North American producers (Ds) of potash (a mineral used in fertilizer) claiming an agreement to raise prices of the product. The parties agree that the potash industry is an oligopoly. In the 1980s a Canadian potash manufacturer owned by the government was producing significantly more potash than global demand, resulting in historically low prices. American companies complained to the Department of Commerce, which resulted in a Suspension Agreement being entered into by many of the Canadian producers. This resulted in a decreased production of potash and a corresponding significant increase in price. Although the price has trended down somewhat since the agreement, Ps claim that the current price level is artificially high and improperly uniform, thus suggesting an illegal agreement among the producers of potash. The district court granted summary judgment for Ds. On appeal, a panel of the circuit court reversed in part, but an en banc rehearing was ordered.

2) **Issue.** Did Ps present sufficient evidence of consciously paralleled pricing and one of the following plus factors: (i) the existence of interim communications between Ds, (ii) that Ds' actions were against self-interest, or (iii) econometric models showing that potash prices would have been substantially lower absent some form of collusion?

3) **Held.** No. Summary judgment affirmed.

   a) Evidence that a business consciously met the pricing of its competitors does not prove an antitrust violation without the existence of certain "plus factors." And then the evidence must tend to exclude the possibility of independent action. The plaintiff has the burden of proving both consciously parallel pricing and one or more plus factors.

   b) Ds exchanged information sporadically and then only about past sales, and no evidence suggested that these exchanges resulted in price increases.

   c) Several Canadian producers signed on to the Suspension Agreement when they could have continued to increase production. But they had a solid business justification for entering into the agreement in that the outcome of the Department of Commerce investigation was uncertain and could have triggered tariffs.

   d) Ps' expert econometric report was fatally flawed because it failed to take into account the antidumping proceedings and relies exclusively on evidence that is not probative of collusion as a matter of law.

4) **Dissent.** Requiring direct evidence of conspriacy to withstand summary judgment is contrary to *Monsanto v. Spray-Rite Service Corp.*, 465 U.S. 752 (1984). Of the "plus factors" that merely makes conspiracy possible, such as motive and opportunity to conspire, Ps produced abundant evidence. Additionally, Ps demonstrated evidence of solicitations to enter into a price-fixing agreement despite being unable to adduce direct evidence that the people on the receiving end of the solicitations accepted them. The price information exchanges were often between high-level executives who were responsible for establishing pricing decisions. In price fixing cases the exchange of sensitive price information can sometimes be circumstantial evidence of the existence of a per se violation. There was no legitimate business purpose for disclosing the price information to competitors. The court's rationale for dismissing the price information exchanges as merely "sporadic" seems to speak to the quantum of proof necessary rather than the quality of it. The evidence of several dozen communications of the type that tends to prove conspiracy creates a genuine issue of material fact.

e. **The European approach to the oligopoly problem.** According to the casebook authors, the EU's Commission and courts focus more on the "ability of dominant firms to exert market power than with the possibility of market-wide collusion." As a result, the impact of a merger on competitors troubles EU authorities more than it would trouble U.S. authorities. And the Commission concerns itself with "concertation," which is somewhat different than "conscious parallelism." The ECJ explained in its *1992 Wood Pulp* decision (ECR 1-1307), "parallel conduct cannot be regarded as furnishing proof of concertation unless concertation constituted the only plausible explanation for the conduct."

C. THE ROLE OF TRADE ASSOCIATIONS AND INFORMATION DISSEMINATION

1. **Information Dissemination.** The dissemination of information about prices, costs, capacity, etc., is a two-edged sword in antitrust terms. On the one hand, it can make markets and firms more efficient. To illustrate, firms armed with accurate information can better plan their production runs, devise their marketing strategies, and make their investment decisions. Markets in which accurate information is readily available (like the organized market of an exchange) provide more appropriate incentives to both producers and consumers. They also economize on the cost

of searching for the highest quality, lowest price producer. On the other hand, the dissemination of information can make it easier for firms to coordinate their activities without engaging in a detectable contract, combination, or conspiracy.

2. **Trade Associations.** Trade associations engage in a host of activities, many of which could not possibly pose any antitrust problem. They frequently engage in data dissemination presumably because the exchange of information between individual firms is unlikely to benefit anyone very much.

3. **Information Exchange Characterized as Price Fixing--American Column and Lumber Co. v. United States,** 257 U.S. 377 (1921).

    a. **Facts.** An association of 400 firms manufacturing hardwood adopted an "open competition" plan, the express purpose of which was stated to be that "knowledge regarding prices actually made is all that is necessary to keep prices at reasonably stable and normal levels." Participation in the plan was optional but in practice 90% of member firms, accounting for one-third of the national output of hardwood, took part. Members were required to provide the secretary of the association with daily reports of sales and deliveries (with copies of invoices), monthly reports of production and stocks, and monthly reports on prices. The secretary of the association collated the material and sent out weekly and monthly reports. In addition, there were regular monthly meetings, and territories were broken up and members therein met weekly. Future estimates of production were asked for. At the meetings, the attempt was made to arrive at "policies," which were strongly urged on members. No specific agreement to restrict output and set prices existed. The district court issued an injunction restricting the operation of the plan.

    b. **Issue.** Is the agreement to share information a violation of the Sherman Act absent specific agreements to reduce output or fix prices?

    c. **Held.** Yes. Decree affirmed.

        1) This network of agreements amounts to an unlawful restraint of trade to fix prices. Agreement is found in the tendency of intelligent men to follow a common course based on elaborate distribution of information and the restraint of business honor and social penalties.

        2) Furthermore, the facts show an actual adverse effect on interstate commerce in that the association developed a policy and members adhered to it in an anticompetitive manner (in the early months of 1919 there was a policy to restrict production; later the policy was to raise prices, which the firms did).

        3) The conduct involved clearly is not that of competitors.

d. **Dissent** (Holmes, J.). Information sharing will of course tend to equalize prices. This is not an unreasonable restraint of trade. The knowledge is not a secret to the public, and the parties are bound to fix their prices. The decree as it stands is surprising in a country of free speech.

e. **Dissent** (Brandeis, McKenna, JJ.). There is no coercion involved in this case. Competition among members was vigorous. It was not an aim of the plan to regulate competition in any way. Surely it is not against the public interest to share trade facts, even in great detail. There is nothing in the Sherman Law that should limit freedom of discussion.

f. **Comment.** In *United States v. American Linseed Oil Co.*, 262 U.S. 371 (1923), the facts were similar to *American Column*, except here there were only 12 firms controlling a very large part of the industry and in addition to the reports and meetings there were penalties assessed for nonattendance and for violation of the agreement. The Court found a violation.

4. **Benign Agreement--Maple Flooring Manufacturers' Association v. United States,** 268 U.S. 563 (1925).

    a. **Facts.** The association (D) computed average costs from information of the individual firms; distributed a freight book showing rates from a central point to thousands of locations; gathered and distributed information on past prices, stock on hand, etc.; and held meetings to discuss conditions in the industry (but there was an express finding that prices were not discussed at these meetings). The district court granted an injunction.

    b. **Issue.** Was this network of agreements a violation of section 1 of the Sherman Act?

    c. **Held.** No. Judgment reversed.

        1) The ultimate result of the association may be to stabilize prices, but this is not in itself unlawful.

        2) There is no evidence of concerted action or actual agreement.

    d. **Comment.** Prices were not uniform among members and they were generally lower than for nonmember competitors in the industry. The Court in *American Column* had said that an information exchange was not necessarily a violation, and in *Maple Flooring* there existed a situation where the good results outweighed the bad.

5. **Protection Against Fraud--Cement Manufacturers' Protective Association v. United States,** 268 U.S. 588 (1925).

    a. **Facts.** Members of the Association (D) submitted monthly reports on production, shipments, and stocks. A freight book involving a basing point system was distributed and periodic meetings were held, but prices were not discussed. Extensive credit information was exchanged, but nothing about credit policies. Above all, information about specific contracts was also exchanged and checkers were employed to determine the exact amount needed on specific jobs (to remedy the problem of buyers ordering their requirements in advance from several firms and having excess cement in rising markets, but canceling their orders in a declining price market).

    b.   **Issue.** May an association exchange data to protect its members from opportunistic buyers?

    c.   **Held.** Yes.

        1)   There is no violation where there is an attempt to protect against buyer fraud.

6.   **Price Exchange and a Ban on Secret Discounts--Sugar Institute, Inc. v. United States,** 297 U.S. 553 (1936).

    a.   **Facts.** The sugar industry was in trouble from overproduction. The practice was to announce price changes, after which firms in the industry either followed and the changes went into effect, or they declined to follow and the change was dropped. The problem was that many firms, having announced their prices, then sold with secret concessions. The Institute (D) was formed, and member firms agreed that once they announced a price they would make no secret concessions, but they could change prices as often as they wanted. The agreement was backed up by several policies, including information gathering and sharing, maintaining a delivered price system, etc. The evidence showed that subsequent to the agreement profits went up even though overcapacity remained a problem.

    b.   **Issue.** Did the agreement in question go beyond price data dissemination and constitute price fixing?

    c.   **Held.** Yes.

        1)   The announcement of price is not the problem. Neither is a system of information gathering and sharing that might tend to stabilize prices.

        2)   The problem is the agreement to not change prices once announced.

7.   **Interseller Price Verification--United States v. Container Corporation of America,** 393 U.S. 333 (1969).

    a.   **Facts.** Eighteen of 51 manufacturers of corrugated containers in the Southeast (Ds), controlling 90% of production, informally agreed to share price information on products (without adhering to a price schedule) and to exchange information concerning specific sales to specific customers. While demand in the industry had been growing, the number of competitors was also growing since entry into the industry was easy. This led to overcapacity and falling prices. The product was undifferentiated; and price competition could have the effect of changing market shares of the competing companies. The district court dismissed the complaint, which had alleged a violation of section 1 of the Sherman Act.

b. **Issue.** Does the exchange of price information violate the Sherman Act?

c. **Held.** Yes. Judgment reversed.

1) This was illegal price data dissemination. Exchange of price information had the effect of stabilizing prices, since Ds seemed to match the prices of their competitors.

2) Here the industry is dominated by relatively few sellers. The product is fungible, and competition is over price. In this situation, the exchange worked to prevent competition.

d. **Concurrence** (Fortas, J.). I agree with the result, but the exchange of price information among sellers is not a per se violation.

e. **Dissent** (Marshall, Harlan, Stewart, JJ.).

1) Ds only amount to 18 of 51 producers, and entry is easy. This is not sufficiently oligopolistic that an extreme danger exists from sharing of price information. The government must prove intent to fix prices or that it had this actual effect. The evidence submitted is insufficient.

2) There is deterrence to maintaining prices because of the large number of competitors.

3) The evidence is that Ds used the price information as they pleased and that it was actually employed to engage in price competition.

4) Ds have shown a downward trend in prices, price variations among themselves, and shifting of accounts.

5) The government has not shown profit levels of Ds or price levels; it relies on theoretical argument that even though there is overcapacity, unusually high profits exist and that prices would have fallen faster except for the sharing of price information.

f. **Comment.** The majority opinion by Justice Douglas was so truncated and abrupt as to lead many commentators to conclude that the Court had made price data dissemination a per se violation, given the absence of detailed analysis. The concurrence presumably represents an attempt by Justice Fortas to distance himself from that view.

8. **Sharing of Price Data.** In *United States v. United States Gypsum Co.*, 438 U.S. 422 (1978), the Court in a footnote addressed the sharing of price data and other information. The Court noted that because these practices could in certain circumstances increase competitiveness, they were not per se violations of the Sherman Act, and that factors such as the structure of the particular industry and the nature of the shared information were to be considered in determining the effect on competitiveness. The Court singled out exchanges of current price information as having the greatest potential for anticompetitive effects, and pointed out that even though not per se violations, these had consistently been held to violate the Sherman Act.

VII. VERTICAL DISTRIBUTION RESTRICTIONS

A. THE ECONOMICS OF VERTICAL RESTRICTIONS

Restrictive distribution systems have become an important element of modern marketing. Antitrust attacks have targeted a number of these restrictions, particularly those relating to resale prices and the number and location of distributors. The principal argument offered in support of the attack on resale price restrictions is that they yield the same effects as horizontal price fixing among dealers (the dealer cartel analogy). In theory at least, such restrictions may also help manufacturers to police their own cartel by, for example, making it easier to detect "cheating." The principal counterargument is that the manufacturer, concerned about prevailing in interbrand competition with other manufacturers, can be depended upon to set the resale price at an efficient level (or at least more efficient than each distributor or a court). Resale price restrictions may serve a number of arguably lawful functions. In particular, they may solve the "free rider" problem. A manufacturer may decide that a particular mix of price and service competition will be the optimum strategy for selling its products in competition with other brands. Dealers will hesitate to make investments in services if rival dealers, unburdened by comparable costs, can afford to offer the same product at lower prices. By solving this problem, the manufacturer may induce the desired level of service and attract dealers. Some commentators have also argued that resale price restrictions may serve two other functions: (i) preserving a product's quality image where lower price may signal lower quality to consumers; and (ii) permitting the survival of small distributors who cannot compete on price.

B. THE INTERPLAY OF COMMON LAW AND ANTITRUST LAWS

1. **Vertical Price Setting--Dr. Miles Medical Co. v. John D. Park & Sons Co.,** 220 U.S. 373 (1911).

    a. **Facts.** Dr. Miles (P) manufactured proprietary medicines under a secret but unpatented formula. Its contracts with wholesalers and retailers prescribed the minimum prices at which the medicines would be sold. John D. Park & Sons (D) obtained the medicines at prices below the minimum. P sued D for inducing P's wholesalers and retailers to breach their distribution contracts.

    b. **Issue.** Are the price clauses in the distribution contracts enforceable?

    c. **Held.** No.

    1) This case does not involve the breach of a consignment contract.

    2) The fact that this product is made under a secret formula does not render the price clauses enforceable.

3) P can fare no better with its plan of identical contracts than could the dealers themselves if they formed a combination and endeavored to establish the same restriction, and thus to achieve the same result, by agreement with each other.

d. **Dissent** (Holmes, J.). What really fixes the price of a product is the competition of conflicting desires. With regard to things like P's medicines the point of most profitable returns marks the equilibrium of social desires and determines the fair price in the only sense in which I can find meaning in those words. P knows better than we what will enable it to do the best business.

e. **Comment.** Manufacturers and distributors wishing to obtain the benefits of resale price maintenance could vertically integrate or distribute goods on consignment.

2. **Vertical Maximum Price Setting No Longer Per Se Illegal--State Oil Co. v. Khan,** 522 U.S. 3 (1997).

a. **Facts.** Khan (P) operated a retail gasoline station that he leased from State Oil (D). P purchased gasoline from D pursuant to a contract that set the price at 3.25¢ less than the retail price suggested by D *unless* P charged his customers a higher price. If he did, he had to pay the difference to D. When P fell behind on lease payments for the service station, D brought eviction proceedings in state court. P then filed suit claiming that D had violated section 1 of the Sherman Act by in effect imposing on P a maximum vertical price restraint. The district court granted summary judgment for D. P appealed and the circuit court reversed and remanded. D appealed and the Supreme Court granted certiorari.

b. **Issue.** Are vertical maximum retail price restraints per se unlawful?

c. **Held.** No. *Albrecht v. Herald*, which held that they were, is overruled, and the circuit court's per se condemnation of D's price restraint is reversed and remanded.

1) *Albrecht* held that vertical maximum retail price restrictions were per se unlawful based in part on *United States v. Arnold, Schwinn & Co.*, which held that vertical territorial restraints were illegal per se. *Continental T.V., Inc. v. GTE Sylvania, Inc.*, overruled *Schwinn* and held that vertical nonprice restrictions would be subject to rule of reason analysis.

2) While some types of restraints are unlawful per se because of their predictable anticompetitive effects and limited potential for procompetitive effects, most restraints require evaluation under the "rule of reason." Vertical maximum price restrictions may have substantial procompetitive effects—promoting interbrand competition,

the primary goal of the antitrust laws—especially when the retailer has an exclusive territory.

3) *Albrecht* expressed concern that maximum price fixing by suppliers could interfere with dealer freedom, but the *Albrecht* rule has actually prompted the elimination of many independent dealers as suppliers integrate forward into distribution in order to avoid the rule. *Albrecht* also expressed concern that maximum prices might be set too low for some dealers to offer consumers essential or desired services, but such conduct is unlikely because it would tend to drive customers away and thus hurt the price-setting manufacturers. In any event, both of these concerns, as well as the third, that vertical maximum price fixing could disguise minimum price fixing, could be satisfactorily addressed under the rule of reason.

3. **Consignment and Its Limitations.** *Simpson v. Union Oil Co.*, 377 U.S. 13 (1964) might be understood as condemning efforts to use the consignment device merely to circumvent the ban on resale price maintenance. The Court held that a supplier may not coerce a retailer in order to maintain prices. It is not clear what the Court meant by "coercion," except that the defendant in that case was doing something that presumably caused the plaintiff to suffer more costs of some kind. Note that citing "coercion" as the basis for condemning resale price setting turns the *Dr. Miles* dealer cartel analogy on its head.

4. **Customer and Territorial Restraints.**

   a. **Introduction.** Territorial and customer restraints serve similar, if not identical, functions as resale price maintenance. In particular, they help solve the free rider problem. Since an agreement between dealers to allocate territories or customers could well violate section one (*see United States v. Topco, supra*), the *Dr. Miles* dealer cartel analogy suggests that these restraints be treated harshly. So, too, does *Simpson*, however it is understood. But that is not how the Court treated these restraints initially. In *White Motor Co. v. United States*, 372 U.S. 253 (1963), the Court declined to extend the dealer cartel analogy, noting that vertical territorial restraints may serve purposes other than the "stifling of competition." The Court said that, "We do not know enough of the economic or business stuff out of which these arrangements emerge to be certain. They may be too dangerous to sanction or they may be allowable protections against aggressive competitors or the only practicable means a small company has for breaking into or staying in business. . . ." Four years later, in *United States v. Arnold, Schwinn & Co.*, 388 U.S. 365 (1967), the Court announced that vertical customer and territorial restraints after sale of a product to a wholesaler or retailer were illegal per se. Virtually identical restraints imposed on bona fide agents or consignees, however, were held subject to a rule of reason. The Court upheld the restraints on

Schwinn's agents (although their arrangements with Schwinn strongly resembled Simpson's arrangements with Union Oil) because other competitive bikes were available to distributors, Schwinn's agents sold other bikes too, and Schwinn's distribution system constituted a response to competitive pressures.

Continental T.V., Inc. v. GTE Sylvania, Inc.

b. **"Rule of reason" applies--Continental T.V., Inc. v. GTE Sylvania, Inc.**, 433 U.S. 36 (1977)

1) **Facts.** After seeing its share of the television set market decline to less than 2%, GTE Sylvania (P) changed its distribution system. Rather than selling to any interested wholesaler or retailer, P sold only to franchised dealers who agreed to abide by a location clause. The clause obligated the dealers to sell P's televisions only at locations specified in the franchise contract. When P contracted with a retailer within one mile of D's store, D protested and asked for permission to sell P's televisions from an additional location near another franchised dealer. P refused permission, but D went ahead. When P sued D to recover the price of televisions previously delivered, D counterclaimed for alleged violations of section 1. Instructed that it was illegal per se for a manufacturer and a distributor to agree to limit the area in which the distributor could resell the manufacturer's product, the jury returned a verdict for D on its counterclaim, and the district court entered a judgment accordingly. The appeals court reversed. The Supreme Court granted certiorari.

2) **Issue.** May a manufacturer and a retailer agree to limit the area in which the retailer can resell the manufacturer's product?

3) **Held.** Yes. Judgment affirmed.

   a) In intent and competitive impact, the contract in the *Schwinn* case (*supra*) between Schwinn and its retailers prohibiting them from selling Schwinn products to unfranchised retailers is indistinguishable from P's location clause.

   b) The market impact of vertical restrictions like P's location clause is complex because of their potential for a simultaneous reduction of intrabrand competition and stimulation of interbrand competition. They may stimulate interbrand competition by permitting the manufacturer to achieve certain efficiencies in the distribution of its products. For example, they may permit a manufacturer to overcome the free rider effect, thereby inducing dealers to invest in and provide promotional activities and service and repair facilities. These efficiency-tending effects do not depend on the passage of title. When interbrand competition exists, as it does among television manufacturers, it provides a significant check on the exploitation of intrabrand market power because of the ability of consumers to substitute a different brand of the same product. Thus, restraints like P's location clause should be evaluated under the "rule of reason."

  c) Application of the per se rule cannot be justified on the ground that the Sherman Act was intended to prohibit restrictions on the autonomy of independent businessmen even though they have no impact on price, quality, and quantity of goods and services. This view is not explicit in *Schwinn*. Competitive economies have social and political as well as economic advantages, but an antitrust policy divorced from market considerations would lack any objective benchmarks. Every agreement concerning trade restrains—to bind, to restrain is of their very essence. Applying the per se rule to restraints like P's location clause may ultimately hurt small businessmen who operate as franchisees. To the extent that a per se rule prevents a firm from using the franchise system to achieve efficiencies that it perceives as important to its successful operation, the rule creates an incentive for vertical integration into the distribution system.

  d) *Schwinn* is overruled.

4) **Concurrence** (White, J.). Sylvania's location clause is not a per se violation of the Sherman Act, but the Court need not overrule *Schwinn*, since it can be distinguished. As to intrabrand competition, Sylvania, unlike Schwinn, did not restrict the customers to whom its purchasers could sell. As to interbrand competition, Sylvania, unlike Schwinn, had an insignificant market share and enjoyed no consumer preference that would allow it to charge a premium price.

5) **Dissent** (Brennan, Marshall, JJ.). The per se rule of *Schwinn* should not be overruled.

6) **Comment.** This decision gives manufacturers a powerful incentive to substitute customer and territorial restraints for pricing restraints whenever it is economical to do so. Both kinds of restraints serve many of the same, if not identical functions. Yet the Court goes out of its way to say that it is not dealing with price restraints, which it argues (not very persuasively) are more likely to cause inefficient effects and are, therefore, illegal per se. As a practical matter, absent an express resale price maintenance clause, it will often be very difficult to distinguish price from nonprice restraints. The Court returned to this issue in the *Sharp* case (*infra*).

c. **Developments after *Sylvania*.**

 1) In *Eastern Scientific Co. v. Wild Heerbrugg Instruments, Inc.,* 572 F.2d 883 (1st Cir. 1978), *cert. denied*, 439 U.S. 833 (1978), the court held that a distributor's agreement not to sell at a discount outside of its assigned area was permissible under a rule of reason analysis, on the theory that this alternative was less restrictive than an outright ban on such sales, which would be permissible under *Sylvania*.

    a)   This decision gives distributors terminated or disciplined for violating customer or territorial restraints a powerful incentive to claim that the restraints were the product of a horizontal agreement. According to the court's opinion, such restraints are still subject to the relatively harsh *Topco* rule even where they serve to overcome the free rider effect, thereby inducing the parties to the agreement to promote a common brand. This decision, however, may undermine the *Topco* rule.

    b)   Although the court makes clear that vertical nonprice restraints are to be evaluated under the rule of reason, it does not make clear what that really means. The difficulty stems from the fact that these restraints stimulate interbrand competition by channeling intrabrand competition away from prices and towards services. The courts have struggled with this problem.

2)   In *Eiberger v. Sony Corp. of America*, 459 F. Supp. 1276 (S.D.N.Y. 1978), *rev'd in part*, 622 F.2d 1068 (2d Cir. 1980), Sony collected from its dealers a "warranty fee," equal to their profit on all sales outside their territory, and remitted the fee to the dealer whose territory it was. The court condemned the practice under the rule of reason as an outright territorial restraint on intrabrand competition and held that the defendant could have realized its permissible business objectives—assuring that users receive warranty service—in a less restrictive fashion.

3)   But in *American Motor Inns, Inc. v. Holiday Inns, Inc.*, 521 F.2d 1230 (3d Cir. 1975), the court stated that "in a rule of reason case the test is not whether the defendant deployed the least restrictive alternative. . . ." Application of the rigid "no less restrictive alternative" test in cases such as this one would place an undue burden on the ordinary conduct of business. Entrepreneurs such as Holiday Inns would then be made guarantors that the imaginations of lawyers could not conjure up some method of achieving the business purpose in question that would result in a somewhat lesser restriction of trade. And the courts would be placed in the position of second-guessing business judgment as to what arrangements would not provide "adequate" protection for legitimate commercial interests.

5.   **Refusal to Deal.** A manufacturer could enforce a vertical restraint by refusing to deal with a non-complying distributor, and the manufacturer could do this

whether or not the restraint was included in a written contract (or for that matter, whether or not there was a written contract). The question is: to what extent, if any, does antitrust law limit such a refusal to deal.

- a. **The seminal case--United States v. Colgate & Co.,** 250 U.S. 300 (1919).

    1) **Facts.** Colgate (D) had a comprehensive resale price maintenance program and all of its products sold at uniform prices across the country. The indictment listed the ways in which such prices had been maintained, including distribution of price lists and an announced policy that D would refuse to sell to anyone who sold at different prices. D demurred. Focusing on the absence of contractual arrangements, the district court sustained the demurrer. P appeals.

    2) **Issue.** May a manufacturer refuse to deal as a means of enforcing resale price maintenance?

    3) **Held.** Yes, absent a purpose to monopolize.

    4) **Comment.** One could interpret this decision as holding that a manufacturer could announce a resale price and enforce it by refusing to sell to those that did not maintain the set prices, as long as there were no explicit contracts between the parties (in theory leaving the distributor free to choose not to maintain the set prices).

- b. **Definition of "agreement" or "combination"--United States v. Parke, Davis & Co.,** 362 U.S. 29 (1960).

    1) **Facts.** Parke, Davis & Co. (D), a manufacturer of drugs, issued price lists with an announcement that it would refuse to deal with wholesalers or retailers who did not maintain D's prices. There were no applicable fair trade laws. Five retail drug chains in these areas refused to maintain the prices. D visited the wholesalers and told them they would be cut off if they sold to price-cutting retailers; they agreed not to. The retailers were also visited and told they would be cut off (and that all other retailers were being similarly informed). The retailers continued price-cutting; D again visited them and worked out an arrangement where they could continue their pricing policy if they would stop advertising cut prices; all agreed. The United States (P) brought an action under the Sherman Act for a combination in restraint of trade.

    2) **Issue.** Does the *Colgate* rule extend to the case where, in addition to refusal to deal, there are accompanying restrictive agreements?

    3) **Held.** No. There is a violation.

        a) In *Colgate* there was only a simple announcement of a price policy and an intention not to deal with price-cutters. There were no agreements, express or implied.

  b) Here D "entwined" the wholesalers and retailers in a program to promote compliance with its price policy; this went beyond "mere announcement" and refusal to deal.

4) Comment. *Parke* appeared to narrow *Colgate* considerably. It seemed to suggest that almost any action taken by a manufacturer to monitor or enforce compliance with its *Colgate* rights would prompt the court to pin the "agreement" label on the manufacturer's restricted distribution arrangements. This interpretation, however, probably did not completely survive the next main case, *Monsanto*.

c. **Complaints by dealers to manufacturer--Monsanto Co. v. Spray-Rite Service Corp.,** 465 U.S. 752 (1984).

 1) Facts. Spray-Rite Service Corporation (P), a discount wholesaler, was the 10th largest distributor of chemical agricultural herbicides produced by Monsanto Company (D). D refused to renew P's distributorship. P sued, claiming that D and its other distributors conspired to fix the resale prices of D's products and terminated P's distributorship in furtherance of the conspiracy. D claimed that it terminated P because P failed to hire trained salesmen and promote sales adequately. The court denied D's motion for a directed verdict. The jury found for P and awarded $3.5 million in damages. The court of appeals affirmed, holding that P could survive the directed verdict motion by showing that D terminated P following complaints by other distributors relating to P's price-cutting practices. The Supreme Court granted certiorari.

 2) Issue. Is evidence of complaints by distributors to a manufacturer about the price-cutting tactics of a particular distributor, followed by the termination of the price-cutting distributor, sufficient proof to support a finding of an antitrust violation?

 3) Held. No. Judgment affirmed, however.

  a) In distributor-termination cases, there are two important distinctions: (i) the distinction between concerted action and independent action, and (ii) the distinction between concerted action to set prices and concerted action on nonprice restrictions. Independent action is permissible; concerted action is not. Concerted action to set prices is per se illegal, but concerted action on nonprice restrictions is judged under the rule of reason.

  b) These basic principles are not always easily applied to a given set of facts because a manufacturer and its distributors frequently exchange specific market information for legitimate reasons. A manufacturer may have legitimate concerns about retail prices so its distributors can afford to provide necessary customer service. Complaints from distributors, by themselves, cannot justify an inference of illegal concerted action. There must also be evidence to exclude the possibility that the manufacturer and nonterminated distributors were acting independently.

    c) In this case, there was evidence that after P was terminated, D approached other price-cutting distributors and stated that their supplies of a new corn herbicide would be reduced if they did not maintain the suggested retail price. One resisted, but complied after D complained to that distributor's parent company. Shortly before P was terminated, another distributor wrote a newsletter to his customers explaining D's attempts to "get the marketplace in order." This evidence supports the inference of concerted action, and the fact that D had relayed to P the complaints about P's price cutting, but never the post-termination justifications, supports the conclusion that D terminated P as part of its concerted action, not independently.

  4) Comment. The approach taken by the court of appeals ignored the danger of eroding the *Sylvania* and *Colgate* doctrines.

d. Price vs. non-price restraints--Business Electronics Corp. v. Sharp Electronics Corp., 485 U.S. 717 (1988).

  1) Facts. Business Electronics Corporation (P) and Hartwell were the Houston area retailers of Sharp Electronics Corporation's (D's) calculators. D suggested minimum retail prices but did not expressly require retailers to charge any specific price. P often undercut the suggested minimum and generally undercut Hartwell. Hartwell complained to D about P's prices and then threatened to stop selling D's calculators unless D terminated P. D complied with this ultimatum. P sought treble damages, claiming that D and Hartwell had violated section 1 by conspiring to terminate P. Instructed that a manufacturer/dealer agreement to terminate another dealer for price cutting is illegal per se, the jury gave P a verdict. The appeals court reversed and remanded, holding that such an agreement is not illegal per se unless the remaining dealer "expressly or impliedly agree[s] to set its price at some level, though not a specific one." The Supreme Court granted certiorari.

  2) Issue. Do a manufacturer and dealer commit a per se offense by agreeing to terminate a second dealer for price cutting if they do not also agree that the first dealer will set its price at some level?

  3) Held. No. Judgment affirmed.

    a) The scope of per se illegality should be narrow for vertical restraints because they may stimulate interbrand competition, "the primary concern of antitrust law." They help overcome the free-rider problem and thereby enable retailers to invest in and provide cost-effective customer services.

    b) P did not show that a manufacturer/dealer agreement to terminate a price cutter almost always tends to restrict competition and reduce output absent a further agreement on the price level to be charged by the remaining dealer.

    c) Because price cutting and some measure of service cutting usually go hand in hand, giving any wider scope to per se illegality for vertical restraints would threaten to undermine *Sylvania* and its effect on interbrand competition.

4) **Dissent** (Stevens, White, JJ.). The agreement to terminate P for price cutting was illegal per se. It could not have been "ancillary" to any vertical non-price restraint because none appeared in D's dealership agreements. This "naked" restraint's sole function was to protect Hartwell from price competition, just like a retail boycott of a manufacturer. That it might have enabled Hartwell to provide better services is of no concern under *Sylvania*, which focused on manufacturer imposed vertical restraints.

5) **Comment.** Despite the Court's efforts to reconcile *Sharp* with antitrust precedent, *Sharp* could undermine several cases: (i) the *Dr. Miles* per se rule against resale price maintenance (effect will partly depend on the meaning courts give to a remaining dealer's "implied . . . agree[ment] to set its price at some level, though not a specific one"); (ii) the *General Motors* and *Klor's* prohibition on retail boycotts; and (iii) the *Topco* condemnation of horizontal restraints designed to overcome the free rider problem (the effect will partly depend on how courts distinguish "horizontal" from "vertical"). In theory, an agreement to terminate a price cutter might still be illegal under the rule of reason, but the reality might be different because such an agreement is likely to stimulate interbrand competition, the "primary concern of antitrust law."

e. **Failure to adhere to vertical agreement on minimum price as "antitrust injury"--Pace Electronics, Inc. v. Cannon Computer Systems, Inc.,** 213 F.3d 118 (3d Cir. 2000).

1) **Facts.** Pace Electronics (P), a wholesale dealer of electronic and computer equipment, entered into a dealer's agreement with Cannon Computer Systems (D). The agreement required P to purchase a certain number of printers. This agreement, unlike an earlier agreement between D and one of P's competitors, did not require that the printers not be sold below a minimum price. Nevertheless, D informed P that it expected P to adhere to the minimum. P started selling the printers at a lower price. D subsequently terminated the agreement with P purportedly because P

failed to order the required minimum number of printers. P claimed that D terminated P because of P's pricing, thereby causing P to lose profits and reduce competition among wholesalers of Cannon products, which resulted in higher printer prices. The district court granted D's motion to dismiss. P appeals.

2) **Issue.** Could D's termination of P's wholesale dealer's contract for P's refusal to acquiesce in an alleged vertical minimum price fixing conspiracy cause antitrust injury?

3) **Held.** Yes. Judgment reversed.

   a) A showing of "antitrust injury" (*i.e.*, an injury of the type the antitrust laws were intended to prevent and that flows from that which makes the defendant's conduct unlawful) is required even in cases where the defendant's conduct constitutes a per se violation of the antitrust laws.

   b) As the Supreme Court noted in *Simpson v. Union Oil* (*supra*), an agreement to set minimum prices can cause antitrust injury in that it deprives independent dealers of the exercise of free judgment. Accordingly, a restriction on dealer independence with respect to pricing decisions is an anticompetitive aspect of vertical minimum price fixing agreements and one that the antitrust laws have an interest in forestalling.

VIII. ADDITIONAL LIMITATIONS ON A SINGLE FIRM EXERCISING MARKET POWER

A. INTRODUCTION

In theory at least, a firm with market power might engage in a variety of conduct designed to deter rivalry, including blocking entry or expansion or "disciplining" competitors. Unfortunately, such conduct will usually resemble precisely the kind of rivalry that section 1 of the Sherman Act is supposed to foster. Thus, the difficult antitrust task is to make the necessary distinction, and to do so at some reasonable cost. Courts often pin the labels "exclusionary" or "predatory" on conduct adjudged bad, sometimes without explaining how it is that judgment was made.

B. MARKET POWER

Broadway Delivery Corp. v. United Parcel Service of America, Inc.

1. **Market Power and the Likely Effect of Challenged Conduct-- Broadway Delivery Corp. v. United Parcel Service of America, Inc.**, 651 F.2d 122 (2d Cir. 1981).

   a. **Facts.** A group of small New York transport firms (Ps) claimed that UPS (D) had attempted to monopolize and had monopolized the delivery of small packages sent by wholesalers in the New York garment district through predatory pricing. Instructed that Ps could not prevail on a monopolization claim "unless [Ps] proved that during the relevant period D controlled at least 50% of the relevant market," the jury found for D. The district court entered judgment for D and Ps appeal.

   b. **Issue.** Did the trial court err in instructing the jury?

   c. **Held.** Yes, but the error was harmless.

   1) Exclusive focus on market share percentages can produce a distorted picture of market power because "the relative effect of percentage command of a market varies with the setting in which that factor is placed. . . . A true picture emerges only from consideration of additional market characteristics, among them, the strength of the competition, the probable development of the industry, and customer demand." Thus the trial court's instruction on market share was erroneous.

   2) The trial court's error was harmless because Ps had not submitted sufficient evidence to put the market power question to the jury in the first place. In the absence of conventional market share data, Ps must produce unambiguous evidence that D

had the power to control prices or exclude competition. D's principal competitor, the United States Postal Service, could not be driven out of business, and entry barriers for new competitors were low. Moreover, Ps failed to prove that D had operated consistently below cost.

2. **Problems of Market Definition--United States v. Eastman Kodak Co.,** 63 F.3d 95 (2d Cir. 1995).

   a. **Facts.** Over the opposition of the United States (D), Eastman Kodak Company (P) moved to terminate a 1921 consent decree barring it from selling private label film and a 1954 consent decree barring it from selling its film bundled with film processing. When P's motion was heard, five "well-financed, billion-dollar, multinational corporations" manufactured all of the amateur color negative film sold in the United States: P, Fuji, Konica, Agfa, and 3M. Only P manufactured film in the United States, but the flow of imported film has been continuous and systematic through the entire United States, and no evidence suggests that transportation costs or tariffs put imported film at a significant cost disadvantage. The films of the five are of comparable quality. P supplied 67% of the film purchased in the United States (75% in dollar terms), Fuji 11%-12%, and private labels, the fastest growing segment of the film market, more than 12%; Worldwide, P sold 36%—43% of the film purchased in Europe and less than 10% of the film purchased in Japan; while Fuji sold 34%, Konica 16%, Agfa 10%, and 3M 4%. A price survey conducted at the behest of D showed that P's average wholesale prices in the United States were higher than in Europe which were higher than in Japan. At mass merchandisers in the United States, which account for approximately 50% of all film sales, Kodak and Fuji film are priced within 1% of each other; sometimes Kodak film is priced higher and sometimes Fuji's. (Five years earlier, Kodak film had commanded a 6.3% price premium at mass merchandisers.) At smaller food and drug stores, which account for the vast majority of other sales, the average price difference between Kodak and Fuji film is 4.5%. This difference resulted from Fuji's policy of undercutting P's price to make its product more attractive to retailers as well as to consumers with a preference for Kodak film. One-half of surveyed consumers said that they would only buy Kodak film, while 40% said that they prefer Kodak film, but would purchase another brand of film. This loyalty reflected the fact that P had earned consumer trust by producing a product that consumers perceive to be superior. Finding that P lacked market power in the worldwide market for film, the district court terminated both consent decrees, and D appeals.

   b. **Issue.** Should P's market power be assessed in the worldwide market for film?

   c. **Held.** Yes. Judgment affirmed.

1) To terminate an antitrust consent decree the antitrust defendant must establish that (i) the primary purposes of the consent decree have been achieved and (ii) the termination of the consent decree would benefit consumers.

2) The relevant geographic market is the area of effective competition in which the supplier operates and to which the purchaser can practically turn for supplies. Here, that is the world since the five manufacturers compete everywhere selling film of comparable quality. While purchasers in the United States say that they prefer Kodak film, their purchasing behavior shows that a large number of them are price sensitive, as indicated in part by the growth of private label film.

3) Since the film produced by P's competitors is of comparable quality to P's film, and since the small, declining price premium that P obtains for its film at some retailers does not show monopolistic pricing, the district court did not fall victim to the *Cellophane* fallacy: finding one product, foreign film, a good substitute for another, Kodak film, only because the price of the latter was set at monopolistic levels.

4) Absent evidence that P's costs are uniform throughout the world, the fact that P charges more for its film in the United States than in other countries cannot show price discrimination that might indicate market power. No evidence showed such uniformity, but it did show that P's marketing and distribution systems differ markedly from country to country. Besides, the data upon which D relied represented P's prices at only a single point in time, which even D's expert acknowledged is not necessarily evidence of systematic price discrimination. Moreover, differing currency exchange rates made D's price comparisons of "limited evidentiary value."

5) The 4.5% average price difference between Kodak and Fuji film at smaller food and drug stores reflects not P's market power, but Fuji's policy of undercutting P's price to make its product more desirable.

6) According to D, P's "own elasticity of demand" is two, meaning that a price increase would cause a drop in sales twice the percentage of the price increase. This indicates, again according to D, that the sales price of Kodak film is twice the short-run marginal cost, from which D infers that P is earning monopolistic profits from the sale of its film, which it could only do if it exercised significant market power in the United States. Even if P's short-run marginal costs equaled one-half of the product's sales price, it does not necessarily follow that P is earning monopolistic profits since many deviations between marginal cost and price reflect other factors such as high fixed costs. P used 8%-9% of its revenues for research and development and produced its film at plants costing hundreds of millions of dollars.

3. **Refusal to Sell at Wholesale Prices.** In *Otter Tail Power Co. v. United States*, 410 U.S. 366 (1973), Otter Tail sold electric power at retail in 465 towns in three states. In 45 towns in this area, municipal systems sold electric power. Where Otter Tail provided retail service, it did so under municipally granted franchises granted for 10- to 20-year periods. When these franchises expired, proposals were made to supplant Otter Tail with municipal systems. These proposals usually failed to materialize because Otter Tail refused to sell power at wholesale to such systems. The Supreme Court held that Otter Tail's refusal constituted a section 2 offense.

4. **Monopolists' Duty to Cooperate With Competitors--Aspen Skiing Co. v. Aspen Highlands Skiing Corp.,** 472 U.S. 585 (1985).

    Aspen Skiing Co. v. Aspen Highlands Skiing Corp.

   a. **Facts.** The Aspen Highlands Skiing Corporation (P) owned and operated a skiing facility on a mountain in Aspen, Colorado. The Aspen Skiing Company (D) owned and operated facilities on three other mountains in Aspen. For 15 years, P and D offered 6-day, 4-area ski tickets and divided the revenues on the basis of the usage of each resort. D then informed P that it would participate only if P accepted a fixed share of the revenues. P reluctantly agreed. The next year, D reduced the fixed share offer. D also made it virtually impossible for P to offer a multi-area package by refusing to sell P any tickets, by refusing to accept vouchers from P's ticket pass, and by discontinuing its 3-day pass, leaving in effect only its 6-day, 3-area pass, thereby eliminating the opportunity for its customers to ski at P's resort. As a result, P's share of the skiing business at Aspen declined from 20% during the last year of the 4-area tickets to 11% four years later. P sued for damages. The district judge instructed the jury that a monopolist is not barred from taking advantage of its efficiencies, and has no duty to cooperate with its business rivals, but it cannot unnecessarily exclude or handicap competitors, or use its monopoly power to further any domination of the relevant market. The jury found for P and awarded $2.5 million in actual damages. The court of appeals affirmed, holding that D had a duty to market jointly with P because the multi-area ticket was an "essential facility," and that there was sufficient evidence to support a finding that D's intent in refusing to market the ticket was to create or maintain a monopoly. The Supreme Court granted certiorari.

   b. **Issue.** Does a monopolist have a duty to market jointly with its competitors if the marketing had originated in a competitive market and had persisted for several years?

   c. **Held.** Yes. Judgment affirmed.

      1) D properly asserts that a monopoly has no general duty to engage in a joint marketing program with a competitor, but the verdict in this case was not based on that proposition. D's refusal to participate in

Antitrust - 93

the combined ticket plan is evidence of its purpose and could give rise to liability. A monopolist does not monopolize by mistake; exclusion that is not the result of superior efficiency is improper and is always deliberately intended.

2) In this case, D did not just reject a new idea proposed by P; D made a significant change in a pattern of distribution that had originated in a competitive market and had persisted for several years. In fact, the 6-day, all-Aspen ticket was created when each mountain was separately owned and operated. Such tickets are available in other multimountain areas, which indicates that a free competitive market would lead to the use of such tickets. By eliminating the ticket, D as a monopolist made an important change in the character of the market.

3) The jury was properly instructed, and its conclusion that D's refusal to deal was not justified by valid business reasons should be upheld as long as it is supported by the evidence. This requires consideration of the effect of D's conduct on consumers as well as on P and D itself.

4) The evidence indicates that the 6-day, 4-area ticket was popular with skiers and was preferred to D's 3-area ticket when both were available. Skiers also desired to ski P's mountain but did not solely because of the inconvenience when it was not included in the ticket. The evidence clearly shows that elimination of the ticket adversely affected P's business. Despite these adverse facts, D was unable to provide any efficiency justification for its practice. Thus, the evidence supports the verdict.

5. **Monopolist Retains Right to Unilaterally Refuse to Deal--Official Airline Guides, Inc. v. FTC,** 630 F.2d 920 (2d Cir. 1980), *cert. denied*, 450 U.S. 917 (1981).

   a. **Facts.** Official Airline Guides, Inc. (D) published a widely used compilation of airline schedules. In showing how to get from one city to another, the guide listed direct flights (no plane change) and connecting flights (one or more plane changes). In its list of connecting flights, however, D listed only those connections between "certified" carriers, and did not show where connections were available on minor airlines known as commuter airlines. The ALJ, affirmed by the full commission, found this to violate section 5 of the FTC Act.

   b. **Issue.** Does a monopolist have a greater duty to deal with others than a nonmonopolist?

   c. **Held.** No, on the facts here presented.

1) It should be noted that in this case the party injured by the refusal (the commuter airline) was not a competitor of the monopolist (D) but only a competitor of another customer of D. Moreover, there was no evidence here that D refused to deal at the favored customers' request.

6. *Aspen* **Distinguished.** In *Olympia Equipment Leasing Co. v. Western Union Telegraph Co.,* 797 F.2d 370 (7th Cir. 1986), Western Union had been circulating to its telex customers a list of terminal equipment vendors. (Telex is a non-voice message transmission service.) Because Western Union became dissatisfied with the pace at which it was liquidating its own inventory of such equipment, it abruptly withdrew this assistance. At trial, Western Union was convicted of monopolization, but the appeals court reversed. The court stated that "since Western Union had no duty to encourage the entry of new firms into the equipment market, the law would be perverse if it made Western Union's encouraging gestures the fulcrum of an antitrust violation. Then no firm would dare to attempt a graceful exit from a market in which it was a major seller. . . . The essential feature of the refusal-to-deal cases—a monopoly supplier's discriminating against a customer because the customer has decided to compete with it—is missing here. . . . Olympia [the plaintiff in the case] analogizes access to all the major mountains at Aspen to Western Union's vendor list, and argues that just as Aspen Highlands could not survive without access to the mountains so Olympia could not survive without the list. The analogy lacks not only plausibility but also evidentiary support. Aspen Highlands could not acquire three more mountains in the Aspen area in order to be able to compete more effectively with the Aspen Skiing Company, but Olympia could and did hire salesmen to substitute for the Western Union sales force that had been helping it. If Western Union had tried to prevent Olympia from making the substitution, it would have been guilty of exclusionary conduct. But Olympia had no right to take a free ride on its competitor's sales force. . . . Conjoined with other evidence, lack of business justification may indicate probable anticompetitive effect. But there is a clear business justification in this case: Western Union wanted to liquidate its supply of telex terminals faster, so it stopped promoting a competitor's supply. . . ."

7. **Duty of Vertically Integrated Monopolist to Deal With Non-vertically Integrated Competitor.** Even when a vertically integrated monopolist *is* required to deal with non-vertically integrated competitors, it may do so on price and/or supply terms that permit the monopolist to realize a competitive advantage.

   a. **Competing services revisited--Paddock Publications, Inc. v. Chicago Tribune Co.,** 103 F.3d 42 (7th Cir. 1997).

      1) **Facts.** Paddock Publications (d/b/a *The Daily Herald*) (P) claimed that the *Chicago Tribune* and the *Chicago Sun-Times* (Ds) violated

Paddock Publications, Inc. v. Chicago Tribune Co.

section 1 by entering into exclusive distribution contracts with providers of supplemental news and features services. These services attracted readers and made the subscribing newspapers distinct from their rivals. The exclusive contracts were terminable at will or on very short notice, but Ds and their providers tended to renew them over a long period. P did not allege a conspiracy among the larger papers or among the supplemental news services. The district court dismissed P's action for failure to state a claim, and P appeals.

2) **Issue.** Given the small number of daily newspapers in the Chicago area (the assumed market), did the exclusive distribution contracts violate section 1?

3) **Held.** No. Judgment affirmed.

   a) Even assuming that general interest newspaper readership in the Chicago area was the relevant market, any firm wishing to enter could compete for an exclusive distribution contract since the contracts are terminable at will or on very short notice.

   b) P had access to hundreds of opinion and entertainment features in the unconcentrated newspaper input market.

   c) Unlike *FTC v. Motion Picture Advertising Service Co.,* 344 U.S. 392 (1953), this case arose under the Sherman Act, involves contracts of short duration, and involves exclusive distribution which, unlike exclusive dealings, cannot restrict entry at any level.

United States v. Microsoft

8. **Business Justifications Versus Exclusionary Conduct in the Technology Sector by a Single Firm--United States v. Microsoft,** 253 F.3d 34 (D.C. Cir. 2001).

   a. **Facts.** Both the United States (P) and several states brought suit against Microsoft (D), which sold 95% of all Intel-compatible PC operating systems. To compete with D, a new entrant would have had to overcome significant barriers, in particular the "applications barrier:" most users want an operating system for which a large number of applications exist and software engineers prefer to create applications for operating systems that have a large customer base. D's conduct helped protect its power in the market for Intel-compatible PC operating systems.

   First, D licensed Windows to computer manufacturers on the condition that they refrain from (i) removing any desktop icons, folders, or "Start" menu entries; (ii) altering the initial boot sequence (the process that occurs the first time a consumer turns on the computer); or (iii) otherwise changing the appearance of the Windows desktop.

Second, D integrated Internet Explorer ("IE") with Windows by (i) writing Windows code so that deleting the IE code would cripple the operating system; (ii) designing the "add/remove programs" feature of Windows so that it could not remove IE; and (iii) designing Windows to override a substitute IE for the user's choice of browser in situations where Netscape's browser, Navigator, would not support the user's actions.

Third, D licensed IE and the IE Access Kit (a software package that allows an Internet Access Provider ("IAP") to "create a distinctive identity for its service in as little as a few hours by customizing the IE title bar, icon, start and search pages") to hundreds of IAPs at no charge. Moreover, D agreed with the 10 largest IAPs to provide easy access to their services from the Windows desktop in return for their agreement to promote IE exclusively and to keep shipments of Internet access software using Navigator under a specific percentage, typically 25%. D also gave these IAPs rebates or cash in exchange for their efforts to upgrade existing subscribers to client software that came bundled with IE instead of Navigator.

Fourth, D entered into similar arrangements with Internet Content Providers ("ICPs"), such as AOL.

Fifth, D entered into agreements with Independent Software Vendors ("ISVs") promising early Windows 98 and Windows NT betas (preliminary versions of the software), certain technical information, and the right to use certain D seals of approval *provided* that the ISVs used IE as their default browser for any software developed with a hypertext-based user interface and that they used D's "HTML Help," which is accessible only with Internet Explorer, to implement their applications' help systems.

Sixth, when Apple made Netscape's browser standard on its computers, D threatened to discontinue producing Mac Office software, which was widely used by owners of Apple's computers. Within a month, D and Apple agreed that D would continue to produce up-to-date versions of Mac Office for at least five years while Apple would (i) bundle the most current version of IE with its operating system; (ii) make IE the default browser on its computers; and (iii) refrain positioning icons for other browsing software on the desktop of its new computers.

Seventh, when Netscape agreed with Sun Microsystems to include Sun's software development platform, Java, with its browser software, D developed its own faster-operating version of Java and included it with IE as well as with its operating system software. D designed its version of Java so that programs designed on it would not run on Sun's version. D purposely misled software engineers about this incompatibility. It also threatened to support chip manufacturers competing with Intel if Intel did not stop supporting Netscape and Sun in their development of Java.

After a trial on the issue of liability, the district court concluded that D had (i) unlawfully maintained a monopoly in the market for Intel-compatible PC operating systems; (ii) attempted to monopolize the market for Internet browsers; and (iii) illegally tied its Windows operating system software to its IE browser software. The court ordered divestiture of D into two separate companies without holding a remedy-specific hearing to resolve disputes about relevant facts. D appealed and asked that the court of appeals remand to a different judge, citing adverse public comments made by the judge during and after the trial and ex parte communications between the district judge and P.

b. Issues.

1) Did Intel-compatible PC operating systems constitute a market for the purposes of antitrust law?

2) If Intel-compatible PC operating systems did constitute a market, could the district court properly infer that D had market power in that market from evidence of market share and barriers to entry?

3) If D had market power, did it unlawfully maintain it?

4) If D unlawfully maintained this market power in part by actions relating to its IE browser software, did such actions constitute an attempt to monopolize the Internet browser market?

5) Did the integration of IE and Windows constitute per se illegal tying?

6) Was the district court obliged to hold a remedy-specific evidentiary hearing before entering its divestiture order?

7) Did the district court judge's ex parte communications and public comments on the merits violate the Code of Conduct for United States Judges and evidence partiality?

c. Held. 1) Yes. 2) Yes. 3) Yes. 4) No. 5) No. 6) Yes. 7) Yes. Divestiture order vacated and judgment affirmed in part and reversed in part. Case remanded to a different trial judge.

1) Intel-compatible PC operating systems constitute a market for antitrust purposes. (*Note*: The court's analysis of this issue does not appear in the casebook.)

2) The district court properly inferred that D possessed monopoly power from the structure of the market: D's 95% share and evidence of significant barriers to entry, including the "applications barrier." "Direct proof" of this power was not required even though (i) firms in the market often compete through innovations for temporary market dominance from

which they may be unseated by the next wave of product advancements, and (ii) competition may be for the field rather than within the field because of "network effects." In any event, some aspects of D's behavior would be difficult to explain unless Windows were a monopoly product, behavior such as setting the price of Windows without considering rivals' prices. That D invested heavily in research and development and may not have priced Windows to maximize short-run profits did not prove otherwise.

3) D maintained its market power in part by (i) licensing Windows to computer manufacturers on the condition that they refrain from installing competing software or altering the Windows desktop; (ii) integrating IE and Windows software code so that deleting the IE code would cripple the operating system; (iii) designing the "add/remove programs" feature of Windows so that it could not remove IE; (iv) purposely misleading software engineers about whether programs designed to run on its version of Java would run on Sun's version; and (v) threatening to support chip manufacturers competing with Intel if Intel did not stop supporting Netscape and Sun on their development of Java D.

4) The conditions in D's Windows' license with computer manufacturers resulted in a reduction of the percentage of computer users using Netscape's browser and thereby helped protect D's operating system monopoly because, if a consumer could have access to the applications he desired, regardless of the operating system he uses, simply by installing a particular browser on his computer, then he could select an operating system other than Windows based solely upon its quality and price.

   a) Prohibiting the removal of desktop icons, folders, and Start menu entries insured that manufacturers could not remove visible means of accessing IE. This deterred some of them from adding Netscape's browser in part because a certain number of novice computer users, seeing two browser icons, would wonder which to use when and would call the manufacturer's support line, thereby causing the manufacturer to incur significant costs. Browser installation by a manufacturer is one of the two most cost-effective methods by far of distributing browsing software. (The other is bundling the browser with Internet access software distributed by an IAP.)

   b) Prohibiting manufacturers from modifying the initial boot sequence caused them to change their practice of inserting Internet sign-up procedures that encouraged users to choose from the manufacturer's list of Internet service providers, many of which used Netscape's browser.

   c) D failed to justify the conditions in these licenses except to invoke its copyrights. Its copyrights justified only the prohibition on automatically launching a substitute user interface upon completion of the boot process, which would drastically alter D's copyrighted work without significantly affecting competition. D failed to substantiate its claim that these license conditions prevented manufacturers from taking actions that would undermine the principal value of Windows as a stable and consistent platform that supports a broad range of applications and that is familiar to users.

- d) That the license restrictions did not completely block Netscape from distributing its browser does not shield D from liability because they did bar Netscape from the cost efficient ones.

5) Integrating IE with Windows deterred some consumers from using other browsers. It also deterred manufacturers from pre-installing other browsers because pre-installing a second browser would increase a manufacturer's product testing costs since a manufacturer must test and train its support staff to answer calls related to every software product pre-installed on the machine; moreover, pre-installing a browser in addition to IE would be a questionable use of the scarce and valuable space on a PC's hard drive.

- a) Writing Windows code so that deleting the IE code would cripple the operating system effectively prevented manufacturers from removing IE and thereby deterred them from installing a second browser because doing so wold have increased product testing and support costs.

- b) Designing the "add/remove programs" feature of Windows so that it could not remove IE reduced the usage share of rival browsers not by making D's own browser more attractive to consumers but, rather, by discouraging manufacturers from distributing rival products.

- c) Designing Windows to override a user's choice of browser by substituting IE in certain situations prevents some people from using other browsers, thereby reducing rivals' usage share and so protecting D's market power.

- d) A monopolist's design changes are not per se lawful. D proffered no justification for commingling browser and operating system code or for designing the "add/remove programs" feature so that it could not remove IE; nor did D argue that these actions achieved any integrative benefit. Evidence did support D's position that Netscape's browser would not support certain user actions, so D had to design Windows to override a user's choice of browser in some situations. P failed to bear its burden of rebutting this justification and demonstrating that it was outweighed by the anticompetitive effect of the challenged action.

6) D's deals with IAPs ensured that the majority of all IAP subscribers were offered IE either as the default browser or as the only browser, thereby helping to keep Navigator usage below the level necessary for it to pose a real threat to D's monopoly. That D wanted to keep developers focused upon its APIs, which is to say it wanted to preserve its power in the operating system

market, did not qualify as a procompetitive justification for these deals, but D proffered no other justification.

7) D's deals with ICPs did not violate section 2 in light of the district court's finding that there was not sufficient evidence to support a finding that D's promotional restrictions actually had a substantial, deleterious impact on Navigator's usage share.

8) D's deal with ISVs, which affected applications used by "millions" of consumers, foreclosed a relatively small channel for browser distribution, but this foreclosure became significant because D's other conduct had largely foreclosed the two primary channels. D did not proffer any procompetitive justification for these deals, only the competitively neutral explanation that it was trying to persuade ISVs to utilize Internet-related system services in Windows rather than Navigator.

9) D's deal with Apple substantially restricted the distribution of rival browsers, thereby reducing their usage share and so protecting D's monopoly. D did not proffer any procompetitive justification for this deal.

10) Deliberately misleading software engineers about whether programs designed on D's version of Java would run on Sun's version resulted in many more applications that required D's, thus protecting D's monopoly from the potential threat posed by Sun's version of Java. D's deal with Intel reinforced this. D offered no procompetitive explanation for this conduct.

11) In an equitable enforcement action, an antitrust plaintiff need not present direct proof that a defendant's continued monopoly power is precisely attributable to its anticompetitive conduct. To require that section 2 liability turn on a plaintiff's ability or inability to reconstruct the hypothetical marketplace absent a defendant's anticompetitive conduct would only encourage monopolists to take more and earlier anticompetitive action. Because Navigator and Java showed potential as middleware platform threats, conduct aimed at excluding them raises significant antitrust concern.

12) D's liability for monopolization of the Intel-compatible PC operating system market does not presumptively indicate that D attempted to monopolize the putative browser market. To prove this attempted monopolization claim, P would have had to show that browsers constitute a relevant market for antitrust purposes and that there was a dangerous probability that D would acquire monopoly power in that market. With respect to market definition, P did not even articulate and identify evidence bearing on (i) what constitutes a browser (*i.e.*, what are the technological components of or functionalities provided by a browser) and (ii) why certain other products are not reasonable substitutes (*e.g.*, browser shells or viewers for individual Internet extensions, such as Real Audio Player or Adobe Acrobat Reader). With respect to dangerous probability of acquiring market power, P failed to establish that the puta-

tive browser market was protected by significant barriers to entry, without which D could not expect to acquire significant market power. P showed no more than that network effects were merely a possible consequence of high market share in the browser market; P failed to show that this consequence was probable or that a barrier to entry resulting from it would be "significant" enough to confer monopoly power.

13) Since this case provides the first up-close look at the technological integration of added functionality into software that serves as a platform for third-party applications, per se condemnation of this tying arrangement would carry a serious risk of harm. Such integration is common in competitive software markets. Moreover, due to the pervasively innovative nature of the platform software markets, tying arrangements in these markets may produce efficiencies that courts have not previously had opportunities to encounter.

14) A hearing on the merits does not substitute for a relief-specific evidentiary hearing where the parties dispute facts relevant to the remedy. That six years had passed since D engaged in the challenged conduct ("an eternity in the computer industry") makes a relief-specific evidentiary hearing especially important because innovations might have made the challenged conduct inconsequential in terms of competition. In any event, the remedial decree must be vacated because the district court failed to provide adequate rationale for it and because the scope of D's liability has been reduced on appeal.

15) Canon 3A(6) of the Code of Conduct for United States Judges prohibits judges from commenting publicly on a pending case and requires them to avoid the appearance of impropriety. The public comments of the district court judge that disfavored D constituted deliberate and flagrant violations of this canon. Section 455(a) of the Judicial Code requires judges to recuse themselves when their impartiality may reasonably be questioned, but the district court judge refused to recuse himself.

9. **Intellectual Property Rights--Image Technical Services, Inc. v. Eastman Kodak Co.,** 125 F.3d 1195 (1997).

   a. **Facts.** Image Technical Services and several independent service organizations (Ps) brought suit against Kodak (D) alleging violations of section 2. D is a leading producer of high speed copy machines and competes with Ps for service contracts for these copiers. Ps provided repair service at a price substantially less than D and according to some customers this service was of higher quality. In an effort to maintain its service contracts, D refused to deal with Ps, thereby preventing them from obtaining necessary replacement parts to service Kodak copiers. Ps sued claiming that D's refusal to sell parts constituted an unlawful attempt to monopolize the service market by tying replacement parts to its repair service. The district court granted summary judgment for D, the court of appeals reversed and remanded, and the Supreme Court affirmed the appellate court's decision. On remand, the jury rendered a verdict for Ps, finding that D possessed market power in Kodak copier parts and had used that power to create a monopoly over the provisioning of service for Kodak copiers. The district court entered a permanent injunction, and D appeals.

b. **Issue.** Does the holder of numerous patents on selected parts of a machine, in a market in which it has market power, violate the antitrust laws when it refuses to sell all parts to competitors in the service market?

c. **Held.** Yes. Judgment affirmed.

1) To interpret section 2 as prohibiting the use of monopoly power "to foreclose competition, to gain a competitive advantage, or to destroy a competitor" does not invite a jury to treat aggressive competition as an offense.

2) Exclusionary conduct, while necessary, is not sufficient to establish D's liability, because such conduct is not actionable if supported by a legitimate business justification. A monopolist's desire to exclude others from its protected work is a presumptively valid business justification. Ps rebutted this presumption, however, by showing that D had refused to sell not only its 65 patented copier parts, but thousands of other copier parts as well.

10. **Refusal to License Patented and Copyrighted Information as Antitrust Violation--Independent Service Organizations Antitrust Litigation v. Xerox Corporation,** 203 F.3d 1322 (Fed. Cir. 2000).

    a. **Facts.** Xerox Corporation (D) refused to sell certain parts that were necessary for repair and maintenance of its high end copiers. To enforce this policy, D instituted a process of end user verification to confirm the identity of those purchasing its parts and where the parts were being used. In 1994, D entered into a settlement agreement with several independent service organizations as part of an antitrust action and ended its restrictive parts policy. Independent Service Organization (P) opted out of the settlement and brought suit against D, claiming that its refusal to sell patented parts and copyrighted software to P for use in repairing D's copiers constituted an unlawful restraint of trade. The district court granted summary judgment for D. P appeals.

Independent Service Organizations Antitrust Litigation v. Xerox Corporation

b. Issue. Does a holder of a lawfully acquired patent or copyright engage in unlawful exclusionary conduct by unilaterally refusing to sell or license its product if its refusal affects more than one market?

c. Held. No. Judgment affirmed.

1) Intellectual property rights do not confer a privilege to violate the antitrust laws, but the antitrust laws do not negate a patentee's right to exclude others from patent property. The possession of market power does not impose on the intellectual property owner an obligation to license the use of that property.

2) A patentee may not bring an objectively baseless infringement suit simply to interfere directly with the business relationship of a competitor, but D's suit was not objectively baseless.

3) The Copyright Act expressly grants a copyright owner the exclusive right to distribute the protected work by transfer of ownership, or by rental, lease, or lending. The owner of the copyright may refrain from dealing with others and effectively exercise a right to exclude others from using its property. It may not use these property rights to extend power in the marketplace beyond what Congress intended, but P failed to discharge its burden of proving that D's refusal to license its protected work did any such thing.

C. ATTEMPT TO MONOPOLIZE

1. **Introduction.** Borrowing from the substantive criminal law, courts have traditionally identified three elements of a section 2 attempt-to-monopolize case: (i) the nature of the conduct; (ii) dangerous probability of success; and (iii) "intent." Of course, it is the conduct that usually constitutes most, if not all, of the proof of the other two elements; and dangerous probability of success supports "intent."

2. **Refusal to Deal--Lorain Journal Co. v. United States,** 342 U.S. 143 (1951).

    a. Facts. Lorain Journal Co. (D) operated a newspaper in Lorain, Ohio, a town of 50,000. The paper reached about 99% of the population. A radio station was set up in a town eight miles away. D then refused to allow advertising in the paper if the customer was also advertising on the radio station; D monitored the radio programs to enforce its policy. The government took action under section 2 of the Sherman Act.

    b. Issue. Was D's refusal to deal illegal?

c. **Held.** Yes. The right to refuse to deal is not absolute; here D's acts amounted to an attempt to monopolize.

3. **Right to Institute Changes.** In *A.H. Cox & Co. v. Star Machinery Co.*, 653 F.2d 1302 (9th Cir. 1981), Star persuaded R.O. Products to allow Star to be the exclusive carrier of R.O. Products line instead of Cox, which had been R.O.'s prior sole distributor of heavy equipment. Driven into bankruptcy, Cox charged a concerted refusal to deal in violation of section 1 and an attempt to monopolize in violation of section 2. The appeals court affirmed summary judgment for Star. The section 1 claim failed because in deciding to switch from Cox to Star, R.O. did not act in concert with any other manufacturer. The section 2 claim also failed because the switch simply replaced one distributor with another. The court held that where "each distributor has only one line, it is particularly appropriate to recognize a right of a distributor to initiate changes; otherwise a weak distributor could continue ineffective promotion of a good brand, while a strong distributor would be forced to continue representing a manufacturer with whom it has poor relations."

4. **Dangerous Probability of Success Required to Show Attempt to Monopolize--Spectrum Sports, Inc. v. McQuillan,** 506 U.S. 447 (1993).

   Spectrum Sports, Inc. v. McQuillan

   a. **Facts.** In 1980, the McQuillans (Ps) became the exclusive dealer of equestrian products using sorbothane, a patented elastic polymer with strong shock-absorbing capacity. Subsequently, the manufacturer of sorbothane (D) selected Ps as a regional distributor for all products made from sorbothane. In early 1982, however, the manufacturer shifted the distribution of medical products made from sorbothane to a single national distributor and, later that year, appointed Spectrum Sports (D), a company run by the son of the manufacturer's CEO, as the sole distributor of athletic sorbothane products. The manufacturer insisted that Ps cease distributing athletic sorbothane products as a condition for retaining the right to distribute equestrian sorbothane products. Ps resisted, but then the manufacturer refused to fill its orders. Ps brought suit claiming that Ds had violated section 2 of the Sherman Act. With respect to the charge of "attempt to monopolize," the judge instructed the jury that it could infer specific intent and dangerous probability of success from Ds' conduct, if deemed "predatory," even if Ps had established neither the relevant market nor the chances that Ds could achieve monopoly power in that market. The jury found for Ps without specifying whether Ds had monopolized, attempted to monopolize, or conspired to monopolize. The trial court refused Ds' motion for judgment notwithstanding the verdict, and the ninth circuit court of appeals affirmed, relying on *Lessig v. Tidewater Oil Co.*, 327 F.2d 459, *cert. denied*, 377 U.S. 993 (1964), and its progeny. Ds appeal.

   b. **Issue.** May the jury find a section 2 offense by inferring probability of success and market power from only evidence of conduct?

    c. Held. No. Judgment reversed and remanded.

        1) Neither the language of section 2 nor the cases interpreting it provide much, if any, support for the notion that proof of "unfair" or "predatory" conduct alone is sufficient to make out the offense of attempted monopolization. Section 2's "any part" of commerce language, upon which *Lessig* placed considerable reliance, applies to charges of monopolization as well as to attempts to monopolize, and the former undoubtedly requires proof of market power in a relevant market.

        2) Because of the difficulty of distinguishing robust competition from conduct with long-term anticompetitive effects and because single-firm activity does not present the same anticompetitive risk as concerted activity covered by section 1, section 2 makes the conduct of a single firm unlawful only when it actually monopolizes or dangerously threatens to do so. The problem of over-deterrence is not solved by inquiring whether the challenged conduct was "unfair" or "predatory" tactics. This problem, the one addressed by the dangerous probability requirement, requires inquiry into the relevant market and the defendant's power in that market. The *Lessig* interpretation is contrary to the purpose and policy of the Sherman Act.

5. Dangerous Probability Element. In *United States v. Empire Gas Corp.*, 537 F.2d 296 (8th Cir. 1976), *cert. denied*, 429 U.S. 1122 (1977), the court found specific intent to monopolize (on the basis of the defendant's behavior) but found no dangerous probability of success, mostly because of the defendant's small market share. The element of dangerous probability seems to be required in all but the Third and Ninth Circuits. In *International Distribution Centers, Inc. v. Walsh Trucking Co., Inc.*, 812 F.2d 786 (2d Cir.), *cert. denied*, 482 U.S. 915 (1987), the Second Circuit explained why. "Eliminating the dangerous probability element from attempted monopolization would . . . extend the coverage of section 2 to behavior already covered by state and federal law. . . . There is no unmet need calling for judicial expansion of section 2 to reach similar behavior. Furthermore, any significant reduction in the antitrust plaintiff's burden of proving that the defendant has a dangerous probability of monopolizing the market might discourage the healthy competition that section 2 is intended to nurture . . . and deter businesses from aggressively expanding into new markets." If the dangerous probability of success element is to serve the function suggested by the Second Circuit, it must be assessed in a fairly predictable manner. For that reason, many courts give considerable attention to the defendant's market share and entry.

D. PREDATORY PRICING

1. Generally. The task of distinguishing lawful from unlawful pricing conduct is formidable. The actor's "intention" helps little because price cuts are always motivated by the desire to win sales at the expense of rivals, and if the cuts work, the actor will no doubt be pleased about the impact. A court might turn to costs as a benchmark because, if a firm were to realize a loss on each sale, its conduct does not correspond to expected business behavior. Unfortunately, there is considerable dispute about which "costs" provide an appropriate benchmark, and measuring those costs is rather difficult (and in some cases impossible). Another possible approach would be to focus on the ability of the actor to recoup the losses it supposedly sustained during the period of predation.

2. **Must Show Prospect of Recoupment to Prove Predatory Pricing--Brooke Group Ltd. v. Brown & Williamson Tobacco Corp.,** 509 U.S. 209 (1993).

   a. **Facts.** In 1980—with overall demand for cigarettes in the United States declining, no immediate prospect of recovery, and substantial excess capacity afflicting all manufacturers—Brooke Group (P), formerly Liggett, pioneered the development of the economy segment of this market by introducing a line of "black and white" generic cigarettes. The economy or "generic" segment comprises: (i) black and whites, which are true generics sold in plain white packages with simple black lettering describing their contents; (ii) private label generics, which carry the trade dress of a specific purchaser, usually a retail chain; (iii) branded generics, which carry a brand name but which, like black and whites and private label generics, are sold at a deep discount and with little or no advertising; and (iv) "Value-25s," packages of 25 cigarettes that are sold to the consumer some 12.5% below the cost of a normal 20-cigarette pack.

   By 1984, when Brown & Williamson (D) entered the generic segment, P's black and whites represented 97% of the generic segment, which in turn accounted for a little more than 4% of domestic cigarette sales. D sold its generics at a price lower than P's, and D offered volume rebates to wholesalers. A price war ensued, which D won. For a year afterwards, list prices for generic cigarettes remained stable, but in June of 1985, P raised its list price, and the other manufacturers followed several months later. From 1986 to 1989, list prices increased twice a year by similar amounts, on generics from $19.75 to $33.75 and on branded cigarettes from $33.15 to $46.15. The increases outpaced increases in costs, taxes, and promotional expenditures. Since the dollar amount of these increases was the same for generic and full-priced cigarettes, a greater percentage price increase in the less expensive generic cigarettes resulted and the percentage gap between the list price of branded and black and white cigarettes narrowed from approximately 38% in 1984, to approximately 27% at the time of trial in 1989. Some of this increase was reflected in a higher net price to the consumer but not all because all firms offered a variety of discounts, coupons, and other promotions directly to consum-

Brooke Group Ltd. v. Brown & Williamson Tobacco Corp.

ers on both generic and branded cigarettes. Moreover, many wholesalers passed portions of their volume rebates on to the consumer. At that time, six manufacturers dominated production as they had for decades: Philip Morris (40% market share), R.J. Reynolds (28%), American Brands, Lorillard, D (12%), and P (5%, up from 2% in 1980). All had entered the economy segment of the market, and five, including P, had introduced so-called "subgenerics," a category of branded generic cigarette that sold at a discount of 50% or more off the list price of full-priced branded cigarettes. The economy segment increased from about 4% of the market in 1984, when the price war between P and D began, to about 15% in 1989. The consumer price of generics had increased along with output.

P filed suit claiming that D cut prices on generic cigarettes below average variable cost and offered discriminatory volume rebates to wholesalers in order to pressure P to raise its list prices on generics, so that the percentage price difference between generic and branded cigarettes would narrow. Thus, according to P, the volume rebates violated section 2(a) of the Robinson-Patman Act in that they amounted to price discrimination that had a reasonable possibility of injuring competition. The jury, using a special verdict form, agreed. The trial judge, however, held that D was entitled to judgment as a matter of law on three separate grounds: (i) lack of injury to competition, (ii) lack of antitrust injury to P, and (iii) lack of a causal link between the discriminatory rebates and P's alleged injury. With respect to the first issue (the only one that reached the Supreme Court), the district court found that no slowing of the growth rate of generics, and thus no injury to competition, was possible absent tacit price coordination in the economy segment of the cigarette market and that a reasonable jury could only conclude that such coordination did not exist. The court of appeals held that the dynamic of conscious parallelism among oligopolists could not produce competitive injury in a predatory pricing setting, which necessarily involves a price cut by one of the oligopolists. In the court of appeals' view, "[t]o rely on the characteristics of an oligopoly to assure recoupment of losses from a predatory pricing scheme after one oligopolist has made a competitive move is . . . economically irrational." The Supreme Court granted certiorari.

    b.   **Issue.** Did the record show that D had a reasonable probability of recouping the losses that it allegedly incurred as a result of allegedly selling its generic cigarettes below cost in an effort to injure P?

    c.   **Held**. No. Judgment affirmed. D is entitled to judgment as a matter of law.

        1)   To establish competitive injury resulting from a rival's low prices, a plaintiff must prove not only that the prices are below an appropriate measure of its rival's costs, but also that the rival had "a reasonable prospect" (or, under section 2 of the Sherman Act, "a dangerous probability") of recouping its investment in below-cost prices. To prove the latter, a plaintiff must show that below-cost pricing could drive rivals from the market

or cause them to raise their prices to supracompetitive levels within a disciplined oligopoly, and that accomplished, that the ensuing price rise would likely compensate for the amounts expended on the predation, including the time value of the money invested in it.

2) For a multi-firm predatory scheme to succeed, the participants must agree on how to allocate present losses and future gains among themselves and each firm must resist powerful incentives to cheat on the allocation. Such a scheme is unlikely to succeed even with an express agreement. Without one, the participants must rely on uncertain and ambiguous signals that are subject to misinterpretation, especially in the context of changing or unprecedented market circumstances. Any attempt to discipline a suspected cheater is likely to produce an outbreak of competition. If one firm does all of the below-cost selling, as D is accused of doing, that firm would have to bear all of the present losses while sharing the later supracompetitive profits with its rivals, including the intended victim, in proportion to their market share.

3) Whatever D's intent in introducing black and whites may have been, the price and output data do not support a reasonable inference that D and the other cigarette companies elevated prices above a competitive level for generic cigarettes. Supracompetitive pricing entails a restriction in output, but after D entered the generic segment, the average rate of growth in that segment doubled. Perhaps it would have grown even faster, but the record does not support that conclusion. An important planning document prepared by D in 1984 predicted that the economy segment would account for 10% of the total cigarette market by 1988 if it did not enter the segment. In fact, in 1988, the generic segment accounted for over 12% of the total market.

4) Because the undisputed evidence showed that during the period in question consumers did not actually pay list prices, a reasonable jury could not have inferred from the changes in those prices that D succeeded in bringing about oligopolistic price coordination and supracompetitive prices in the generic category sufficient to slow its growth, thereby preserving supracompetitive branded profits and recouping its predatory losses. Especially in an oligopoly setting, in which price competition is most likely to take place through less observable and less reputable means than list prices, it would be unreasonable to draw conclusions about the existence of tacit coordination or supracompetitive pricing from data that reflect only list prices.

5) During the relevant period, the price difference between the highest priced branded cigarette and the lowest priced cigarettes in the economy segment grew substantially as P pioneered "subgeneric" cigarettes, which were priced at discounts of 50% or more from the list prices of normal branded cigarettes, and four of its five rivals followed suit. It is still possible that transaction prices rose because the cumulative discounts attributable to subgenerics and the various consumer promotions might not have cancelled out the full effect

of the increases in list prices, but a rise in price does not itself permit an inference of collusion, even in a concentrated market, when output also rises and P's own officers and directors deny that P or its rivals priced their cigarettes through tacit collusion or reaped supracompetitive profits.

6) Declining demand, substantial excess capacity, and the introduction of new products (generic and subgeneric cigarettes) made supracompetitive pricing in the economy segment highly unlikely since tacit coordination is facilitated by a stable market environment, fungible products, and a small number of variables upon which the firms seeking to coordinate their pricing may focus.

7) Even if all the cigarette companies had been willing to participate in a scheme to restrain the growth of the generic segment—and P conceded that R.J. Reynolds was not—they could not have coordinated their actions unless they understood that D entered the segment to discipline rather than to compete with P. A misinterpretation by even one rival would almost certainly have prompted an outbreak of competition. P argued that D signaled that it did not intend to attract additional smokers to the generic segment by its entry by maintaining list prices while offering substantial rebates to wholesalers. But a reasonable jury could not conclude that this pricing structure eliminated or rendered insignificant the risk that the other firms might misunderstand D's entry as a competitive move. The likelihood that D's rivals would have regarded its pricing structure as an important signal is low, given that P itself was already using similar rebates, as was R.J. Reynolds in marketing its Doral branded generic.

d. **Dissent** (Stevens, White, Blackmun, JJ.). From the succession of price increases after 1985, the jury was entitled to infer that D's below-cost pricing disciplined P, permitting the six largest cigarette manufacturers to charge supracompetitive prices. In any event, the jury was entitled to infer that "D's predatory plan, in which it invested millions of dollars for the purpose of achieving an admittedly anticompetitive result, carried a reasonable possibility of injuring competition."

3. **The Cost Standard and Areeda & Turner.** Areeda and Turner argue that predatory pricing is highly unlikely behavior because it holds out the promise of sufficient recoupment only where the predator has far greater financial staying power than rivals and where entry barriers are substantial. Thus, the court should concern itself with overdeterrence when it evaluates claims of such conduct. The authors assert that marginal cost pricing is the economically sound division between acceptable, competitive behavior and predation, but they advocate using average variable cost as a proxy because of the extreme difficulty of ascertaining marginal cost. (Marginal cost is the increment to

total cost that results from producing an additional increment of output. Variable costs are those that vary with output changes.) Their approach is to presume that prices above average variable cost are lawful, and that those below average variable cost are unlawful.

4. **Alternative Approaches.**

   a. **Scherer.** Scherer argues that Areeda and Turner's proposals are too narrow and suggests a more complex analysis keyed to long-term economic welfare.

   b. **Baumol.** Baumol criticizes the Areeda-Turner failure to consider timing.

   c. **Posner.** Posner also believes the Areeda-Turner formula is too narrow and would also include sales below long-run marginal cost.

   d. **Jeshow & Keevorick.** Jeshow and Keevorick propose a two-level approach: Is a market ripe for predatory behavior; and, has there been such behavior?

   e. **Bolton, Brodley, and Riordan.** They criticize the Areeda and Turner rule for its static approach to predatory pricing issues and urge a dynamic approach reflecting strategic considerations and modern game theory. They argue that in a number of scenarios predatory pricing would be rational.

5. **"Intent" Standards.** In *McGahee v. Northern Propane Gas Co.*, 865 F.2d 1274 (11th Cir. 1988), the court reversed a grant of summary judgment in favor of a defendant accused of predatory pricing. The district court had found that new entrants to the propane market did not have to overcome trade secrets, patents, or licenses and that the plaintiff had not produced any evidence that the defendant sold propane below its average variable cost. The district court had ignored evidence of the defendant's subjective intent: (i) the defendant's investigation of the plaintiff's financial position; (ii) the defendant's new policy of rent-free tanks designed to take advantage of the plaintiff's weak financial position; and (iii) the defendant's internal memo stating that the goal of the defendant's local office was to "contribute to [the plaintiff's] financial problems." The appeals court opined that "when an antitrust defendant moves for judgment as a matter of law, the test for predatory pricing must consider subjective evidence and should use average total cost as the cost above which no inference of predatory intent can be made...."

E. **TYING**

1. **The Clayton Act.** Section 3 of the Clayton Act provides as follows: "That it shall be unlawful for any person engaged in commerce, in the

course of such commerce, to lease or make a sale or contract for sale of goods, wares, merchandise, machinery, supplies or other commodities, whether patented or unpatented, for use, consumption or resale . . . or fix a price charged therefor or discount from or rebate upon, such price, on the condition, agreement or understanding that the lessee or purchaser thereof shall not use or deal in the goods, wares, merchandise, machinery, supplies, or other commodity of a competitor or competitors of the lessor or seller where the effect of such lease, sale, or contract for sale or such condition, agreement or understanding may be to substantially lessen competition or tend to create a monopoly in any line of commerce."

2. **Definition.** "Tying" may take many forms in addition to the refusal to sell or lease one product unless the buyer also buys or leases another. These include contractual provisions either forbidding the buyer from handling a rival's products or requiring the buyer to obtain a product from a particular supplier. Tying may also take the form of selling two or more products at a price below the total price that the buyer would have had to pay had the buyer purchased each separately. Because tying may take this form, almost every sale involves a tie. The antitrust problem is to distinguish unlawful from lawful tying, which in principle requires that the objections to tying be articulated. This is the same problem that arises in connection with concerted refusals to deal.

3. **Introduction to the Case Law--United Shoe Machinery Corp. v. United States,** 258 U.S. 451 (1922).

    a. **Facts.** United Shoe Machinery Corporation (D) controlled 95% of the shoe machinery business in the United States. Its machines were covered by patents. It leased its machinery; as part of the lease it had every type of tying contract imaginable (to lease any machinery one must lease all from D; use of a competitor's machinery was a basis for cancellation of leases; all supplies used with the machines had to come from D, etc.).

    b. **Issue.** Did this network of patents and leases so prevent lessees from using other products as to violate section 3?

    c. **Held.** Yes. Violation of section 3 of the Clayton Act.

        1) D here controls nearly the entire industry and the tying arrangements clearly tend to create a monopoly.

4. **Quality Control--International Salt Co. v. United States,** 332 U.S. 392 (1947).

    a. **Facts.** International Salt Company (D) leased two patented machines designed for using salt in industrial processes. D obliged itself to maintain these machines. For proper functioning, these machines required salt with an average sodium chloride content of 98.2%. The leases provided that the user had to purchase its salt from D, which was the nation's leading producer of industrial salt. With respect to the much more widely used machine, the leases released the user from the obligation to buy salt from D if D would not match a lower price from another supplier. In one year, D sold $500,000 worth of salt to users of its machines. The Department of Justice (P) challenged the salt-buying clauses as violations of section 1 of the Sherman Act and section 3 of the Clayton Act. P obtained summary judgment, and D appeals.

b. **Issue.** Do the salt-buying clauses unreasonably restrain trade or "tend to substantially lessen competition or create a monopoly"?

c. **Held.** Yes. Judgment affirmed.

   1) Patent law provides no antitrust immunity for a tying arrangement with an unpatented product.

   2) It is unreasonable per se to foreclose competitors from any substantial market. The volume of business affected by these contracts cannot be said to be insignificant or insubstantial and the tendency of the arrangement to accomplishment of monopoly seems obvious. Agreements are forbidden that "tend to create a monopoly," and it is immaterial that the tendency is a creeping one rather than one that proceeds at full gallop; nor does the law await arrival at the goal before condemning the direction of the movement.

5. **Market Power Required--Times-Picayune Publishing Co. v. United States**, 345 U.S. 594 (1953).

   a. **Facts.** Times-Picayune Publishing Company (D) published the only morning newspaper in New Orleans, and one of the two evening newspapers. It only sold advertising for publication in both papers. D controlled about 40% of the advertising space in the relevant market. An action was brought under sections 1 and 2 of the Sherman Act.

   b. **Issue.** Does D's refusal to sell advertising for publication in each of its papers separately unreasonably restrain trade?

   c. **Held.** No.

      1) The Clayton Act condemns tying where *either* the seller enjoys a monopolistic position in the market for the tying product, *or* a substantial volume of commerce in the tied product is restrained. ***Both*** conditions must be met to satisfy the Sherman Act. P failed to show that D enjoyed a monopolistic position.

      2) Advertising in both papers was really only one product.

   d. **Comment.** Note that the Government did not proceed under the Clayton Act, probably because the Clayton Act, section 3, is inapplicable to tying contracts for the sale of services (it applies only to goods, wares, etc.). Thus, there was an important issue as to whether section 3 applied to advertising.

6. **The Market Power Requirement Diluted--Northern Pacific Railway v. United States,** 356 U.S. 1 (1958).

   a. **Facts.** Northern Pacific Railway (D) sold 40 million acres of land under contracts that required the buyer to ship by D's railroad all product manufactured on the land, provided that D's rates were no higher than those of competing carriers. The government (P) brought a Sherman Act action.

   b. **Issue.** Did the preferential shipping clause in the land sale contracts unreasonably restrain trade?

   c. **Held.** Yes.

      1) Tying contracts are per se illegal where D has sufficient economic power with respect to the tying product and a not insubstantial amount of interstate commerce is affected. (Note that this standard is less than the "monopoly position" required in *Times-Picayune*.) Here D had the requisite power.

      2) The very existence of a tying arrangement is compelling evidence of the required market power, at least where there is no other business explanation. (Note that the Court seems to be referring here to the possible defense suggested in *International Salt*.)

   d. **Comment.** In *United States v. Loew's, Inc.*, 371 U.S. 38 (1962), the Court asserted that the requisite power could be inferred from the uniqueness or desirability of the tying product, which could be presumed in the case of a copyrighted product.

7. **Per Se Illegality and Business Justifications.** Despite the repeated use of the "per se" language, most tying remains lawful. In *United States v. Jerrold Electronics Corp.*, 187 F. Supp. 545 (E.D. Pa. 1960), *aff'd per curiam*, 365 U.S. 567 (1961), the defendant was a new company selling and installing community television antenna systems, and tying these systems to maintenance contracts. The tying was upheld since the equipment was not fully proven and was of a highly sensitive nature; any other arrangement would have threatened the development of a bad reputation for the defendant. The court noted that at some point the restriction would not be reasonable any longer (as the defendant became better established and technical requirements of the systems became better and more widely known). Cases like *Jerrold* leave open the question: Under which circumstances may a tying defendant invoke business justifications to defeat liability? In particular, do the costs of using alternatives to tying count?

8. **Two Approaches to Tying Arrangements--Jefferson Parish Hospital District No. 2 v. Hyde,** 466 U.S. 2 (1984).

   a. **Facts.** Hyde (P), a board certified anesthesiologist, sought admission to the medical staff of a hospital within the Jefferson Parish Hospital District No. 2 (D). D refused the application because of an exclusive contract for anesthesiological services between the hospital and Roux & Associates, a four-person firm of anesthesiologists. The court of appeals held that the contract was illegal per se. The Supreme Court granted certiorari.

   b. **Issue.** Must a firm have market power in the tying product market before a tying arrangement may be considered illegal per se?

   c. **Held.** Yes. Judgment reversed.

      1) Tying arrangements are per se unreasonable because they present an unacceptable risk of stifling competition. Not every refusal to sell two products separately restrains competition, however. When each product could be purchased separately in a competitive market, a combined package would not restrain competition.

      2) The essential element of an invalid tying arrangement is the use of market power in the tying product to force buyers to take the tied product. The impairment of competition in the market for the tied product is the violation of the Sherman Act.

      3) Application of the per se rule depends first on the requirement that the volume of commerce foreclosed must be substantial, then on the likelihood of anticompetitive forcing taking place. When a patent is used to force buyers to purchase separate tied products, the per se rule applies. The focus is on the markets for the two products involved because there must be two separate product markets to have a tying arrangement.

      4) In this case, the focus is on D's sale of services to its patients, including anesthesiological services. D claims it provides a functionally integrated package of services, but the evidence demonstrates that consumers differentiate between anesthesiological services and the other services provided by D. Thus, there are two markets. However, the hospital P applied to handles only 30% of the patients in its area, which is insufficient market power to permit forcing. For that reason, the per se rule does not apply.

      5) D's practice could still violate the Sherman Act if it unreasonably restrained competition, but the evidence in this case does not establish how the practice affected consumer demand for separate arrangements with anesthesiologists such as P.

d. **Concurrence** (Brennan, Marshall, JJ). We have long held that tying arrangements are subject to evaluation for per se illegality, and there is no reason to depart from that principle in this case.

e. **Concurrence** (O'Connor, J., Burger, C.J., Powell, Rehnquist, JJ.).

   1) The per se rule should not be used in tying cases because it requires analysis of the economic effects of the tying arrangement before it can be applied. In effect, the court must conduct a rule of reason inquiry before determining whether the per se rule applies. This has the result of ignoring economic benefits that a particular arrangement may have.

   2) Instead, the courts should apply the rule of reason and determine whether (i) the seller has power in the tying product market; (ii) there is a substantial threat that the tying seller will acquire market power in the tied-product market; and (iii) there is a coherent economic basis for treating the tying and tied products as distinct, such that consumers would wish to purchase the tied product separately without also purchasing the tying product. Once these requirements are met, the arrangement would be held illegal only if its anticompetitive impact outweighs its contribution to efficiency.

   3) In this case, the third element was not satisfied because there is no sound economic reason to treat surgery and anesthesia as separate services. Patients purchase anesthesia only as part of hospital services. At the same time, the arrangement confers significant benefits on patients by insuring availability, and by making the hospital responsible to select and monitor anesthesiologists.

   4) Even though the contract with Roux is exclusive dealing, it does not unreasonably enhance the hospital's market position relative to other hospitals, or unreasonably permit Roux to acquire power relative to other anesthesiologists. Thus it is permitted under the rule of reason.

f. **Comments.**

   1) **Number of products.** This case demonstrates that the question of how many products there are for the purposes of the law of tying cannot be answered by reference to physics, but only by reference to policy. In particular, before one can say how many products there are, one must have some idea of what it is about tying that makes it an antitrust offense.

   2) **Market power.** The majority opinion may indicate a threshold of market power significantly higher than that indicated by earlier Court decisions.

3) **O'Connor's concurring opinion.** This opinion may prove more influential than many other concurring opinions for two reasons. First, the majority opinion commanded only five votes. Second, the majority opinion struggles to reconcile the outcome in this case with the nearly irreconcilable outcomes in earlier cases. As a result, its logic is not as compelling as the logic of the concurring opinion. Since the concurring opinion does provide an explanation of the result reached, lawyers in subsequent tying cases may turn to it as the true explanation for the decision reached.

9. **Tie Between Parts and Repair Service--Eastman Kodak Co. v. Image Technical Services, Inc.,** 504 U.S. 451 (1992).

   a. **Facts.** Image Technical Services and several independent service organizations (Ps) brought suit against Kodak (D) alleging violations of section 2. D is a leading producer of high speed copy machines and competes with Ps for service contracts for these copiers. Ps provided repair service at a price substantially less than D and, according to some customers, this service was of higher quality. In an effort to maintain its service contracts, D refused to deal with Ps, thereby preventing them from obtaining necessary replacement parts to service Kodak copiers. Accordingly, Ps sued claiming that D's refusal to sell parts constituted an unlawful attempt to monopolize the service market by tying replacement parts to its repair service. The district court granted summary judgment for D, and the court of appeals reversed. The Supreme Court granted certiorari.

   b. **Issue.** Does D's lack of market power in the primary equipment market preclude, as a matter of law, the possibility of market power in the derivative aftermarkets of replacement parts and service?

   c. **Held**. No. Ps have raised sufficient evidence to preclude granting summary judgment for D and thus the court of appeal's reversal of the district court's entry of summary judgement is affirmed.

   1) A tie is an agreement by a party to sell one product on the condition that the buyer also purchase a different product, or at least agrees he will not purchase that product from any other supplier. These arrangements violate the Sherman Act when the seller has appreciable economic power in the tying product market if the arrangement affects a substantial volume of commerce in the tied market.

   2) In order to survive D's motion for summary judgment Ps must establish that service and parts are two distinct products and that D has tied the sale of the two products. Service and parts are distinct products because there is sufficient consumer demand to make it efficient for a firm to provide service separately from parts. Many customers would purchase parts directly and only use Ps for ser-

vice. The record also supports finding a tying arrangement as D would only sell parts to a third party if they agreed not to purchase service from Ps.

    3) Market power is the power to force a purchaser to do something that he would not do in a competitive market. Some customers testified that they would have preferred to patronize Ps because their service was better and cheaper than D's. The existence of such power is often inferred from a seller's possession of a predominant market share. D argues that its lack of market power in the product market precludes a finding of market power in the parts or service markets. D argues that if it was extracting exorbitant prices in the service arena, then it would lose sales of its products and the absence of this shift suggests a lack of market power. But customers faced high information costs associated with projecting lifetime service costs when purchasing the initial product and thus often became locked in and unable to switch products without facing huge costs.

  d. Dissent (Scalia, O'Connor, Thomas, JJ.). The extension of per se condemnation to a manufacturer for its activities in its single brand aftermarket when the manufacturer is without market power at the interbrand level extends the antitrust laws beyond their original intent. Every manufacturer of durable goods with distinctive parts possesses the type of power condemned by the majority.

F. PARTIAL VERTICAL INTEGRATION BY CONTRACT: EXCLUSIVE SELLING AND EXCLUSIVE DEALING

1. Exclusive Selling--Valley Liquors, Inc. v. Renfield Importers, Ltd., 678 F.2d 742 (7th Cir. 1982).

  a. Facts. Renfield Importers (D) had sold its wine and liquor to several wholesalers in each county where it did business. D's sales had not been growing as rapidly in Illinois as in the rest of the country, so it decided to adopt a system of restricted distribution whereby it would sell to one, or at most two, wholesalers in each county. Although Valley Liquors (P) was D's largest wholesaler in McHenry and Du Page counties, accounting for some 50% of D's total sales there, the new plan terminated P and all of D's other distributors in the two counties except Continental and Romano (who were terminated in some other areas). P had been selling D's products at prices 5% below those charged by D's other distributors in the two counties. P's termination followed discussions between D and Continental and between D and Romano in which Continental and Romano had expressed unhappiness with D for terminating them in other areas. P claimed that D and the other two wholesalers conspired to increase the wholesale prices of D's products in the two counties in violation of section 1. The district judge denied a preliminary injunction against D's termination of P because he did not think that P had demonstrated that it was likely to win the case if tried in full.

b. **Issue.** Did the trial judge abuse his discretion by refusing to preliminarily enjoin a manufacturer's termination of a price-cutting dealer pursuant to the adoption of a restricted distribution plan when the terminated dealer was the manufacturer's largest in the area and when the remaining non-price-cutting dealers had complained to the manufacturer about being terminated in other areas?

c. **Held.** No. Order affirmed.

    1) No direct evidence suggests that Continental and Romano agreed to raise the prices of D's products and to that end persuaded D to terminate P.

    2) The fact that they each separately expressed unhappiness at being terminated elsewhere did not compel the court to infer that they demanded and received, as a quid pro quo, the termination of P, their major competitor in the two counties. D may have had independent reasons for terminating P despite the fact that P was D's largest and lowest price wholesaler in the two counties. The adoption of a restricted distribution system implies a decision to emphasize non-price competition over price competition. While parsing D's motives seems a bit unreal, in this case it is enough that P did not prove an improper motive by D.

    3) That P's termination reduced price competition among wholesalers of D's products does not establish a prima facie case of unreasonable restraint of trade that would shift to D the burden of showing an offsetting increase in competition between D's products and the products of D's competitors. The elimination of a price cutter who is taking a free ride on the promotional efforts of competing distributors will tend to stimulate non-price competition among the distributors at the same time that it dampens price competition among them, so that the net effect on intrabrand competition need not be negative.

    4) In any event, presuming illegality from a reduction in intrabrand competition is inconsistent with the test courts apply in restricted distribution cases (like *Continental T.V. v. GTE Sylvania*), which requires a balancing between intrabrand and interbrand effects. Because this test is hard to apply, courts say that the balance tips in the defendant's favor if the plaintiff fails to show that the defendant has significant market power. A firm without such power is unlikely to adopt policies that disserve its consumers; it cannot afford to do so. And if it blunders, market retribution will be swift. Here, no market was defined, no evidence of market

share was presented, and P did not try to establish D's market power in some other way.

2. Exclusive Dealing.

    a. Introduction. Section 3 of the Clayton Act, studied in connection with tying contracts, applies to an exclusive dealing arrangement where the buyer agrees to buy only from a certain supplier. Note that to be unlawful such a contract must be something more than simply a contract to buy some goods; every contract excludes other suppliers as to the quantity purchased.

    b. Substantial lessening of competition--Standard Fashion Co. v. Magrane-Houston Co., 258 U.S. 346 (1922).

        1) Facts. Standard Fashion Co. (P), a manufacturer of patterns for clothes, signed a contract with Magrane-Houston Co. (D) that P would supply patterns and D would resell them, and no others, for a period of two years. D has dropped P's line and begun to sell a competitor's. P sought an injunction. The case was dismissed by the district court, and affirmed by the circuit court.

        2) Issue. Is such an exclusive dealing arrangement legal?

        3) Held. No. Judgment affirmed.

            a) P controls 40% of the outlets for patterns.

            b) Section 3 reaches agreements in their incipiency that "may substantially lessen competition." "May" means "probably will," since the lessening of competition must be "substantial."

            c) The contract is a violation of section 3 of the Clayton Act.

    c. A quantitative test--Standard Oil Co. of California v. United States, 337 U.S. 293 (1949).

        1) Facts. Standard Oil Co. of California (D) was the largest refiner and supplier of gasoline in the western states. It sold gas through its own stations and independent dealers, selling 7% of the market's volume through the dealers and 7% in its own stations. There were six other major competitors and 70 small ones. D used exclusive-supply contracts with the dealers (as did all competing companies with their dealers). The independent dealers constituted 16% of the stations in the area. Sixty million dollars worth of gas was sold in 1947 through these dealers. The contracts were from year to year. The government (P) brought a section 3 action.

2) **Issue.** Did this network of exclusive dealing arrangements violate section 3?

3) **Held.** Yes. D has violated section 3.

   a) Where tying contracts are involved (such as in *International Salt*) all that need be shown is that a "not insubstantial amount of business" is involved. But requirement contracts serve purposes that are not necessarily anticompetitive. Often both the buyer and seller wish to use such a contract. By such a contract buyers can be assured of a source of supply, protect against price rises, avoid the risk of storage, etc. Sellers can reduce selling expense, plan production, etc.

   b) Thus, requirement contracts might justify a rule of reason analysis. Here D has not increased market share in the past several years, but it might have lost market share without such contracts. In short, courts are not set up to conduct such detailed economic analysis.

   c) Therefore, section 3 is violated when competition has been foreclosed as to a "substantial amount" of business. Here no one will disagree that a substantial amount of business was involved.

d. **Length of time of the contract.** Note that the length of time that the requirements contract is to run can be a determinative factor, since this reflects on whether there is really a barrier to entry to other competing firms. The longer the contract the more restrictive. Thus, in *FTC v. Motion Picture Advertising Service Co.*, 344 U.S. 392 (1953), in dictum, the Court suggested that where a requirements contract was a necessity for doing business, that such a contract, if limited to a period of less than one year, would probably not be unreasonable. Therefore, where contracts are terminable at will or after a short notice period, this would be an important factor to consider.

e. **A qualitative test--Tampa Electric Co. v. Nashville Coal Co.,** 365 U.S. 320 (1961).

   1) **Facts.** Tampa Electric Co. (P) is an electrical utility in Tampa, Florida, supplying electricity to an area of the state. It built a new plant and contracted with Nashville Coal Co. (D) for all its requirements for a 20-year period, to be not less than 225,000 tons per year. Just prior to delivery D refused to perform. It was estimated that the total requirements of P would reach 2,250,000 tons annually; the contract was worth about $128 million over its life. P sued D to enforce performance. The lower court held that the relevant market was Florida, where the tons of coal used was 700,000 (outside of P's needs) and that the contract lessened competition.

   2) **Issue.** Did the lower court properly define the market?

Tampa Electric Co. v. Nashville Coal Co.

Antitrust - 121

3) **Held.** No. Lower court reversed.

   a) The first question is the "relevant market." Here it is the geographical area of the seven states where producers of coal compete for customers. Here P's requirements amount to less than 1% of total output.

   b) Second, there must be a determination of product market; here the market is for coal.

   c) Third, there must be a determination of a substantial lessening of competition. Several factors should be considered: (i) the probable effect of the contract on the relevant area of effective competition; (ii) the percentage of the total volume of commerce involved; (iii) the probable effects on competition of the share of commerce involved being preempted; and (iv) the fact that the amount of commerce quantitatively is of little consequence, standing alone. The contract here does not substantially lessen competition.

   d) The case is distinguished from *Standard Fashion* in that there the defendant had 40% of the market. It is distinguished from *Standard Oil* in that there the whole industry was using requirement contracts and a large number of retail outlets was involved (over 6,000 stations).

4) **Comment.** This case rejects the approach of *Standard Oil* (a purely quantitative amount of business), but it does not give anything much more concrete.

   a) Note the critical importance of the definition of the relevant market.

   b) In *Tampa*, the coal company was trying to get out of an unfavorable contract, which they had aggressively pursued, because the market price of coal had shot up. Thus it was clear that the contract had not given D any market power.

f. **Exclusive dealing revisited.**

1) Exclusive dealing may serve a host of business purposes, many of which, ironically, are catalogued in the *Standard Oil of California* opinion. For example, in *Tampa Electric*, exclusive dealing helped a public utility with an obligation to provide service to cope with the risk of price fluctuations.

2) *Jefferson Parish Hospital District No. 2 v. Hyde, supra,* may have implications for the antitrust treatment of exclusive dealing. Note that the four-vote concurring opinion would have treated the challenged arrangement

in that case as exclusive dealing. In *Roland Machinery Co. v. Dresser Industries, Inc.*, 749 F.2d 380 (7th Cir. 1984), the court opined: "The exclusion of competitors is cause for antitrust concern only if it impairs the health of the competitive process itself. Hence, a plaintiff must prove two things to show that an exclusive dealing agreement is unreasonable. First, he must prove that it is likely to keep at least one significant competitor of the defendant from doing business in a relevant market. If there is no exclusion of a significant competitor, the agreement cannot possibly harm competition. Second, he must prove that the probable (not certain) effect of the exclusion will be to raise prices above (and therefore reduce output below) the competitive level, or otherwise injure competition; he must show in other words that the anticompetitive effects (if any) outweigh any benefits to competition from it."

3) *United States v. Colgate & Co., supra*, may insulate some exclusive dealing from antitrust scrutiny. In *Roland Machinery Co.*, the court observed that the defendant's preference for exclusive dealers, its efforts to find out whether its dealers were exclusive dealers, and its terminating the plaintiff when it found out that the plaintiff no longer was its exclusive dealer did not support an inference both "that the distributor communicated its acquiescence or agreement" to exclusive dealing "and that this was sought by the manufacturer."

g. Federal Trade Commission's power--FTC v. Brown Shoe Co., 384 U.S. 316 (1966).

1) **Facts.** The FTC (P) brought an action against Brown Shoe Company (D), the second largest manufacturer of shoes, enjoining D from continuing its "franchise" contracts with 650 shoe stores to sell D shoes and "no other competing lines." The franchise could be canceled on short notice. D also provided some special services to shoe stores accepting the franchise (low-cost group insurance, special marketing assistance, etc.). D argued that there had to be a showing that there was a substantial lessening of competition. The Commission found that the restriction was an unfair method of competition, but the court of appeals reversed. The Supreme Court granted certiorari.

2) **Issue.** Does the FTC have the power to enjoin unfair methods of competition without a showing of a substantial lessening of competition?

3) **Held.** Yes. Judgment reversed; P's action upheld.

   a) P can bring an action for unfair competition against practices that conflict with the central policies of the Sherman or Clayton Act even though specific proof of the elements required by these acts is not shown.

4) **Comment.** It seems unfortunate to have different standards for the various acts applied to the same facts. Also, it seems unclear what this case stands for, since the opinion is not clearly written.

U.S. Healthcare, Inc. v. Healthsource, Inc.

h. ***Tampa* applied to exclusive dealing contracts--U.S. Healthcare, Inc. v. Healthsource, Inc.,** 986 F.2d 589 (1st Cir. 1993).

1) **Facts.** U.S. Healthcare, Inc. (P), an operator of HMOs, was interested in expanding its operations into New Hampshire. In response, Healthsource (D), the only non-staff HMO in that state, solicited from its participating physicians an exclusive dealing provision in their contracts in exchange for a slightly higher payment per patient seen. A physician who signed obligated himself to see only HMO patients affiliated with D, although the physician could continue to treat all other non-HMO patients. A physician who so obligated himself could escape the obligation on 30 days' notice. About 87% of D's physicians opted for exclusivity. P brought suit claiming that the exclusivity clause violated sections 1 and 2 of the Sherman Act. The judge found for D on all counts, and P appeals.

2) **Issue.** Does D's exclusive dealing clause with its physicians violate the Sherman Act?

3) **Held.** No. Judgment affirmed.

   a) Vertical agreements like D's exclusive dealing arrangements with its participating physicians are not per se illegal.

   b) *Tampa* requires that the court determine the probable effect of the exclusive contract on the relevant area of effective competition, taking into account the probable immediate and future effects that preemption of that share of the market might have on effective competition therein. The 30-day escape clause coupled with the absence of any showing that P was foreclosed in any substantial manner from hiring other physicians requires the conclusion that D's arrangements were "reasonable."

IX. MERGERS

A. HORIZONTAL MERGERS

1. **Introduction.** Horizontal mergers may create a firm with market power. In the two decades following the passage of the Sherman Act, the Department of Justice challenged a number of these mergers under both section 1 and section 2 and prevailed in some of the ensuing litigation. But horizontal mergers may also leave the remaining firms in a market in a much better position to coordinate their behavior without engaging in a detectable conspiracy. The parties to these mergers rarely, if ever, arrange them for that purpose (too "iffy"). This, along with the fact that it is difficult to sort out all of the potential effects of a merger, contributed to the Department of Justice's lack of success in attacking sizable, but not monopoly-creating, mergers. Against this backdrop, especially the Government's loss in *United States v. Columbia Steel Co.*, 334 U.S. 495 (1948), Congress amended section 7 of the Clayton Act.

2. **Clayton Act.** Section 7 provides:

   That no person engaged in commerce or in any activity affecting commerce shall acquire, directly or indirectly, the whole or any part of the stock or other share capital and no person subject to the jurisdiction of the Federal Trade Commission shall acquire the whole or any part of the assets of another person engaged also in commerce or in any activity affecting commerce, where in any line of commerce or in any activity affecting commerce in any section of the country, the effect of such acquisition may be substantially to lessen competition, or to tend to create a monopoly. . . .

   This section shall not apply to persons purchasing such stock solely for investment and not using the same by voting or otherwise to bring about, or in attempting to bring about, the substantial lessening of competition. Nor shall anything contained in this section prevent a corporation engaged in commerce or in any activity affecting commerce from causing the formation of subsidiary corporations for the actual carrying on of their immediate lawful business, or the natural and legitimate branches or extensions thereof, or from owning and holding all or a part of the stock of such subsidiary corporations, when the effect of such formation is not to substantially lessen competition . . . .

3. **Presumptive Illegality--United States v. Philadelphia National Bank,** 374 U.S. 321 (1963).

   a. **Facts.** Philadelphia National Bank (D), the second largest of the 42 commercial banks with head offices in the Philadelphia metropolitan area, agreed to merge with Girard Trust Corn Exchange Bank, the third largest such bank. Each had its headquarters in the city, but state law permitted them to open branches in the three contiguous counties. Consummation of the merger would have created a bank with 36% of the area banks' total assets, 36% of deposits, and 34% of net loans. Where before the merger the two largest area banks had controlled approximately 44% of the area's commercial banking business, afterwards, they would have controlled 59% (a 33% increase). The four largest would have controlled 79%. The bank resulting from the merger, with its greater prestige and increased lending limit, would have been better able to compete with large out-of-state (especially New York) banks, would have attracted new business to Philadelphia, and generally would have promoted economic development in the area. Although commercial banking was subject to intensive government regulation, there was plenty of room for the free play of competitive forces. The Department of Justice (P) sought to enjoin the merger as violative of section 1 of the Sherman Act and section 7 of the Clayton Act. The district court gave judgment for D, and P appeals.

b. **Issue.** Does a merger producing a firm controlling at least 34% of the relevant market and resulting in a 33% increase in the share of the market controlled by the two largest firms tend to substantially lessen competition within the meaning of section 7?

c. **Held.** Yes, in the absence of evidence clearly showing that the merger is not likely to have such anticompetitive effects. The district court's judgment is reversed.

1) The product market is commercial banking services. The geographical market is the four-county area. Geographical markets are determined by supplier-customer relations, and banking is primarily based on convenience of location. The market definition here is not perfect since some larger borrowers do banking nationwide and smaller customers bank in their neighborhood. But this is the best market definition possible.

2) Because of the difficulty of predicting a merger's impact on competitive conditions in the future and the business community's need for certainty, the courts ought to simplify the test of illegality where it is possible to do so without subverting congressional intent. Thus, a merger producing a firm controlling an undue percentage of the market and resulting in a significant increase in concentration of the market is inherently likely to lessen competition and will be enjoined unless there is a clear showing that the merger is not likely to have anticompetitive effects.

a) Here the merger would result in a firm controlling more than 30% of the market and result in an increase in concentration of like amount. This is large enough to raise the inference of illegality. We do not indicate what the smallest percentage would be to raise such an inference.

b) There is no evidence to rebut the inference of anti-competitiveness. Entry is unlikely because of barriers erected by federal and state government. That some officers of small area banks testified in favor of the merger adds nothing because "in an oligopolistic market, small companies may be perfectly content to follow the high prices set by the dominant firms, yet the market may be profoundly anticompetitive."

3) The merger cannot be justified on the ground that "only through mergers can banks follow their customers to the suburbs and retain their business." This does not seem particularly related to the instant merger, and in any event it has no merit. There is an alternative to the merger route: the opening of new branches in the areas to which the customers have moved. One premise of section 7 is that corporate growth by internal expansion is socially preferable to growth by acquisition.

4) The merger cannot be justified on the ground that "the increased lending limit of the resulting bank will enable it to compete with the large out-of-state banks." If anticompetitive effects in one market could be justified by procompetitive consequences in another, the logical upshot would be that every firm in an industry could embark on a series of mergers that would make it in the end as large as the industry leader.

5) The merger also cannot be justified on the ground that "Philadelphia needs a bank larger than it now has in order to bring business to the area." A merger otherwise violative of section 7 is not saved because, on some ultimate reckoning of social or economic debits and credits, it may be deemed beneficial. A value choice of such magnitude is beyond the ordinary limits of judicial competence, and in any event, it has been made for us already by Congress when it enacted section 7.

d. **Comment.** Note that the Court in *Brown Shoe Co. v. United States, infra,* apparently considered more factors than market share and industry concentration. *Brown Shoe* indicated that the Court would follow a policy of attempting to qualitatively assess the effect on competition of the merger. This case indicates that, when the market share of the merged firms gets large enough, a presumption of illegality will be made, thus shifting to the defendant the burden to prove that section 7 is ***not*** violated. Note also in all of these cases that the definition of the relevant market is incredibly important to the outcome. This case may follow the notion that a geographical market is ***any submarket*** where there is a substantial number of consumers that would prefer to do business in their "local" area.

United States v. Continental Can Co.

4. **Product Market--United States v. Continental Can Co.,** 378 U.S. 441 (1964).

   a. **Facts.** Continental Can Company (D) was the second largest producer of metal containers; it acquired Hazel-Atlas, the third largest producer of glass containers.

   b. **Issue.** Under the applicable definition of relevant market, is this merger unlawful?

   c. **Held.** Yes. The merger is unlawful.

      1) The geographical market is nationwide; the product market is metal and glass containers. While many users did not consider changing the type of containers they used based on price shifts (because they already owned machinery for packing one type of container or because their products had specific requirements for metal or glass), there were situations where one type of container had supplanted the other. The result was that there was continuous competition of substantial proportions between the two, and each considered the pricing of the other in setting its own prices.

      2) D has 22% of the market; Hazel has 3.1%. The six largest firms have 70%. This is enough to bring it within the presumption of the *Philadelphia Bank* case.

   d. **Dissent** (Harlan, J.). Relevant market discussion is spurious. The Court is holding that mergers between two large companies in related industries are presumptively illegal.

United States v. Pabst Brewing Co.

5. **Geographical Market--United States v. Pabst Brewing Co.,** 384 U.S. 546 (1966).

   a. **Facts.** Pabst Brewing Company (D), the nation's 10th largest brewer, acquired Blatz, the 18th largest. Combined they had 24% of the Wisconsin market, 11% in the three-state area of Wisconsin, Illinois, and Michigan, and 4.5% of the nation's sales.

   b. **Issue.** Under the applicable definition of geographic market, is this merger unlawful?

   c. **Held.** Yes. The merger is unlawful.

      1) A relevant geographic market is "any section of the country" where the Government can show a substantial lessening of competition.

      2) Here there is a lessening of competition because the number of breweries is down from 714 to 229 in five years, the number of compa-

nies from 206 to 162, and the percentage share of the market controlled by the leading brewers is going up.

6. **The Meaning of Concentration--United States v. Von's Grocery Co.,** 384 U.S. 270 (1966).

   a. **Facts.** The market was defined as the retail grocery business in the Los Angeles area. Von's Grocery Company (D) had 4.7% of the market; the acquired company had 4.2% (they were the third and sixth largest chains). The four largest had 24%; the eight largest had 41%; the 12 largest had 49%. Ten years previously, the corresponding percentages had been 26%, 34%, and 39%. The number of single-store grocers had dropped in the same period from 5,300 to 3,800; the number of two-store-or-more chains had increased from 96 to 150; nine of the top 20 firms had acquired in the aggregate 126 stores. Both D and the acquired company were very aggressive and had grown substantially in the past five years.

   b. **Issue.** Will a trend toward concentration condemn a merger in an otherwise unconcentrated market?

   c. **Held.** Yes. Violation of section 7.

      1) Section 7 looks to the possible future effect on competition. The purpose of the Act is to maintain many small competitors. A trend toward concentration is to be arrested in its incipiency.

      2) Here, there is a merger between two large firms in a market that is becoming increasingly concentrated.

   d. **Concurrence** (White, J.). In a market that is moving toward concentration, any merger between the largest firms (or between one of the largest and a lesser company) is unlawful where the top eight firms have 40% or more of the market.

   e. **Dissent** (Stewart, Harlan, JJ.). The majority relied simply on counting the decline in the number of stores. This is too simple a rationale; it must look behind these numbers to determine the actual state of and trend of competition in the market. The decline in the number of single-store owners is a result of the combined supermarket. The acquisitions that took place by the largest 20 firms were mostly of failing firms. There have been numerous new one-store start-ups. Seven of the top 20 firms were not even in existence 10 years ago. And there are no barriers to entry into the market.

   f. **Comment.** Would a showing of economic efficiency through the merger be a defense? What is the majority really holding? The dissent is probably correct—that it is dangerous to rely simply on one factor (declining number of firms). A group of factors should be looked at together::

(i) The number of firms;

(ii) The trend among the top eight or 10 firms;

(iii) The reasons for the trends; and

(iv) The share represented by the combined firms.

This opinion is considered by many to be the high (or low) water mark in antimerger activity. Subsequent opinions, most notably *General Dynamics* (below), give defendants considerably greater room to argue that the merger is not anticompetitive.

United States v. General Dynamics Corp.

7. **Rebutting the *Philadelphia National Bank* Presumption--United States v. General Dynamics Corp.,** 415 U.S. 486 (1974).

a. **Facts.** From World War II onward, coal had become increasingly less able to compete with other sources of energy. The electric utility industry had become by far the principal customer for coal, purchasing it under long-term requirements contracts at predetermined prices. In 1959, Material Service Corporation bought control of United Electric Coal Companies. Material Service produced coal from deep shaft mines; United from strip mining. In 1966, General Dynamics Corporation (D) gained control of Material Service, and therefore of United as well. Claiming that the 1959 acquisition substantially reduced competition in the sale of coal in Illinois or in the Eastern Interior Coal Province Sales Area (Illinois, Indiana, and parts of Kentucky, Tennessee, Iowa, Minnesota, Wisconsin, and Missouri), the Department of Justice (P) challenged it as violative of section 7. In these regions the industry showed high concentration and a trend toward concentration:

	Region		Illinois	
	1957	1967	1957	1967
Top 2 firms	29.6%	48.6%	37.8%	52.9%
Top 4 firms	43.0	62.9	54.5	75.2
Top 10 firms	65.5	91.4	84.0	98.0

Also, the number of coal producing firms in Illinois dropped from 144 to 39, and the combined firm's share of the coal market was increased.

	Region			**Illinois**		
	Rank	Year	%	Rank	Year	%
Material Service	2	1959	7.6	2	1959	15.1
United	6	1959	4.8	5	1959	8.1
Combined	2	1959	12.4	1	1959	23.2
Material Service	5	1967	6.5	2	1967	12.9
United	9	1967	4.4	6	1967	8.9
Combined	2	1967	10.9	2	1967	21.8

Of the coal reserves held by producers in Illinois, Indiana, and western Kentucky, United controlled less than 1%. It had "neither the possibility of acquiring more nor the ability to develop deep coal reserves." The district court entered judgment for D, and P appeals.

b. Issue. Did sufficient evidence support the district court's conclusion that the *Philadelphia National Bank* presumption was rebutted?

c. Held. Yes. Judgment affirmed.

1) P introduced sufficient evidence statistics to invoke the *Philadelphia National Bank* presumption, but the presumption is not conclusive.

2) Because the focus of competition in the coal market was the procurement of new long-term supply contracts, statistical evidence of coal production did not fairly indicate the competitive strength of the merging firms. United's "unpromising" coal reserve prospects indicated that it had little strength. Coal's increasing vulnerability to other energy sources only confirms this conclusion.

3) The district court did not err by giving consideration to post-acquisition evidence of market developments because these developments could not reflect a decision by the merged firms to refrain from anticompetitive conduct pending trial.

4) The district court did not apply—correctly or incorrectly—the "failing company" doctrine. D's showing of United's weak reserves position did not prove that United would have gone out of business but for the merger, but rather that P's statistics were not reliable indicators of competitive strength.

5) That United might have subsequently purchased new strip reserves or acquired deep mining expertise does not show that the acquisition might tend to substantially lessen competition because many firms might have done the same thing.

6) The district court was justified in holding that the merger would not have tended to substantially reduce competition in either of the relevant markets advocated by P.

d. **Dissent** (Douglas, Brennan, White, Marshall, JJ.). Coal is the relevant product market (it has distinct customers who are not price sensitive); the geographical market is the state of Illinois or the region, as P suggests (Material Service and United sold at least one-half of their output to the same customers). The argument that United had no substantial reserves to sell is the "failing company" defense; but this must be assessed at the time of merger, not at the time of trial, and United did not qualify at that time. No time of merger findings as to competitive effect were made. Also, it appears that many companies bought new coal reserves in the 1960s, and United had an additional 27 million tons of deep shaft reserves. Five years previous to the merger it had been mining deep reserves. The record of the district court is devoid of the findings necessary to make a decision in this case; it should be remanded.

e. **Comment.** The Court went out of its way to avoid treating this case as if it simply raised a market definition question. Apparently, the Court wished to signal that the *Philadelphia National Bank* presumption could be rebutted, and to suggest how it might be done.

8. **The Failing Company Doctrine.**

a. **Introduction.** The legislative history of the 1950 amendments to section 7 of the Clayton Act cite with approval *International Shoe Co. v. FTC*, 280 U.S. 291 (1930), involving the acquisition of a company whose resources were so depleted and its prospects for rehabilitation so remote that "it faced the grave probability of a business failure" and there were no other prospective purchasers available. Nothing more was said by Congress concerning this possible defense.

b. **Narrow defense--Citizen Publishing Co. v. United States,** 394 U.S. 131 (1969).

1) **Facts.** Two newspapers, the only ones in the city, entered a joint operating agreement to manage many departments together and to split profits. One of the papers had several losing years, since it had 50% of the market but had only 33% of the advertising.

2) **Issue.** Is an otherwise objectionable merger permissible if one of the merging companies is in difficulty?

3) **Held.** No, not on these facts. Violation of section 7.

a) The failing company doctrine is a very narrow defense. It applies only if rehabilitation is so remote that business failure is

Citizen
Publishing
Co. v.
United
States

probable and (after good faith efforts) there appears to be no other prospective purchasers available. Here, the merged company had not sought other purchasers.

- c. **1992 DOJ/FTC horizontal merger guidelines.** The guidelines adopt this restrictive approach to the defense. In fact they provide that it is available only if the allegedly failing firm would not be able to reorganize successfully through bankruptcy proceedings, and only if, absent the merger, the assets of the failing firm would exit from the market. A restrictive approach to a failing company defense may reflect, in part, the difficulty of determining whether a business failure really is imminent.

- d. **Newspaper Preservation Act.** This 1970 statute permits newspapers in "probable danger of financial failure" to merge if they keep their editorial functions separate. [15 U.S.C. §1801-04]

- e. **"Failing" company and the *General Dynamics* defense.** Even if a firm is not on the brink of bankruptcy, its financial position may be so weak or its capacity to compete so diminished (for example, because of depleted financial resources, lack of access to an essential raw material, or weakened distribution) that its market share measured by percentage of past sales may overstate its competitive significance.

9. **Ease of Entry and the *Philadelphia National Bank* Presumption.** Conditions of entry have implications not only for the appraisal of mergers, but for other antitrust doctrine as well, including potential competition theory. Because easy entry conditions would almost surely upset any scheme for cartelization or monopolization, the existence of these conditions would strongly suggest that an antitrust defendant is not engaged in such a scheme. Thus, easy entry conditions might prompt a court to characterize the defendant's conduct benignly.

10. **Hospital Acquisitions Under the Clayton Act--Hospital Corporation of America v. FTC,** 807 F.2d 1381 (7th Cir. 1986).

    - a. **Facts.** In 1982, Hospital Corporation of America (D), the largest for-profit hospital chain in the United States, acquired two corporations that owned hospitals in Chattanooga, Tennessee. Prior to the acquisitions, D owned one hospital in this region; afterwards, it owned three and managed two others. Six other hospitals served the region. The four largest hospitals held 91% of the market. The acquisitions raised D's market share from 14% to 26%. The FTC (P) brought suit under section 7 of the Clayton Act claiming that the acquisitions facilitated collusion. Although subsequent to the initiation of litigation D lost one management contract, the Commission held that D violated the Clayton Act when acquiring its competitors. D appeals.

Hospital Corporation of America v. FTC

b. **Issue.** Does substantial evidence support the Commission's conclusion that D's acquisition of hospitals is likely to foster collusive practices harmful to consumers?

c. **Held.** Yes. Judgment affirmed.

1) The acquisitions reduced the total number of competing hospitals in the market from 11 to seven. Although the acquisitions involved 12% of the market, they almost resulted in the four largest entities controlling almost the entire market.

2) Moreover, due to Tennessee's certificate-of-need law, entry into the market is difficult and time consuming. The law's requirement of notice of steps to increase capacity renders it difficult, if not impossible, for members of a cartel to "cheat."

3) Finally, the competing hospitals have closely cooperated in determining reimbursement levels from insurers or the government. These findings show that the merger creates an appreciable danger of collusion in the future.

11. **Antitrust Injury and Mergers.**

a. **Loss due to continued operation of defaulting competitor--Brunswick Corp. v. Pueblo Bowl-O-Mat, Inc.,** 429 U.S. 477 (1977).

1) **Facts.** Brunswick (D), one of two large United States bowling equipment manufacturers, had sold a lot of bowling center interiors on credit, and when the bowling boom went bust, many of these centers defaulted and D acquired them in lieu of what it was owed. D operated some of these centers. One of these acquisitions was challenged under section 7 by three bowling centers (Ps) located in the same community. They established damages by showing that if D had allowed the defaulters to close, Ps would have earned more. A jury returned a verdict for Ps. The appeals court reversed and remanded, but argued that a properly instructed jury could have concluded that when a "giant" like D entered a "market of pygmies," retail competition might decline. The Supreme Court granted certiorari.

2) **Issue.** May Ps recover the sort of damages proven?

3) **Held.** No. The district judge is directed to enter judgment for D notwithstanding the verdict.

a) Ps' injuries bear no relationship to the size of either the acquiring company or its competitors.

b) The damages Ps obtained would give them the profits that they would have realized had there been less competition. Awarding damages for this type of injury would be inimical to the purposes of the law. Plaintiffs must prove ***antitrust*** injury, which is to say injury of the type the antitrust laws were intended to prevent and that flows from that which makes the defendants' acts unlawful.

b. **Lowering of prices by merged firm--Cargill, Inc. v. Monfort of Colorado, Inc.,** 479 U.S. 104 (1986).

    Cargill, Inc. v. Monfort of Colorado, Inc.

1) **Facts.** Cargill (D), the second largest beef packer in the country, proposed to merge with the third largest. Monfort (P), the fifth largest, challenged the proposed merger under section 7, claiming that absent an injunction it would likely suffer injury when the merged firm, taking advantage of multiplant efficiencies, would lower its prices to some level at or slightly above its costs in order to compete with other packers for market share, and P would have to lower its prices. The district court enjoined the proposed merger and the appeals court affirmed. The Supreme Court granted certiorari.

2) **Issue.** May P challenge this merger on its claim of possible injury?

3) **Held.** No. Judgment reversed and the case remanded.

a) In order to seek injunctive relief under section 16, a private plaintiff must allege threatened loss or damage of the type the antitrust laws were designed to prevent and that flows from that which makes the defendant's acts unlawful.

b) Taking advantage of multiplant efficiencies to lower price in order to obtain greater market share is not activity forbidden by the antitrust laws. Therefore, P may not challenge the merger if its only claim of injury is the profits it would forgo as a result.

c) If, as the appeals court thought, P had claimed that the merged firm would attempt to drive P out of business through sustained predatory pricing, P could have challenged the merger. But P did not make this claim to the district court.

4) **Comment.** The Court pointedly rejected the United States's amicus argument that the "danger of allowing a competitor to challenge an acquisition on the basis of necessarily speculative claims of post-acquisition predatory pricing far outweighs the danger that any anticompetitive merger will go unchallenged."

c. **May a "target" firm invoke section 7 against a hostile takeover?** The arguments for a "no" answer are even stronger than the arguments for denying this right to a competitor. In *Consolidated Gold Fields PLC v. Minorco, S.A.,*

Antitrust - 135

871 F.2d 252 (2d Cir. 1989), the court answered "yes." "[The target firm's] wholly owned United States mining subsidiary . . . is threatened with curtailment of its production. . . . Surely [the target's] loss of independence is causally linked to the injury occurring in the marketplace, where the acquisition threatens to diminish competitive forces. Though what happens to [the target] and what happens to competition may not be precisely the same type of injury, there is a common element in that the independent existence of a major competitor is being eliminated." Notice that one's answer to the question may depend on one's conception of the purpose of the antitrust laws.

12. **Remedies.** Fashioning remedies for illegal mergers can raise a host of practical and legal issues, especially where the remedy of choice is divestiture. In *California v. American Stores Co.,* 495 U.S. 271 (1990), the Supreme Court held that divestiture is available in private litigation.

13. **Department of Justice Horizontal Merger Guidelines.**

   a. **Introduction.** A crucial element of merger law under section 7 is the policy followed by the Justice Department and the FTC in challenging mergers. In 1968, the Department issued its first set of "Merger Guidelines." In 1982, the Department rewrote them completely, only to revise them in 1984 and again in 1992. The FTC joined the 1992 version. Although the standards set forth in the guidelines do not have the force of law and are not binding on the courts, a number of courts have accepted them in analyzing mergers. [*See, e.g.,* Allis-Chalmers Manufacturing Co. v. White Consolidated Industries, 414 F.2d 506 (3d Cir. 1969)]

   b. **Policy.** Mergers should not be permitted to create or enhance "market power" or to facilitate its exercise.

   c. **"Market power" defined.** Market power is the ability of one or more firms profitably to maintain prices above competitive levels for a significant period of time.

   d. **Product market definition.** Taking the products of the merging firms as a beginning point, the product market will also include those products that the merging firms' customers view as good substitutes at prevailing prices. The Agency will add additional products to the market if a significant percentage of the buyers of products already included would be likely to shift to those other products in response to a small but significant and nontransitory increase in price.

   1) **Provisional market and the profitability test.** Ordinarily, the Agency will hypothesize a price increase of 5% and ask how many buyers would be likely to shift to the other products within one year. The provisional market of products will continue to expand until a hypothetical firm that made all sales of those products in that

area could increase its profits through a small but significant and nontransitory increase in price.

2) **Example.** Are balloons a market? Under the profitability test, if producers of balloons tried to raise their price by 5% after they had combined effectively into a single seller, could they profitably exercise such market power? If the answer is yes, balloons are a market. If the answer is no—because buyers of balloons would switch away to confetti or party favors—then balloons are not a market. In the latter case confetti or party favors should be included in the provisional market before the test is applied again.

3) **Predicting how buyers would respond to a price increase.** An Agency will consider, among other things:

   a) Evidence that relative changes in price or other competitive variables have prompted buyers to purchase other products or to consider doing so;

   b) Evidence that, in making business decisions, sellers take into account the prospect that relative changes in price or other competitive variables would prompt buyers to purchase other products;

   c) "The influence of downstream competition faced by buyers in their output markets;" and

   d) The "timing and costs of switching products."

4) **Prospect of price discrimination may narrow product market.** One or more uses of a product by specified buyers may constitute a relevant product market if a hypothetical monopolist could profitably impose on them a "small but significant and nontransitory" price increase. Whether a hypothetical monopolist could do so would depend on its ability to identify "targeted buyers" who would not defeat the price discrimination by purchasing substitute products and the ability of other buyers to defeat the price discrimination through arbitrage (*i.e.*, buy at the lower price and resell to targeted buyers).

e. **Geographic market definition.** For each product market in which the merging firms participate, the Agency will determine the geographic market(s) in which the firms sell.

   1) **Geographic market—profitability test.** The geographic market is a geographic area such that a hypothetical firm that was the only present or future producer of the relevant product in that area could profitably raise its price. If, however, a raise in price would result in buyers shifting to firms located elsewhere to purchase the relevant product, then the price

increase could not be profitably carried off, and the geographic market would have been defined too narrowly. Ordinarily, the Agency will use a 5% increase in price.

2) **Predicting how buyers would respond to a price increase.** An Agency will consider the same sort of things that it would consider in connection with defining the product market, except of course, that it will consider evidence that, in making business decisions, sellers take into account the prospect that relative changes in price or other competitive variables would prompt buyers to purchase not other products, but the same products in other geographic locations.

3) **Prospect of price discrimination may narrow geographic market.** If a hypothetical monopolist could profitably engage in geographic price discrimination, the Agency will use a narrower geographic market.

f. **Identification of firms that participate in the relevant market.** Participants include firms then selling or producing in the relevant market, including (i) firms that do, or likely would, produce or sell used, reconditioned, or recycled substitutes, and (ii) vertically integrated firms. Participants also include firms that could sell or produce in the relevant market without incurring significant sunk costs of entry and exit *if* a "small but significant and nontransitory" price increase would probably prompt them to enter within one year. ("Sunk costs" are the acquisition costs of tangible and intangible assets that cannot be recovered through the redeployment of these assets outside the relevant market, *i.e.*, costs uniquely incurred to supply the relevant product and geographic market. Examples of sunk costs may include market-specific investments in production facilities, technologies, marketing (including product acceptance), research and development, regulatory approvals, and testing. A significant sunk cost is one that would not be recouped within one year of the commencement of the supply response, assuming a "small but significant and nontransitory" price increase in the relevant market.) If such an "uncommitted entrant" would probably not enter (say because of "difficulties in achieving product acceptance, distribution, or production"), it would not be considered to be a market participant. The competitive significance of supply responses that require more time or that require firms to incur significant sunk costs of entry and exit are considered in entry analysis.

g. **Calculating market shares.** Ordinarily, the Agency will calculate market shares for all firms (or plants) identified as market participants based on the total sales or capacity currently devoted to the relevant market together with that which likely would be devoted to the relevant market in response to a "small but significant and nontransitory" price increase. The Agency will measure market share in whatever terms—the dollar value or quantity of sales, shipments, production, capacity, or reserves—the Agency believes best indicates the firms' future competitive significance.

h. Concentration and market share. Market concentration is a function of the number of firms in a market and their respective shares. Concentration increases as the number of firms decreases and their market shares increase.

1) **The Herfindahl-Hirshman Index.** As an aid to the interpretation of market data, the Agencies use the HHI, the sum of the square of each participant's market share.

    a) **Example.** A market consisting of four firms with market shares of 30%, 30%, 20%, and 20% has an HHI of 2,600 ($30^2 + 30^2 + 20^2 + 20^2 = 2,600$). The HHI ranges from 10,000 (in the case of a pure monopoly) to a number approaching zero (in the case of an atomistic market).

    b) **Compare.** Unlike the traditional four-firm concentration ratio used in the 1968 guidelines, the HHI reflects both distribution of the market shares of the top four firms and the composition outside the top four firms.

    c) **Change in the HHI.** The increase in concentration as measured by the HHI can be calculated independently of the overall market concentration by doubling the product of the market shares of the merging firms. For example, the merger of firms with shares of 5% and 10% of the market would increase the HHI by 100 (5 x 10 x 2 = 100; or $5^2 + 10^2 = 125$; $15^2 = 225$; $225 - 125 = 100$).

i. Enforcement policy.

1) **Post-merger HHI below 1,000.** The Agencies are unlikely to challenge mergers falling in this region.

2) **Post-merger HHI between 1,000 and 1,800.** Generally, the Agencies are unlikely to challenge mergers producing an increase in HHI of less than 100 points. They are more likely than not, however, to challenge mergers in this region that produce an increase in HHI of more than 100 points.

3) **Post-merger HHI above 1,800.** For mergers producing an increase in the HHI of less than 50 points, a challenge is unlikely. Where the increase in the HHI is more than 100 points, a challenge is likely.

4) **Factors affecting the significance of market shares and concentration.** These factors are: (i) recent or ongoing changes in a market that indicate that the current market share of a particular firm either understates or overstates the firm's future competitive significance; and (ii) the degree of difference between the products and locations in the market and substitutes outside the market.

5) **The prospect of "committed" entry and other nonmarket share/market concentration factors relevant to assessing the threat posed by a merger.**

   a) "Committed entry" (*i.e.*, new competition requiring significant sunk costs of entry and exit) might reduce or eliminate the potential adverse impact of a merger. To do so, the new committed entrants would have to "achieve significant market impact within a timely period," so the Agencies will assess how likely that is. The Agencies will also assess whether committed entry would be profitable and therefore likely. In making this assessment, the Agencies assume that these potential entrants evaluate the profitability of entry on the basis of long-term participation in the market, because the underlying assets will be committed to the market until they are economically depreciated. Entry that is sufficient to reduce or eliminate the potential adverse impact of a merger will cause prices to fall to their premerger levels or lower. Thus, according to the Agencies, the profitability of such committed entry must be determined on the basis of premerger market prices over the long-term. Finally, the Agencies will assess whether the timely entry that is likely would pack enough competitive wallop to return market prices to their premerger levels.

   b) The firm created by a merger is more likely to find a price rise/output reduction profitable if the participants in its market (i) produce highly differentiated products so that competition is "non-uniform (*i.e.*, localized), [with] individual sellers compet[ing] more directly with those rivals selling closer substitutes" or (ii) "face binding capacity constraints that could not be economically relaxed within two years or if existing excess capacity is significantly more costly to operate than capacity currently in use."

   c) Post-merger market conditions that facilitate or complicate the tasks required for express or tacit collusion include: (i) reaching terms of coordination, (ii) detecting deviations from those terms, and (iii) punishing such deviations. These conditions might include "the availability of key information concerning market conditions, transactions, and individual competitors; the extent of firm and product heterogeneity; pricing or marketing practices typically employed by firms in the market; the characteristics of buyers and sellers; and the characteristics of typical transactions."

6) **Merger-generated efficiencies.** The Agencies will not challenge a merger if the "cognizable" efficiencies that the merger is likely to generate would probably "reverse the merger's potential to harm consumers in the relevant market." In assessing the efficiencies that the merger is likely to generate, the Agencies will count only those unlikely to be generated in the "absence of either the merger or another means having comparable anticompetitive effects" (*i.e.*, "merger-specific" efficiencies). And the Agencies will count these only if the merging firms substantiate these efficiencies so that the Agencies

"can verify by reasonable means the likelihood and magnitude of each asserted efficiency, how and when each would be achieved (and any costs of doing so), how each would enhance the merged firm's ability and incentive to compete, and why each would be merger-specific."

7) **Failing firm defense.** This established but ambiguous defense will usually not be challenged when the allegedly failing firm:

a) Probably would be unable to meet its financial obligations in the near future;

b) Probably would not be able to reorganize successfully under chapter 11 of the Bankruptcy Act; and

c) Has made unsuccessful good faith efforts to elicit reasonable alternative offers of acquisition that would keep it in the market and pose a less severe danger to competition than does the proposed merger.

14. **Horizontal Merger Resulting in Duopoly in Concentrated Market--FTC v. H.J. Heinz Co.,** 246 F.3d 708 (D.C. Cir. 2001).

FTC v. H.J. Heinz Co.

a. **Facts.** Three firms dominate the baby food market: Gerber (65% market share); Heinz (17.4% market share); and Beech-Nut (15.4% market share). Gerber enjoys unparalleled brand recognition and loyalty. Its products are found in over 90% of domestic supermarkets. Heinz (D) is found in only 40%; it markets itself as a "value brand" selling for several cents below Gerber. Beech-Nut is carried at approximately 45% of domestic grocery stores; it markets itself as a premium brand comparable to Gerber selling for roughly the same amount. Most stores sell only two brands of baby food, so D and Beech-Nut often competed with each other for this second position. As a result of refurbishing its baby food plant, D manufactured its product much more efficiently than Beech-Nut, but still lagged in terms of taste. D proposed to acquire Beech-Nut. The FTC (P) filed for a preliminary injunction, which the district court denied. P appeals.

b. **Issues.**

1) Did the market share statistics entitle P to the *Philadelphia National Bank* presumption?

2) If so, did evidence of pre-merger competition or post-merger efficiencies rebut the presumption?

c. **Held.** 1) Yes. 2) Yes. Judgment reversed and remanded.

1) The pre-merger Herfindahl-Hirschmann Index ("HHI") for the domestic baby food market was 4775, which the merger would have

Antitrust - 141

raised by 510 points. These statistics entitled P to the *Philadelphia National Bank* presumption. In addition, P demonstrated that there are high barriers to market entry as reflected by the district court's finding that there have been no significant entries in decades.

2) D's claim that it has not competed with Beech-Nut at the retail level fails to take into account the wholesale competition that currently exists for the "second shelf" position next to Gerber. The efficiencies that D claims will result from the merger can be achieved without the loss of a competitor by either company investing in its production.

B. **JOINT VENTURES, POTENTIAL COMPETITION, AND CONGLOMERATE MERGERS**

United States v. El Paso Natural Gas Co.

1. **Acquiring a Firm Competing for the Market--United States v. El Paso Natural Gas Co.,** 376 U.S. 651 (1964).

   a. **Facts.** El Paso Natural Gas (D) bought the stock of Pacific, another natural gas company with the only other important interstate pipeline west of the Rockies. D supplied 50% of the natural gas to the California market; Pacific had tried to get a license to serve the California market and had competed with D on some large utility contracts, causing D to lower its prices. The Federal Power Commission rejected Pacific's application, but Pacific still had large gas deposits in surrounding states and had the management capability to enter the California market.

   b. **Issue.** Would this acquisition tend to substantially lessen competition in the California natural gas market?

   c. **Held.** Yes. Competition in natural gas is for the new increments of demand.

United States v. Penn-Olin Chemical Co.

2. **Joint Ventures--United States v. Penn-Olin Chemical Co.,** 378 U.S. 158 (1964).

   a. **Facts.** Pennsalt (D) had $100 million in assets, manufactured and sold chemicals, and had 9% of the sodium chlorate industry, with a plant in the Northwest. Olin (D) had $860 million in assets and seven divisions, one of which produced chemicals. It did not manufacture sodium chlorate but sold it in the Southeast for Pennsalt. It had a process, which it licensed to paper manufacturers, that made use of the chemical in the bleaching process. Because of this process, the demand for the chemical was growing fast. Two other companies, Hooker and American Potash, controlled 90% of the sodium chlorate market in the Southeast and were worth $200 million and $100 million, respectively. Both Ds had done studies about building a plant in the Southeast; they formed a joint venture and built the plant. The next year another company entered the market in the Southeast with a new plant. The district court found that each D had the resources and the expertise to enter the market by itself, and that each thought the venture could be profitable. But the court held that the issue was whether both Ds would have entered the market if the joint venture had not been formed; only if both would have entered would competition have been foreclosed.

b. **Issue.** Could the formation of this joint venture tend to substantially lessen competition even if both parties to it would not have entered?

c. **Held.** Yes. Judgment vacated and remanded for new findings.

   1) The district court should make findings about whether even one firm would have entered the market, with the other remaining as a potential competitor.

   2) If the district court finds that this was probable, then it must be determined whether there could be a substantial lessening of competition because the two formed a joint venture and thus foreclosed the probable competitive state that would have existed. Factors to consider:

      a) Number and power of competitors in the markets;

      b) Market power of the joint venturers;

      c) The relationship of the line of commerce of the joint venturers;

      d) Reasons and necessities for the joint venture; and

      e) The adaptability of the lines of commerce of the joint venturers to anticompetitive activity.

d. **Comments.**

   1) On remand, the district court found that neither D would have entered the market by itself; thus, there was no violation.

   2) Perhaps the problem confronting the Court can best be understood by viewing the *Penn-Olin* situation in the context of a continuum of somewhat similar situations. If neither party to a joint venture would have entered independently, the joint venture increases market competition—an unmitigated plus in antitrust terms. If both would have entered, this plus is mitigated. Depending on the time horizon for entry, consumers might be better off if the joint venture were blocked. A court would have to strike a difficult balance, made all the more difficult because of the need to guess about the likelihood of entry (which itself would depend

on future market developments). What if absent the joint venture, one would have entered? The analysis must turn, in part, on what the other firm would have done. If entry by the first would have caused the other to lose interest in the market, there would be little reason to block the joint venture on antitrust grounds (apparently, the parties are willing to bet that they can compete most effectively by combining their efforts). But if after the first firm entered, the second firm would have remained a likely potential entrant, the court would have to resort to balancing. The argument for blocking the joint venture, however, would be significantly weaker than it would be in the case of dual entry for the same reasons that underlie the old proverb about the bird in the hand and the two in the bush. Whenever a court engaged in this balancing, it would presumably consider the sort of factors that bear on the legality of horizontal mergers. It would ask itself: Will this merger significantly increase the chances that the firms operating in the market could coordinate their behavior without committing a detectable section 1 offense?

3. **Conglomerate Mergers.**

   a. **Efficiencies.** In some instances where a company makes a product extension merger, there may be efficiencies involved in the acquisition, even though the two firms sell different products. For example, the products may be close enough (although not substitutes) that the distribution system used by one company can be used for both products (*i.e.*, the customers are the same), such as for soap and bleach. In other instances, there is absolutely no way that marketing efficiencies can result; the products involved may be entirely different (movies and insurance). There are possible economic efficiencies involved in conglomerate mergers, even where there is no relationship in the marketing processes. For example, there are management personnel efficiencies; or size may be such that the cost of capital comes down.

   b. **Product line extension merger--FTC v. Procter and Gamble Co.,** 386 U.S. 568 (1967).

   FTC v. Procter and Gamble Co.

   1) **Facts.** Procter and Gamble Co. (D) bought Clorox, the leading manufacturer of liquid bleach with 48.8% of the market and sales of $40 million. The next largest competitor had 16%; the top four firms had 65%; the top six had 80%; and the remaining 20% was held by 200 firms. Clorox has $12 million in assets; only eight firms had more than $1 million. All bleach is chemically the same; advertising is the key to sales. It is marketed through grocery stores. D had over $500 million in sales and 55% of all detergent sales. Detergent is also sold by advertising, to the same customers as bleach, and through the same outlets. Advertising by D was $80 million per year. D had been considering entering the bleach market, but it found

that buying Clorox was better. It expected to be able to expand Clorox's market share (which it did, to 52%, in the four years after the merger).

2) **Issue.** Would this product extension merger tend to substantially reduce competition in the bleach market?

3) **Held.** Yes. Violation of section 5 of the FTCA. The FTC's (P's) findings are upheld.

   a) Substitution of D with its huge assets and advertising advantages for the already dominant Clorox would dissuade new entrants and discourage active competition from the firms already in the industry due to fear of retaliation by D. Retailers might be induced to give Clorox preferred shelf space since it would be manufactured by D, which also produced a number of other products marketed by the retailers. (This is known as the "entrenchment" theory.)

   b) D might underprice Clorox to drive out competition and subsidize the underpricing with revenue from other products.

   c) The acquisition eliminated D as a potential competitor in the bleach market. This might tend to substantially reduce competition even though there was no evidence that D's management had ever intended to enter the industry independently. D was the most likely entrant; the barriers to entry by a firm of D's size and with its advantages were not significant; and the number of potential entrants was not so large that the elimination of one would be insignificant.

4) **Concurrence** (Harlan, J.).

   a) The state of economic knowledge about conglomerate mergers is not at the point where rules of thumb can be used to decide cases. There are both beneficial aspects (a merger allows one company to sell out; it allows the buying company to diversify to protect against fluctuations; etc.) and harmful aspects; a full analysis is required.

   b) Four guides should be relied on:

      (1) An analysis of premerger market structure;

      (2) A presumption may be made that the market operates according to generally accepted economic principles, but the defendant must be given the chance to show that in fact it does not (*i.e.*, the defendant might argue that there is no price leadership even though the structure is made up of only a few firms);

      (3) A showing of reasonable probability that there will be a change in market structure allowing the exercise of substantially greater market power is a prima facie case; and

(4) The defendant may show that there are countervailing economies from the merger that should be weighed against the adverse effects.

United States v. Falstaff Brewing Corp.

c. **The perceived potential competition theory--United States v. Falstaff Brewing Corp.,** 410 U.S. 526 (1973).

1) **Facts.** Falstaff Brewing Corporation (D) bought Narragansett Brewing Company. Narragansett had 20% of the New England beer market. The eight largest firms had 81% of this market, up from 74% five years before. D had 6% of the national market (fourth largest) but did no business in New England. It had studied the possibility of entering the New England market, but decided on the merger instead. At the time of the acquisition, competition was vigorous, and it did not diminish afterward. Narragansett's market share declined from 21.5% to 15.5%. The district court found that since D would not have entered the market without a merger, there was no violation.

2) **Issue.** Could a conglomerate geographical extension merger with a relatively large firm tend to substantially reduce competition if the extending firm would not have entered independently?

3) **Held.** Yes. Judgment reversed and case remanded.

   a) The acquisition might have tended to substantially reduce competition even though D would not have entered the market de novo. Because of D's financial capabilities and conditions in the market, others operating there may have reasonably perceived D as a potential entrant and modified their behavior accordingly.

   b) Because we remand for proper assessment of D as an on-the-fringe potential competitor, it is not necessary to reach the question of whether section 7 bars a market-extension merger by a company whose entry into the market would have no influence whatsoever on the present state of competition in the market—that is, the entrant will not be a dominant force in the market and has no current influence in the marketplace. We leave for another day the question of the applicability of section 7 to a merger that will leave competition in the marketplace exactly as it was, neither hurt nor helped, and that is challengeable only on grounds that the company could, but did not, enter de novo or through a "toe-hold" acquisition and that there is less competition than there would have been had entry been in such a manner.

4) **Comment.** The Court's perceived potential competitor theory did not survive *Marine Bancorporation* (*infra*) intact.

d. The actual potential competitor theory--United States v. Marine Bancorporation, Inc., 418 U.S. 602 (1974).

1) **Facts.** The National Bank of Commerce (D), a national bank with its principal office in Seattle, having $1.8 billion in assets (second largest in the state) and 107 branches, bought Washington Trust Bank, a bank located in Spokane (where D had no branches), with assets of $112 million. The five largest banks in the state had 75% of the market. In the Spokane market, the top two banks held 74%, and Washington Trust had an additional 19%. State law prevented banks from branching except in the city of their headquarters; in effect, mergers were the only way for expansion into new markets, but after a merger no branching was permitted. The Government (P) challenged the merger under section 7, claiming that it would tend to substantially lessen competition in the Spokane and Washington commercial banking markets by: (i) eliminating each bank as a potential competitor of the other, and (ii) creating a statewide system of interlocking oligopolies that would lead to parallel practices and a reduction in competition. The district court found for D, and P appealed.

2) **Issues.**

   a) Does the state of Washington constitute a relevant geographic market?

   b) Does this geographical extension merger tend to substantially lessen competition because it eliminates the prospect for long-term deconcentration of an oligopolistic market that in theory might result if the acquiring firm had to enter de novo or through a toe-hold acquisition?

3) **Held.** a) No. b) No. Judgment affirmed.

   a) In a potential competition case the geographic market is the area in which the firms actually compete.

   b) Even assuming that, despite the anti-branching laws, D could have succeeded in sponsoring and then acquiring a new bank in Spokane at some indefinite time in the future, this method of entry would not significantly affect the market because D could not have lawfully branched from its sponsored bank. The same is true of P's possible acquisition of one of the two small state-chartered commercial banks operating in Spokane (even assuming that one would have been available for sale) for the same reason.

   c) P did not demonstrate that the alternative means of entry offered a reasonable prospect of long-term structural improvements or other benefits in the target market.

d) Since the preconditions for P's principal potential competition theory are not met, we do not reach it or the question reserved in *Falstaff*.

e) Because P failed to establish that D had alternative methods of entry that offer a reasonable likelihood of producing procompetitive effects, it is improbable that D, by "standing in the wings," exerts any meaningful procompetitive influence since rational commercial bankers in Spokane are presumably aware of the key regulatory barriers.

4) **Comments.**

a) In *United States v. Citizens & Southern National Bank*, 422 U.S. 86 (1975), the Department of Justice challenged Citizens & Southern's acquisition of five banks that it had sponsored in order to circumvent Georgia's anti-branching law. The Court rejected the challenge, stating: "[T]he proposed acquisition will extinguish no present competitive conduct or relationships. . . . As for future competition, neither the District Court nor the FDIC could find any realistic prospect that denial of these acquisitions would lead the defendant banks to compete against each other."

b) The power of the potential competition theory ought to vary directly with the strength of entry barriers. Thus *Marine Bancorporation* may be a bad omen for the theory in practice.

e. **The time horizon of potential competition--BOC International Ltd. v. FTC,** 557 F.2d 24 (2d Cir. 1977).

1) **Facts.** BOC (D), the world's second largest producer of industrial gases, acquired Airco, the third largest in the United States (16% of market), where D had not previously marketed. D had never exerted any "in the wings" effect. The FTC (P) found a violation of section 7, because it concluded D would "eventually" have entered on its own.

2) **Issue.** Does section 7 reach mergers between potential competitors without regard to the probable length of time before independent entry?

3) **Held.** No. Judgment reversed.

a) The "eventual" test is too harsh, using the actual potential entry principle.

4) **Comment.** The court left unanswered whether actual potential entry, if imminent rather than eventual, is a basis for condemnation.

f. **1984 Department of Justice merger guidelines: horizontal effect from non-horizontal mergers.**

1) **General approach.** Although non-horizontal mergers are less likely than horizontal ones to create competitive problems, they are not invariably innocuous. If the merger effectively removes the acquiring firm from the edge of the market, or it could eliminate a significant present competitive threat that constrains the behavior of the firms already in the market, this could result in an immediate deterioration in market performance; or it could eliminate the possibility of entry by the acquiring firm in a more procompetitive manner, and thereby forfeit a chance for improvement in market performance resulting from the addition of a significant competitor. Because of the close relationship between perceived potential competition and actual potential competition, the Department evaluates mergers that raise either type of concern under a single structural analysis analogous to that applied to horizontal mergers. (The 1992 merger guidelines, which amended the horizontal provisions of the 1984 guidelines, did not amend the vertical or conglomerate merger provisions.)

2) **Factors considered.**

   a) Market concentration;

   b) Conditions of entry generally;

   c) The acquiring firm's entry advantage;

   d) The market share of the acquired firm; and

   e) Efficiencies.

C. **INTEGRATION THROUGH VERTICAL MERGER**

1. **Functions Served.** Integration by merger may economize on market transaction costs, the costs of shopping, negotiating, and monitoring and enforcing compliance with contractual obligations. Integrated firms may experience advantages in producing component parts and in responding rapidly to external changes.

2. **Supplier Buys Controlling Stock Interest in Customer--United States v. E.I. du Pont de Nemours & Co.,** 353 U.S. 586 (1957).

   a. **Facts.** In 1917, E.I. du Pont de Nemours & Company (D) bought 23% of the common stock of General Motors ("GM") and began supplying GM with finishes and fabrics. An action was brought under section 7. It was shown that GM has 50% of the car market; in one year it bought $18 million worth of car finishes from D (67% of its needs) and $3 million worth of fabrics (52% of its needs). In

United States v. E.I. du Pont de Nemours & Co.

1947, D's finish sales to GM constituted 3.5% of all sales of finishes to industrial users, and its fabric sales to GM constituted 1.6% of the total market for the type of fabric used by the automobile industry. The district court dismissed the complaint and the Department of Justice appeals.

b. **Issues.**

1) Do automobile finishes and fabrics constitute relevant product markets?

2) Did this acquisition tend to substantially lessen competition in the markets for automobile fabrics and finishes because of the supply relationship between the parties?

c. **Held**. 1) Yes. 2) Yes. Judgment reversed.

1) Automobile finishes and fabrics have sufficient peculiar characteristics and uses for them to constitute product markets.

2) Section 7 applies to vertical acquisitions.

3) Section 7 applies not only to the acquisition of stock, but its subsequent use as well. The idea is to arrest the creation of monopolies in their incipiency, here meaning when the acquisition threatens to ripen into a prohibited effect.

4) The bulk of D's production has always supplied the largest part of the requirements of the one customer in the automobile industry connected to D by a stock interest. D employed its stock to pry open the GM market to entrench itself as the primary supplier of GM's requirements for automotive finishes and fabrics.

d. **Dissent** (Burton, Frankfurter, JJ.). The Government did not show that the identical products were not used on a large scale for many other purposes in many other industries. Nor did the Government show that the automobile industry in general or GM in particular comprised a large or substantial share of the total market. What evidence there is in the record affirmatively indicates that the products involved do have wide use in many industries, and that an insubstantial portion of this total market would be affected even if an unlawful preference existed or were probable. Section 7, prior to its amendment in 1950, did not apply to vertical acquisitions; the Government failed to prove that there was a reasonable probability at the time of the stock acquisition of a tendency toward monopoly; and the Government failed to prove that D's competitors have been or may be foreclosed from a substantial share of the relevant market.

e. **Comment.** It is not clear that du Pont would have found it in its own self-interest to force GM to buy finishes and fabrics from it. Perhaps this explains why it is that du Pont did not supply 100% of GM's requirements.

3. **The Test for "Substantially Lessen" Competition--Brown Shoe Co. v. United States,** 370 U.S. 294 (1962).

   a. **Facts.** Brown Shoe Co. (D) bought Kinney Shoe Co.; both were manufacturers and retailers of shoes (men's, women's, and children's). D was the fourth largest manufacturer (4%); Kinney was the twelfth largest (0.5%). D was the third largest retailer (6%); Kinney was eighth (2%). The Government (P) brought suit to enjoin the acquisition. The district court found the following:

      (i) Men's, women's, and children's shoes are generally produced in separate factories;

      (ii) There is a definite trend in the industry towards manufacturers acquiring retailers;

      (iii) There is a definite trend towards fewer and fewer manufacturers;

      (iv) There is a definite trend towards manufacturers' supplying an increasing percentage of shoes to owned retail outlets;

      (v) D was involved in each of these trends itself;

      (vi) At the time of the merger Kinney did not buy any of its retail shoes from D; and

      (vii) At the time the action was brought D supplied 8% of Kinney's needs.

      The district court found that the merger violated section 7 of the Clayton Act. D appeals.

   b. **Issues.**

      1) Do men's, women's, and children's shoes constitute relevant product markets?

      2) Did this acquisition tend to substantially lessen competition in the retail product markets because of the supply relationship between the parties?

   c. **Held.** 1) Yes. 2) Yes. Judgment affirmed.

      1) The relevant product market is defined by reasonable interchangeability or cross-elasticity of demand between the product and substitutes. Submarkets may be defined based on practical indicia such as industry or public recognition, a product's peculiar characteristics and uses, unique production facilities, distinct customers, distinct prices, and specialized vendors. Section 7 prohibits lessening of competition in any of these submarkets. The relevant product mar-

kets are men's, women's, and children's shoes. D argues for price/quality and age/sex distinctions, but none of these would help its case.

2) The relevant geographical market is the entire nation. Manufacturers can distribute on a nationwide basis.

3) In this industry, no merger between a manufacturer and an independent retailer could involve a larger potential market foreclosure. It is apparent both from past behavior of D and from the testimony of D's president that D would use its ownership of Kinney to force D's shoes into Kinney stores.

4) This acquisition is made more suspect by the fact that the trend in this industry is toward vertical integration and that the acquiring manufacturers become increasingly important sources of supply for their acquired outlets.

5) Not only must we consider the probable effects of the merger upon the economics of the particular markets affected, but also we must consider its probable effects upon the economic way of life sought to be preserved by Congress. Congress was desirous of preventing the formation of future oligopolies with their attendant effects upon local control of industry and upon small business. Where an industry was composed of numerous units, Congress appeared anxious to preserve this structure.

6) This merger creates a large national chain, which is integrated with a manufacturing operation. The retail outlets of integrated companies, by eliminating wholesalers and by increasing the volume of purchases from the manufacturing division of the enterprise, can market their own brands at prices below those of competing independent retailers.

d. **Comments.**

1) Note here that the Court indicated that the integrated company might be able to market its own brands at lower prices than the competition, which might benefit the consumer but injure competitors, and that even though the Act protected competition and not competitors, still another purpose of the Act was to insure that markets, even though less efficient, were characterized by many competitive units. This is a very confused handling of the issues. If D could have shown that economic efficiencies would have resulted and consumers would be better off, and the market was still competitive, then D presumably should have been allowed this merger.

2) Note that the majority opinion obscures some important questions on market shares. First, most of D's retail locations were "franchises," not owned by D. Second, in computing Kinney's retail sales, all of Kinney's retail purchases were lumped together; but it might have been more proper

to consider what percent of Kinney's purchases represented the independent manufacturer's sales, since this would be a more accurate reflection of the market share foreclosed by the merger.

4. **Backward Integration--Ford Motor Co. v. United States,** 405 U.S. 562 (1972).

   a. **Facts.** Champion had 50%, Autolite had 15%, and GM had 30% of the spark plug market. Champion sold to Ford (D), and Autolite sold to Chrysler. Normally, the aftermarket replaced the same type of plug put in as original equipment. D was going to start its own manufacture of plugs, but bought Autolite instead. D represented 10% of the users of the plug market. The district court found a violation of section 7 of the Clayton Act.

   b. **Issue.** Did this acquisition tend to substantially lessen competition in the spark plug industry?

   c. **Held.** Yes. Judgment affirmed.

   1) D was a potential entrant and exerted a moderating influence on the other spark plug manufacturers not only because it could enter, but also because it was a major customer of Champion.

   2) D might someday enter via internal expansion, and thus deconcentrate the market.

   3) That the acquisition might make Autolite a stronger competitor against Champion and General Motors is immaterial.

   4) The merger foreclosed 10% of the plug market to other sellers. The tie with the original equipment totally controlled the aftermarket; to allow the acquisition would mean that the plug market would become exactly like the concentrated car market. Entry by any new firms would be impossible.

   d. **Comments.**

   1) In addition to divestiture, the district court ordered D to purchase half of its total annual requirements of spark plugs from the divested plant under the Autolite label for five years; enjoined D from manufacturing spark plugs for 10 years; prohibited D from using its own trade names on spark plugs for five years; and required D to continue its policy of selling spark plugs to its dealers at prices no less than its prevailing minimum suggested jobbers' selling price for 10 years. Over a dissent, the Supreme Court upheld these remedial provisions.

   2) If foreclosure were of concern because of its ultimate impact on consumers, then it would be difficult to understand why the Court

Ford Motor Co. v. United States

Fruehauf
Corp. v.
FTC

invoked the concept to condemn this acquisition when the acquiring firm was one of those consumers. It would also be difficult to understand the remedy.

5. **Realignment, Not Foreclosure--Fruehauf Corp. v. FTC,** 603 F.2d 345 (2d Cir. 1979).

   a. **Facts.** Fruehauf (D) manufactured 25% of the truck trailers in the country and bought 5.3% of the heavy duty wheels (HDWs) used on trailers and similar equipment. Kelsey manufactured 15% of HDWs sold nationwide. D acquired Kelsey. The FTC (P) found a violation of section 7 and D appeals.

   b. **Issue.** Did this acquisition tend to substantially lessen competition in the truck trailer market because in the event of an HDW shortage, the wheel manufacturing party would favor the truck trailer manufacturing party?

   c. **Held.** No. Judgment reversed.

   1) The FTC's decision is based on several assumptions lacking any appreciable evidentiary support. Kelsey has not been a significant and substantial supplier of HDWs to D's competitors.

   2) At the time of the merger, D did not plan to have Kelsey divert HDWs to it in the event of a shortage. A spokesman for one of D's competitors testified that he did not believe that is what would happen. And it would not have been in D's self-interest to do so because such a strategy would risk retaliation by customers following the shortage when they could shift patronage not only of HDWs but of other products made by Kelsey.

   3) While the HDW market is significantly concentrated and the initial capital outlay required to begin production at an efficient level of output is high, the potential foreclosure from this acquisition would not preclude any existing competitor from continuing to operate economically or any potential competitor from entering the market.

   4) The decision cannot be sustained on the FTC's ephemeral theory that, although D was not a potential entrant into the HDW market, it had a procompetitive effect on the market through its collaborative efforts to develop new types of heavy duty wheels and by virtue of its ability to draw new entrants into production of conventional wheels by offering to deliver its patronage. D's new product adventures had been failures. D was not unique in its ability to elicit new competition; in fact, other customers (*e.g.*, the auto giants) could probably do more.

6. **Department of Justice Merger Guidelines for Vertical Mergers.** In a significant departure from its 1968 guidelines, the Department of Justice announced in its 1984 guidelines that, for the most part, it would use the same ultimate standard for evaluating vertical mergers as it used for horizontal ones. This is why the guidelines explain how vertical mergers might make it easier for firms in one or both of the affected markets to coordinate their pricing and output behavior without engaging in a detectable section 1 offense. The 1992 guidelines, which amended the horizontal merger provisions, did not amend the vertical or the conglomerate merger positions.

   a. **How market entry is slowed.** Vertical mergers may slow entry in one of several ways:

   1) The vertical integration might be so extensive that entrants to a primary market would also have to enter a secondary market simultaneously;

   2) The requirement of entry at the secondary level makes entry at the primary level less likely to occur; and

   3) Increased difficulty of entry into the primary market might perpetuate or enhance noncompetitive performance in that market.

   b. **Criteria used to recognize objectionable barrier.**

   1) **Minimal unintegrated capacity.** Minimal unintegrated capacity exists if unintegrated capacity in the secondary market is insufficient to service two minimum-efficient-scale plants in the primary market.

   2) **High costs.** High costs occur if secondary market entry significantly increases the cost of primary market entry.

      a) **Cost of capital.** Capital cost increases as capital assets become more specialized, because the cost of specialized capital is difficult to recover in the event of business failure.

      b) **Economies of scale.** When minimum-efficient-scale plants in the secondary market have greater capacity than a minimum-efficiency-scale plant in the primary market, operating costs may create an entry barrier, particularly if there is no outside secondary market.

   3) **Market structure and performance.** Barriers are more likely to arise in a highly concentrated primary market (HHI above 1800).

   c. **Facilitating collusion in a highly concentrated upstream market through vertical merger.**

1) **Retail level.** When there is vertical integration by upstream firms into associated retail markets, prices are more visible and subject to monitoring. This facilitates collusion. The Department is unlikely to challenge a merger on this ground unless a large percentage of the upstream product would be sold through vertically integrated retail outlets after merger.

2) **Elimination of a disruptive buyer.** If a disruptive downstream buyer creates a rivalry between upstream sellers, the elimination of that disruptive buyer through vertical merger could promote collusion within the upstream market. The Department, however, is unlikely to challenge a merger on this ground unless the disruptive firm differs substantially in volume of purchases or other relevant characteristics from other firms in its market.

7. **Interlocking Directorates.** Section 8 of the Clayton Act prohibits a person from being a director of two or more corporations when any one of them has capital and surplus in excess of $10 million if such corporations are competitors so that elimination of competition between them by agreement would be a violation of the antitrust laws.

X. FOREIGN COMMERCE AND THE U.S. ANTITRUST LAWS

A. JURISDICTION OVER FOREIGN COMMERCE

1. **Foreign Commerce Before 1982.**

    a. **Limited reach of Act and immunity of sovereign--American Banana Co. v. United Fruit Co.,** 213 U.S. 347 (1909).

    American Banana Co. v. United Fruit Co.

    1) **Facts.** American Banana Company (P) succeeded to the interest of McConnell, who had been harmed by actions of Central American governments. The actions were allegedly prompted by United Fruit Company (D), the prominent American banana grower. P sued D for violation of the Sherman Act, and lost at trial and in the circuit court of appeals.

    2) **Issues.**

        a) May a United States court exercise jurisdiction over the behavior of a United States national in another country?

        b) If so, is the behavior actionable?

    3) **Held.** a) No. b) No. Judgment affirmed.

        a) The general rule, not to be overturned here, is that the legality of an act is wholly a function of the law of the country where the act takes place.

        b) Even if jurisdiction existed, it is by no means improper to persuade a sovereign to do what it is lawfully entitled to do, and the sovereign act itself is lawful by definition.

    4) **Comment.** In *Alcoa*, the Court rejected the first element of the analysis and announced that the Sherman Act reaches all behavior, wherever undertaken, with domestic effects.

    b. **The Sherman Act and conduct occurring outside the United States--United States v. Aluminum Co. of America,** 148 F.2d 416 (2d Cir. 1945).

    United States v. Aluminum Co. of America

    1) **Facts.** In 1928, Aluminum Company of America ("ALCOA") (D), organized a Canadian subsidiary, "Limited" (D), to hold and operate almost all of its non-U.S. assets. The United States (P) claimed, among other things, that Ds had violated section 1 by participating in the Alliance, a Swiss corporation created pursuant to a 1931 agreement between Limited and others, all of whom became shareholders. (P also claimed that ALCOA

Antitrust - 157

had monopolized aluminum in violation of section 2. The portion of the opinion dealing with this claim appears at III.A.3., *supra*.) The trial judge found that ALCOA was not a party to the Alliance and held that ALCOA did not bear liability for the conduct of the Alliance simply because ALCOA's controlling shareholders were also Limited's controlling shareholders.

The 1931 agreement provided that the Alliance would from time to time fix a production quota for each Alliance share. Each shareholder could set its own price, but the Alliance fixed a price every year at which it would purchase any unsold part of a shareholder's quota. The agreement prohibited each shareholder from buying, borrowing, fabricating, or selling aluminum produced by any non-shareholder except with the consent of the board of governors, which could not be "unreasonably withheld." The agreement did not expressly provide whether this prohibition extended to sales in the United States, but it did provide that a shareholder "might exceed his quota to the extent that he converted into aluminum in the United States or Canada any ores delivered to him in either of those countries by persons situated in the United States."

In 1936, the shareholders entered into a new agreement that provided that for production exceeding each shareholder's quota, that shareholder would have to pay a royalty—graduated progressively in proportion to the excess—to the Alliance. The Alliance would divide the royalties among the shareholders in proportion to their shares. Unlike the first agreement, this one did not contain an express promise that the Alliance would buy any undisposed of stock at a fixed price, although it may have impliedly recognized such an obligation. But "the last price fixed under the agreement of 1931 was understood to remain in force." Like the 1931 agreement, this agreement did not expressly address imports into the United States, but when that question arose during its preparation, all the shareholders agreed that such imports would be included in the quotas. The trial judge found that the purpose of the agreement was not to "suppress or restrain the exportation of aluminum to the United States for sale in competition with ALCOA."

For the years 1932-1935, average imports, including ALCOA's, were about 15 million pounds while the average domestic ingot manufacture was about 96 million pounds; for 1936, 1937 and the first quarter of 1938, average imports were about 33 million pounds while average domestic ingot manufacture was about 262 million. Citing the increase in imports, the trial judge found that the 1936 agreement failed to "materially affect the foreign trade or commerce of the United States."

2) **Issue.** Does section 1 apply to the 1936 production quota/royalty agreement between Limited and five other foreign firms?

3) **Held.** Yes. Judgment reversed and remanded.

   a) When interpreting the general words of the Sherman Act, a court should not assume that Congress meant to disregard the limitations customarily observed by nations upon the exercise of their powers much less that Congress intended to punish conduct having no consequences within the United States. Congress could impose liabilities—even on foreigners—for agreements made outside U.S. borders having consequences inside them, applying the Sherman Act to such agreements when the parties did not intend to affect imports to or exports from the United States would cause such international complications that it is safe to assume that Congress did not intend that the Act cover them.

b) The Sherman Act does cover agreements made outside U.S. borders having consequences inside them if the parties intended to affect imports from or exports to the United States—regardless of whether the parties send agents into the United States to perform part of the agreement. The 1936 agreement made changes in the 1931 agreement for the purpose of affecting United States imports. (The trial judge's finding that it was not the purpose of the agreement to suppress or restrain the exportation of aluminum to the United States for sale in competition with ALCOA must mean that the agreement was not specifically directed to ALCOA because it only applied generally to the production of the shareholders.)

c) Substantial evidence does not support the trial judge's finding that the 1936 agreement failed to "materially affect the foreign trade or commerce of the United States." That gross imports of ingot increased in 1936, 1937, and the first quarter of 1938 does not show that the agreement failed to restrict imports, especially in light of the fact that the proportion of imports to domestic ingot decreased from about 15.6% to 12.6%. That the proportion of imports to domestic ingot decreased does not show that the 1936 agreement did have an impact on the foreign trade or commerce of the United States, so whether section 1 reaches this agreement depends on which party bears the burden of proof on this factual issue.

d) Once P showed that the parties to the 1936 agreement intended to affect imports to the United States, the burden of proof on the actual effects shifted to Limited.

   (1) All else being equal, a reduction in output will "distribute its effect evenly upon all markets."

   (2) Since the parties took the trouble to make the agreement applicable to the United States, it is reasonable to suppose that they expected that it would have some effect, which it could have only by reducing imports to less than they would have been otherwise. If the parties had other incentives that trumped the ones created by their agreement, they are in a much better position to marshal the evidence proving it.

   (3) Moreover, there is an especial propriety in demanding this of Limited because it was Limited that procured the inclusion in the agreement of 1936 of imports in the quotas.

Antitrust - 159

Continental Ore Co. v. Union Carbide and Carbon Corp.

c. **Act permitted by government not immune--Continental Ore Co. v. Union Carbide and Carbon Corp.,** 370 U.S. 690 (1962).

   1) **Facts.** Continental Ore Company (P), a vanadium manufacturer and refiner, charged that Union Carbide and Carbon Corporation's (D's) wholly owned Canadian subsidiary had violated the Sherman Act by excluding P from the Canadian market. D's subsidiary had been appointed by the Canadian government as exclusive administrator of Canadian sales and purchase of vanadium. The trial court and court of appeals held D's subsidiary's behavior as beyond the reach of the Sherman Act.

   2) **Issue.** Does the exercise of authority granted by a foreign sovereign immunize the exercising private enterprise from Sherman Act exposure?

   3) **Held.** No. The lower court opinion is vacated.

      a) D's subsidiary was authorized, but not required, to cut off P. It did so out of a private business animus (at its corporate parent's request), which enjoys no Sherman Act immunity.

      b) No act of the Canadian government is challenged here, nor is that government a party.

d. **Foreign sovereign permitted to sue.** In *Pfizer, Inc. v. Government of India*, 434 U.S. 308 (1978), the Court held that a foreign sovereign "otherwise entitled to sue in our courts is entitled to sue for treble damages" under the Clayton Act, section 4.

Zenith Radio Corp. v. Hazeltine Research, Inc.

e. **International exports--Zenith Radio Corp. v. Hazeltine Research, Inc.,** 395 U.S. 100 (1969).

   1) **Facts.** Zenith Radio Corporation (D) is a Delaware corporation that manufacturers radio and television sets for export. In so doing it must negotiate with various patent holders to obtain the appropriate licenses. Hazeltine Research, Inc. (P) owned numerous patents and was in the business of selling licenses to them. D determined that it did not need to renew its licenses with P, and P brought suit claiming patent infringement. D counterclaimed for antitrust violations relating to agreements entered into by P with foreign patent pools whereby D was refused a license and its exportation of products to Canada was interfered with unless it agreed to manufacture in Canada. D prevailed in the district court on all counts and was awarded treble damages and injunctive relief on its antitrust complaint. The court of appeals reversed and the Supreme Court granted certiorari.

   2) **Issue.** Did D present sufficient facts to support the damage award and injunctive relief by establishing that P's conduct in refusing to license its patents caused harm to D?

3) **Held.** Yes. Judgment of court of appeals reversed.

    a) P entered into an agreement with a Canadian patent pool and this group required D to purchase a license; however, the license would not give D the right to export products unless they were manufactured in Canada. Furthermore, the group actively contacted dealers and warned them not to deal with unlicensed products such as D's. Accordingly, D had a difficult time entering the market and although it eventually did, the evidence suggests that the Canadian patent pool's interference substantially hampered D's efforts and affected D's profits. Thus D satisfied its burden of establishing that the actions of P and its fellow pool members hampered D's efforts to enter the Canadian market.

    b) Additionally, the court of appeals erred when it concluded that injunctive relief was not proper. It is well established that Congress intended for equitable relief to be available when the plaintiff has established threatened injury even though the plaintiff has yet to suffer actual injury.

2. **The Foreign Trade Antitrust Improvements Act ("FTAIA") of 1982.** With respect to the Sherman Act, the FTAIA (which similarly amended the Federal Trade Commission Act) provides that sections 1 to 7 of Title 15 do not apply to conduct involving trade or commerce (other than imports) with foreign nations unless:

(1) such conduct has a direct, substantial, and reasonably foreseeable effect

    (A) on trade or commerce which is not trade or commerce with foreign nations, or on import trade or import commerce with foreign nations; or

    (B) on export trade or export commerce with foreign nations, of a person engaged in such trade or commerce in the United States; and

(2) such effect gives rise to a claim under the provisions of sections 1 to 7 . . . other than this section.

If sections 1 to 7 apply to such conduct only because of the operation of paragraph (1)(B), then sections 1 to 7 of this title shall apply to such conduct only for injury to export business in the United States.

    a. **The FTAIA and "Comity."** The legislative history of the FTAIA specifies that Congress was not taking a position on the question whether the exercise of judicial power should also be tempered by "comity."

Hartford Fire Insurance Co. v. California

b. **Antitrust jurisdiction and the interests of other nations--Hartford Fire Insurance Co. v. California,** 509 U.S. 764 (1993).

1) **Facts.** Providers of commercial general liability ("CGL") insurance use standard policy forms developed by Insurance Services Office, Inc. ("ISO") (D), an association of approximately 1,400 domestic property and casualty insurers (including the primary insurer defendants, Hartford Fire Insurance Company, Allstate Insurance Company, CIGNA Corporation, and Aetna Casualty & Surety Company (Ds)). For each such form, ISO supplies actuarial and rating information: it collects, aggregates, interprets, and distributes data on the premiums charged, claims filed and paid, and defense costs expended with respect to each form, and on the basis of this data it predicts future loss trends and calculates advisory premium rates. ISO is the almost exclusive source of these critical support services in the United States for CGL insurance. Most ISO members cannot afford to continue to use a form if ISO withdraws these services.

For 1984, Hartford requested that ISO eliminate the form providing for traditional "occurrence" CGL insurance, which obligates the insurer "to pay or defend claims, whenever made, resulting from an accident or 'injurious exposure to conditions' that occurred during the [specific time] period the policy was in effect," and replace it with a form providing for "claims-made" CGL insurance, which obligates the insurer to pay or defend only those claims made during the policy period. Hartford along with Allstate also requested that this "claims-made" policy (i) contain a "retroactive date" provision, which would restrict coverage to claims based on incidents that occurred after a certain date, (ii) eliminate coverage of "sudden and accidental" pollution, and (iii) provide that legal defense costs be counted against the policy limits. A majority of the members of the relevant ISO committees rejected the request.

The four primary insurers then enlisted the help of reinsurers from whom they and most other CGL insurers purchase insurance to cover a portion of the risk that they assume from their customers. (Reinsurers, in turn, often purchase "retrocessional reinsurance" to cover part of the risk that they assume from the primary insurer.) Because "reinsurance" protects its purchaser from catastrophic loss and allows the purchaser to sell more insurance than its own financial capacity might otherwise permit, "[t]he availability of reinsurance affects the ability and willingness of primary insurers to provide insurance to their customers." The four primary insurers persuaded the reinsurers, including key actors in the London reinsurance market (Ds), an important provider of reinsurance for North American risks, to withhold reinsurance for coverages written on the 1984 forms. The ISO executive committee then voted to include a pollution coverage from both this and the "occurrence" policy forms. The reinsurers then collectively refused to write new reinsurance contracts for primary insurers who used the new "occurrence" policy form, and they amended their reinsurance contracts to cover only claims made before a "sunset date" thus eliminating reinsurance for claims made on occurrence policies after that date.

California and several other states (Ps) brought suit claiming that Ds had engaged in an illegal boycott. Ds moved to dismiss on the grounds that the McCarran-Ferguson Act afforded them immunity. The district court granted the motion, rejecting the argument that the conduct complained of fell within the section 3(b) exception to immunity for "boycotts, coercion, or intimidation." The district court also dismissed the three claims that named only certain London-based defendants invoking international comity. The court of appeals reversed on the grounds that (i) because the activities of the foreign reinsurers could not be "regulated by state law" within the meaning of section 2(b), they did not fall within that section's grant of immunity; (ii) the domestic insurers forfeited their section 2(b) exemption when they conspired with the nonexempt foreign reinsurers; and (iii) in any event, the challenged conduct fell within the section 3(b) exception. The court of appeals also held that international comity did not bar Sherman Act scrutiny of the challenged conduct. Ds appeal.

2) **Issue.** If extraterritorial conduct is lawful under, but not compelled by, the law of the nation in which the conduct takes place, is that conduct subject to antitrust scrutiny by a United States court? (*Note*: The "boycott" exception issue is addressed at V.A.4., *supra*.)

3) **Held.** Yes. Case remanded.

   a) The District Court had jurisdiction over these Sherman Act claims, as the London reinsurers apparently concede. ("Our position is not that the Sherman Act does not apply in the sense that a minimal basis for the exercise of jurisdiction doesn't exist here. Our position is that there are certain circumstances, and that this is one of them, in which the interests of another State are sufficient that the exercise of that jurisdiction should be restrained.")

   b) That the challenged extraterritorial scheme was consistent with the comprehensive regulatory regime over the London reinsurance market established by Parliament does not bar application of United States antitrust laws unless British law requires the conduct. While application of American antitrust laws to the London reinsurance market would lead to significant conflict with English law and policy, a reason to decline the exercise of jurisdiction, as the court of appeals noted, other factors, including the London

Antitrust - 163

purpose to affect United States commerce and the substantial nature of the effect produced, outweighed the supposed conflict and required the exercise of jurisdiction.

4) **Dissent** (Scalia, J.). The real issue is whether Congress asserted regulatory power over the challenged extraterritorial conduct when it enacted the Sherman Act. (It is not proper to treat the conduct as something less than extraterritorial because some of the British corporations are subsidiaries of American corporations.) While the Act has extraterritorial reach, the Court still ought to interpret it, if possible—as it would any other act of Congress—as complying with the "the law of nations," or customary international law, which includes limitations on a nation's exercise of its jurisdiction. The Court should not interpret the Sherman Act as regulating conduct that: (i) occurred in London, (ii) was engaged in by British corporations generally doing business outside the United States, and (iii) was and is legal under a comprehensive British regulatory scheme—particularly in light of the limited United States interest evidenced by the McCarran-Ferguson Act, which allows state regulatory statutes to override the Sherman Act in the insurance field, subject only to the "boycott" exception set forth in section 3(b). To permit United States courts to scrutinize extraterritorial conduct under the Sherman Act unless the conduct is compelled by the law of another nation, will bring the Sherman Act and other laws into sharp and unnecessary conflict with the legitimate interests of other countries—particularly our closest trading partners.

c. **International activity in criminal prosecution--United States v. Nippon Paper,** 109 F.3d 1 (1st Cir. 1997).

United States v. Nippon Paper

1) **Facts.** In 1995, a grand jury returned an indictment against Nippon Paper (D) alleging that D and several co-conspirators held meetings in Japan that resulted in an agreement to fix the price of thermal fax paper imported into the United States. The United States (P) initiated criminal prosecution under section 1 of the Sherman Act. D moved to dismiss claiming that because all the conduct complained of occurred entirely in Japan, it did not constitute an offense under the Sherman Act. The district court granted the motion and P appeals the dismissal.

2) **Issue.** Does section 1 of the Sherman Act reach wholly extraterritorial conduct in the criminal context?

3) **Held.** Yes. Judgment reversed and remanded.

a) The Supreme Court has established that the Sherman Act applies to wholly foreign conduct that has an intended and substantial effect in the United States in civil cases.

b) The settled norms of statutory construction dictate that section 1 in the criminal context is co-extensive with section 1 in the civil context.

4) **Concurrence.** Most people recognize that there is a distinction between civil and criminal liability. However, the exercise of jurisdiction is reasonable in this case.

d. **Sufficiency of conduct to support jurisdiction under the FTAIA--Den Norske Stats Oljeselskap As v. HeereMac Vof,** 241 F.3d 420 (5th Cir. 2001).

Den Norske Stats Oljeselskap As v. HeereMac Vof

1) **Facts.** HeereMac Vof and others (Ds) provide heavy-lift barge services throughout the world. Heavy-lift barges are immense vessels with cranes capable of hoisting and transporting offshore oil platforms weighing in excess of 4,000 tons. Only six or seven of these barges exist in the world, and during the period of 1993-97, Ds owned all of them. Den Norske (P), a Norwegian oil company that owns and operates oil and gas drilling platforms exclusively in the North Sea, used heavy-lift barge services. P alleged that Ds conspired to fix bids and allocate territories, with some companies getting exclusive access to the Gulf of Mexico and others working only in the North Sea. P alleged that, as a result, it paid inflated prices for barge services for its projects in the North Sea, which compelled it to charge higher prices for the crude oil it exported to the United States. P does not conduct any business in the United States or with barge companies incorporated here. The district court dismissed for lack of subject matter jurisdiction. P appeals.

2) **Issue.** Was the connection between Ds' alleged conduct and P's injury sufficient under the Foreign Trade Antitrust Improvements Act ("FTAIA") to invoke the jurisdiction of United States federal courts?

3) **Held.** No. Judgment affirmed.

a) The FTAIA provides that United States antitrust laws do not apply to non-import commerce with foreign nations unless (i) the challenged conduct has a "direct, substantial, and reasonably foreseeable effect" on domestic commerce and (ii) such effect gives rise to a claim under United States antitrust laws.

b) Ds' alleged conduct had a direct, substantial, and reasonably foreseeable effect on the United States market in that consumers had to pay supracompetitive prices for oil. But this effect on United States commerce did not "give rise" to its antitrust claim, namely that, as a result of the alleged conspiracy, P had to pay more for barge services for its North Sea operation. The FTAIA's plain language and legislative history require that the specific conduct complained of gives rise to the alleged antitrust injury to the plaintiff. In this case the domestic conduct complained of was the agreement to artifi-

Antitrust - 165

cially increase the cost of barge services in the Gulf of Mexico. Although quite possibly connected to the claim that P had to pay increased prices in the North Sea, it is not sufficiently connected to support a claim. Any domestic effect of increased crude oil prices stemming from increased costs of barge services is an injury suffered by United States consumers and not P and thus cannot be used to support a claim.

  4) Dissent. The FTAIA requires that the effect on United States commerce, not the plaintiff's claim, give rise to a claim. Permitting P to invoke the jurisdiction of the federal courts would not frustrate the purpose behind the FTAIA, which is to protect American exporters who monopolize or restrain export trade if they do harm to United States commerce. If conspirators are liable only to plaintiffs injured by the conspiracy's effects on the United States, deterrence may fail.

 e. Note. The Export Trading Company Act of 1982 permits the establishment under United States law of companies designed principally to export goods and services, and grants such companies certain antitrust immunity upon certification by the Secretary of Commerce.

3. Comity and Cooperation.

 a. Act of state doctrine: comity--Timberlane Lumber Co. v. Bank of America, N.T. & S.A., 549 F.2d 597 (9th Cir. 1976).

  1) Facts. An Oregon partnership (P) purchased a Honduran lumber mill to produce lumber to export to the United States. The purchased mill competed with two larger mills heavily financed by a California bank (D). The two large mills, allegedly at D's behest, obtained court orders injurious to P's Honduran mill's business. P sued alleging violations of the Sherman Act; the trial court granted D's motion to dismiss on the ground that D's behavior was shielded from antitrust immunity by the act of state doctrine.

  2) Issue. Does the act of state doctrine provide a blanket immunity for all foreign government acts?

  3) Held. No. Judgment reversed.

   a) The basis for the act of state doctrine is not notions of foreign sovereignty, but concern for possible interference with the conduct of foreign affairs by the political branches of government. Thus the doctrine confers no "blank check" immunity and here (where the "act of state" is issuance of orders by a local court at D's request) clearly does not require dismissal.

b) Whether the United States law should be accorded extraterritorial reach is not a simple question of whether there is any United States effect but instead requires the following three-part test:

(1) Does the restraint have the purpose or effect of affecting United States foreign commerce?

(2) Is the restraint a violation of the Sherman Act, jurisdictional questions aside?

(3) As a matter of international comity and fairness, should the extraterritorial jurisdiction of the United States be asserted?

4) Comments.

a) The act of state doctrine does not lend itself to easy application. *Occidental Petroleum Corp. v. Buttes Gas and Oil Co.*, 331 F. Supp. 92 (C.D. Cal. 1971), *aff'd*, 461 F.2d 1261 (9th Cir.), *cert. denied*, 409 U.S. 950 (1972), involved a challenge to a decree by the Ruler of Sharjah asserting his proprietary claim as sovereign to land and oil under coastal waters between two mainlands. The claimant alleged that the decree was the product of a conspiracy with United States oil companies to deprive it of the value of oil concessions granted to it by a neighboring sheikdom. Invoking the act of state doctrine, the court declined to adjudicate the claim. *International Association of Machinists v. Organization of Petroleum Exporting Countries*, 649 F.2d 1354 (9th Cir. 1981), *cert. denied*, 454 U.S. 1163 (1982), involved a labor union's claim that OPEC's price fixing had resulted in fewer and lower paying jobs for its members. The appeals court held that the challenged conduct fell within the commercial activity exception of the Foreign Sovereign Immunities Act, but that the act of state doctrine insulated it from antitrust attack. *W.S. Kirkpatrick & Co. v. Environmental Tectonics Corp.*, 493 U.S. 400 (1990) involved a bribe paid to officials of the Nigerian government to secure a construction contract. Invoking the act of state doctrine, the district court granted summary judgment, noting that it was disinclined to inquire into the "motivation of a sovereign act." The appeals court reversed, citing a letter from the State Department's Legal Advisor that such an inquiry would not produce "unique embarrassment" for United States foreign policy. The Supreme Court affirmed, observing that the doctrine applies only where a United States court might have to invalidate a foreign sovereign's act within its own territory.

b) The Justice Department in 1988 published an Antitrust Guide for International Operations, announcing among other things its enforcement intentions with respect to foreign firms. According to the guide, the Justice Department will consider several but not all of the factors suggested in *Timberlane*.

b. DOJ/FTC international guidelines.

    1) Comity. In determining whether to assert jurisdiction, to investigate or bring an action, or to seek particular remedies in a given case, according to these guidelines, the enforcement agencies take into account whether significant interests of any foreign sovereign would be affected. In performing a "comity" analysis, the Agencies first identify the laws or policies of the arguably interested foreign jurisdictions implicated by the conduct in question. If these conflict with United States antitrust law, the Agency then considers (i) whether one country encourages a certain course of conduct, leaves parties free to choose among different strategies, or prohibits some of those strategies, (ii) the impact of the Agencies' enforcement activities on related enforcement activities of a foreign antitrust authority, and (iii) whether the objectives sought to be obtained by the assertion of United States law would be achieved in a particular instance by foreign enforcement. Factors considered by the Agencies may include: (i) the relative significance to the alleged violation of conduct within the United States, as compared to conduct abroad; (ii) the nationality of the persons involved in or affected by the conduct; (iii) the presence or absence of a purpose to affect United States consumers, markets, or exporters; (iv) the relative significance compared to the effects abroad; (v) the existence of reasonable expectations that would be furthered or defeated by the action; and (vi) the degree of conflict with foreign law or articulated foreign economic policies.

    2) Foreign sovereign immunity.

        a) Foreign Sovereign Immunity Act ("FSIA"). Subject to the treaties in place when Congress enacted the FSIA, the Act gives foreign governments immunity unless the foreign government has (i) explicitly or implicitly waived its immunity, (ii) expropriated property in violation of international law, (iii) acquired rights to United States property, (iv) committed certain torts within the United States, (v) agreed to arbitration of a dispute, or (vi) engaged in "commercial activity."

            (1) "Commercial activity." The FSIA provides that "commercial activity" is to be determined by the "nature of the course of conduct or particular transaction or act, rather than by reference to its purpose." Under the FSIA, a foreign government is not immune in any case in which the action is based on (i) a commercial activity carried on in the United States by the foreign state; (ii) an act performed in the United States in connection with a commercial activity of the foreign state elsewhere; or (iii) an act outside the territory of the United States in connection with a commercial activity of the foreign state elsewhere and that act causes a direct effect in the United States.

- **(2) "Commercial" vs. "sovereign."** To distinguish commercial from sovereign activity, courts have considered whether the conduct being challenged is customarily performed for profit and whether the conduct is of a type that only a sovereign government can perform. As a practical matter, most activities of foreign government-owned corporations operating in the commercial marketplace will be subject to United States antitrust laws to the same extent as the activities of foreign privately-owned firms.

b) **Acts of state.** Federal courts will abstain from entertaining a suit against a foreign government if, but only if, the specific challenged conduct is a public act of the foreign sovereign within its territorial jurisdiction on matters pertaining to its governmental sovereignty. The act of state doctrine arises when the validity of the acts of a foreign government is an unavoidable issue in a case.

c) **Foreign sovereign compulsion.** The Agencies will refrain from taking enforcement action on the grounds of foreign sovereign compulsion only if the foreign government, acting in its sovereign, not its commercial capacity, compelled the suspect conduct under circumstances in which a refusal to comply would give rise to the imposition of penal or other severe sanctions. Ordinarily, this defense is available only when the foreign government compels conduct that can be accomplished entirely within its own territory.

d) *Noerr-Pennington.* A genuine effort to obtain or influence action by governmental entities in the United States is immune from antitrust challenge even if the intent or effect of that effort is to restrain or monopolize trade.

XI. PRICE DISCRIMINATION

A. INTRODUCTION

1. **Motivation of Sellers.** The most profitable way to sell a product is to sell for the price that reflects its value to each customer. In many cases, this type of pricing is impossible since the purchaser getting the lowest price would sell to others. This "arbitrage" does not pose as great an obstacle when it comes to services, like medical care.

2. **Price Discrimination in Economics.** In economics, price discrimination refers to a relationship between prices charged and costs incurred in connection with selling to different customers. One common definition is: a seller price discriminates when the ratio between price and marginal cost is different for different customers.

3. **Price Discrimination in the Robinson-Patman Act.** The Act does not fully embrace the economics definition of price discrimination. The Act tends to focus on price differences, which in economics may or may not indicate discrimination.

B. THE ROBINSON-PATMAN ACT

1. **Basic Provisions of the Act.**

    Section 2(a). That it shall be unlawful for any person engaged in commerce, in the course of such commerce, either directly or indirectly, to discriminate in price between different purchasers of commodities of like grade and quality, where either or any of the purchasers involved in such discrimination are in commerce, where such commodities are sold for use, consumption, or resale . . . and where the effect of such discrimination may be substantially to lessen competition or tend to create a monopoly in any line of commerce, or to injure, destroy, or prevent competition with any person who either grants or knowingly receives the benefit of such discrimination, or with customers of either of them;

    Provided, that nothing herein contained shall prevent differentials which make only due allowance for differences in the cost of manufacture, sale, or delivery resulting from the differing methods of quantities in which such commodities are to such purchasers sold or delivered;

    Provided, however, that the Federal Trade Commission may, after due investigation and hearing to all interested parties, fix and establish quantity limits, and revise the same as it finds necessary, as to particular commodities or classes of commodities, where it finds that available purchasers in greater quantities are so few as to render differentials on account thereof unjustly discriminatory or promotive of monopoly in any line of commerce; and the foregoing shall then not be construed to permit differentials based on differences in quantities greater than those so fixed and established. . . .

Section 2(b). Upon proof being made, at any hearing on a complaint under this section, that there has been discrimination in price or services or facilities furnished, the burden of rebutting the prima facie case thus made by showing justification shall be upon the person charged with a violation of this section, and unless justification shall be affirmatively shown, the Commission is authorized to issue an order terminating the discrimination;

Provided, however, that nothing herein contained shall prevent a seller rebutting the prima facie case thus made by showing that his lower price or the furnishing of services or facilities to any purchaser or purchasers was made in good faith to meet an equally low price of a competitor, or the services or facilities furnished by a competitor. . . .

Section 2(f). That it shall be unlawful for any person engaged in commerce, in the course of such commerce, knowingly to induce or receive a discrimination in price that is prohibited by this section.

2. **Other Sections of the Act.** Sections 2(c), (d), and (e) will be outlined *infra*. Section 3 is a separate law.

3. **Major Issues.**

   a. **Interstate commerce required.** In *Gulf Oil Corp. v. Copp Paving Co., Inc.*, 419 U.S. 186 (1974), the plaintiffs charged the defendant (a California manufacturer of asphalt for sale to California interstate road contractors) with price discrimination. There was no allegation that interstate sales were made. "In commerce" means that at least one of the sales must occur "in" commerce; the Court rejected the broader and more easily satisfied "effect on commerce" test used in the Sherman Act cases.

   b. **The requirement of a "commodity."** Section 2(a) applies only if a tangible product is involved.

   c. **What conduct and which effects are proscribed by the Act?**

   d. **What must the alleged discriminator show to invoke the cost justification or meeting competition defenses?**

   e. **Like grade and quality.** Section 2(a) bears on discrimination involving goods of like grade and quality. *FTC v. Borden Co.*, 383 U.S. 637 (1966), involved a defendant's sale of evaporated milk under both its own nationally advertised brand name and various private brand names owned by the defendant's customers. All of the milk was chemically identical, but the defendant sold its own brand at a higher price than the private brands. The Supreme Court held that the products were of like grade and quality. On remand, however, the appeals court exonerated the defendant because of lack of injury to competition, citing evidence of a strong consumer preference for the defendant's own brand.

    f.   Proof of damages. Treble damage claimants must show that the challenged conduct injured them in their business or property, which can be rather difficult in price discrimination cases. In *J. Truett Payne Co. v. Chrysler Motors Corp.*, 451 U.S. 557 (1981), the Supreme Court rejected the "automatic damage theory," pursuant to which injury could be inferred upon a showing of substantial price discrimination. A claimant could show actual injury by proving that the favored purchaser reduced its price as a result of the discrimination and took sales away from the claimant, or that the claimant was less able to compete because it had less funds available for capital expenditures or advertising.

C. THE EFFECTS OF PRICE DISCRIMINATION

1. Primary-Line Effects of Price Discrimination.

    a.   Introduction. "Primary-line" effects are those experienced by a rival of the firm doing the discriminating at the same level of the distribution system.

    b.   Proscribed conduct--Utah Pie Co. v. Continental Baking Co., 386 U.S. 685 (1967).

        1)   Facts. Utah Pie Company (P) is in the frozen dessert pie business, with a plant in Utah. Continental, Carnation, and Pet (Ds) are large companies in the same business with their closest plants in California. The Utah market grew 500% in four years. P maintained about 45% of the market and its volume, sales, earnings, and profits grew. P sold to several grocery chains under brand labels and sold under its own brand. The major competitive weapon in the market was price, and during the four-year period the price in the market dropped about 33%. Pet sold its pies in Utah to Safeway at prices lower than it sold in markets closer to its California plant and lower than its other sales in Utah. Safeway had 6% of the Utah market. For seven of the 44 months, it sold its own label pies at prices in Utah cheaper than in other areas closer to its plant. A jury found for Ds on a conspiracy charge under sections 1 and 2 of the Sherman Act, and for P on a price discrimination charge under section 2(a) of the Robinson-Patman Act. The court of appeals reversed. The Supreme Court granted certiorari.

2) **Issue.** Could a jury find Ds guilty of geographic price discrimination, which could result in primary-line injury to its competition, P?

3) **Held.** Yes. Judgment reversed.

   a) There is evidence from which the jury could have found that for periods of several months Pet was charging less in Salt Lake City than in the California and other closer markets. With respect to sales to Safeway, the burden of proof of proving cost justification is on Pet. Pet only showed evidence of such justification for one year; this evidence was not particularized for the Salt Lake City market. The jury could have found this evidence insufficient to prove cost justification. The jury could have found that Pet's action amounted to a reasonable possibility of lessening of competition. It makes no difference whether P itself would have gotten the Safeway business, or whether P itself was the company that suffered from the anticompetitive actions (although there was evidence that showed that Pet's actions were aimed at P, such as information in Pet's files that it considered P an unfavorable factor, and it had sent an industrial spy into P's plant).

   b) Continental had 1.8% of the market in 1960. In 1961 it cut its prices below what it was selling in other areas and got 8.3%. It sold pies to some of the same chains where P had been selling pies. Its prices were below direct cost plus overhead allocation. The jury could have found this to be anticompetitive. It makes no difference that P's sales volume grew; it had to cut its price to a point it would not otherwise have done.

   c) Carnation sold at less than its costs and at lower prices than in other markets closer to its plants. It was possible for the jury to find a violation.

   d) An injury may be found even though sales volume of the plaintiff is growing and the plaintiff continues to operate at a profit. Nor is it necessary that it be shown that the price discriminators are consistently undercutting the plaintiff's prices (although there was some evidence of predatory intent here by Ds against P). Here the destructive impact of price discrimination was on the price structure of the market.

4) **Dissent** (Stewart, Harlan, JJ.). The majority is protecting competitors, not competition. In 1958, P had 66% of the market. In 1961, it still had 45%, but the market was more competitive than previously. In short, there was no lessening of competition.

5) **Comment.** Note that on the facts, a substantial lessening of competition was found where Utah Pie had the lowest prices, the largest share of the market, and its sales and profits were increasing. There is something to the argument of the dissent.

Antitrust - 173

Anheuser-
Busch, Inc.
v. FTC

c. **Competitive responses--Anheuser-Busch, Inc. v. FTC,** 289 F.2d 835 (7th Cir. 1961).

   1) **Facts.** Anheuser-Busch, Inc. (D) was the leading brewer in the United States with 7% of the market. Most local markets, however, were dominated by local companies. The St. Louis market had four other competitors; in 1953 D was last with 12.5% of this market. After a new labor contract was signed at the end of 1953, D raised its prices, except in St. Louis. D's St. Louis competitors did not raise their prices. D began to lose sales all over the nation; it tried to cut its prices but wholesalers would not pass the savings on. In St. Louis, D cut its prices since it had no wholesalers and the retailers passed the savings on. Over a two-year period D cut prices again and its market share went to 36%; then it raised its price above that of its competitors and introduced a lower price beer under a different label. Its market share fell to 17%. It also raised advertising expenditures and changed its sales distribution system.

   2) **Issue.** Does price cutting violate section 2(a) when it is apparently nothing more than a response to the behavior of competition?

   3) **Held.** No. No violation.

      a) Market share rose, but this alone is not enough. Nor was the rise over the long term very substantial. D's major competitors still controlled over 75% of the market.

      b) D's price changes were made necessary by competitive conditions.

      c) Change in market shares can be accounted for by other factors taking place with D's competitors. Also, one competitor, Falstaff, rose from 29% to 43% of the market.

      d) There is no predatory misconduct shown on D's part, aimed at destroying a competitor. There is no proven use of profits in another area to subsidize price competition in St. Louis.

   4) **Comment.** This case can be seen as one where the court goes back to the original intent of the Robinson-Patman Act and rationalizes the decision on the basis of whether there have been acts that appear to have been motivated by a "predatory intent." In addition, the amount of business diverted to D was small, and the market remained very competitive.

d. **Meaning of "predatory pricing."** Some controversy surrounds the question of whether the same standards apply to a Robinson-Patman Act claim and a Sherman Act predatory pricing claim. Some tribunals and commentators answer "no," citing the different statutory language and the arguably different purposes served by each.

e. **Prospect of recoupment.** (*See Brooke Group v. Brown & Williamson Tobacco*, briefed *supra* at p. 107.)

f. **Conflict in policy.** Note that there is an inherent conflict in the Robinson-Patman Act and the policy of the antitrust laws. Antitrust policy favors a vigorous price competition; yet vigorous enforcement of the Robinson-Patman Act may impair such competition. Note also that a policy that prevents an interstate firm from cutting prices to enter a local market against local competitors (unless the interstate firm cuts prices in all its markets) insulates these local markets.

2. **Secondary-Line Effects.**

   a. **Introduction.** Here the charge is that price discrimination by a seller to a buyer affects competition at the buyer level.

   b. **Proving substantial injury to competition--FTC v. Morton Salt Co.**, 334 U.S. 37 (1948).

   FTC v. Morton Salt Co.

   1) **Facts.** Morton Salt (D) sold table salt for a basic price of $1.60 per case. For carload quantities, the price dropped to $1.50 per case; for very large quantities bought over the course of a year, the price could go as low as $1.35 per case. The discounts permitted the high quantity buyers to resell the salt at a price advantage over smaller buyers. Most buyers were able to take advantage of the carload discount, but only five buyers, all chain stores, ever bought enough salt to qualify for the maximum discount. No justification based on cost savings was offered for the discounts. The FTC found price discrimination in violation of the Robinson-Patman Act; the court of appeals reversed.

   2) **Issue.** Do these facts present a sufficient quantum of proof to show competitive injury at the secondary-line level?

   3) **Held.** Yes. Judgment reversed.

      a) All that need be shown is a "reasonable possibility" of a substantial lessening of competition.

      b) Where goods are sold "substantially cheaper" to one buyer over another, there is evidence that this is a substantial lessening of competition. (Note that "substantially cheaper" is enough that the price difference would cause a buyer to switch to the cheaper product.)

   4) **Comment.** Note the analogy to the tying cases. If there is a substantial difference in price to buyers, there is really no further inquiry into the amount of commerce involved. Any amount of com-

Antitrust - 175

merce (above a de minimis amount) is substantial enough to be a "substantial lessening of competition."

c. **Factors to consider.** The following factors would be relevant in proving anticompetitive effects (the opposites would tend to indicate that there was little anticompetitive effect):

1) Substantial difference in price;

2) Standardized product;

3) Product sold to competing buyers selling to the same market; and

4) There is keen competition among the buyers for their sales and profit margins are low.

D. **FUNCTIONAL DISCOUNTS**

1. **Introduction.** Historically, there have been several distinct levels in the distribution system, from supplier to customer. Each level has performed certain specific tasks and taken certain risks that other levels did not. Each level was rewarded differently; for example, the wholesaler got a larger price discount from the supplier than the retailer. Each level also dealt with a specific class of customer; *i.e.*, the wholesaler sold only to retailers, and retailers only to customers. Therefore, price differences from the supplier to the wholesaler or the retailer could differ and there was no antitrust violation. However, in more recent years these distinctions in the distribution systems have blurred and the antitrust questions are much more difficult. For example, many wholesalers are also retailers, and vice versa.

2. **Functional Discounts as Unlawful Price Discrimination--Texaco Inc. v. Hasbrouck,** 496 U.S. 543 (1990).

a. **Facts.** From 1972 to 1981, Texaco (D) sold gasoline to Hasbrouck and other owners of Spokane area retail stations (Ps) at a price ("RTW" price) higher than D charged two distributors operating in the area, Gull Oil Co. ("Gull") and Dompier. Gull, headquartered in Seattle, distributed petroleum products in four western states under its own name. In Spokane, it purchased its gas from D at prices that ranged from six cents to four cents below D's RTW price. Gull resold that product under its own name; the fact that it was being supplied by D was not known by either the public or the respondents. In Spokane, Gull supplied about 15 stations. Some were "consignment stations" where the station operator set the retail prices, and some were "commission stations" where Gull set the prices—at a penny less than the prevailing price for major brands—

Texaco Inc. v. Hasbrouck

176 - Antitrust

and paid the operator a commission. At both, Gull retained title to the gasoline until it was pumped into a motorist's tank. Gull employed two truck drivers (and one supervisor) in Spokane who picked up product at D's bulk plant and delivered it to the Gull stations.

Dompier paid a higher price for D's gasoline than did Gull (3.95 cents to 3.65 cents below the RTW price), but unlike Gull, Dompier resold its gas under the Texaco brand name. It supplied eight to 10 Spokane retail stations. Prior to October 1974, Dompier's president owned two of them. With the encouragement of D's representatives, Dompier itself acquired four stations in 1974 and 1975. Like Gull, Dompier picked up D's product at D's bulk plant and delivered directly to retail outlets. In return for this service, D paid Dompier what it paid common carriers, thereby permitting Dompier to make a profit on its hauling function. Unlike Gull, Dompier owned a bulk storage facility, but seldom used it because its capacity was less than that of many retail stations.

Gull and Dompier grew and prospered, which D's executives attributed to "the magnitude of the distributor discount and the hauling allowance." At the same time, D's throughput sales in the Spokane market declined from a monthly volume of 569,269 gallons in 1970 to 389,557 gallons in 1975. D's independent retailers' share of the market for D's gas declined from 76% to 49%. By the end of 1978, seven of the Ps were out of business.

Ps brought suit claiming that D had engaged in price discrimination in violation of the Robinson-Patman Act and won a jury verdict. D moved for JNOV on the grounds that the price differences were justified by cost savings, were the product of a good faith attempt to meet competition, and were "functional" discounts. D claimed that, as a matter of law, its discounts did not adversely affect competition with the meaning of the Act because any injury suffered by Ps was attributable to decisions made independently by Dompier. The district court denied D's motion and awarded Ps treble damages. The court of appeals affirmed. The Supreme Court granted certiorari.

b. **Issue.** Did substantial evidence support a finding that the different prices that D charged Ps and its two Spokane distributors constituted price discrimination that adversely affected competition?

c. **Held.** Yes. Judgment affirmed.

1) A supplier need not satisfy the rigorous requirements of the cost justification defense to prove that a particular functional discount is reasonable and accordingly did not cause any substantial lessening of competition between a wholesaler's customers and the supplier's direct customers. But no substantial evidence showed that the discounts to Gull and Dompier constituted a reasonable reimbursement for the value to D of their actual marketing functions. In fact, Dompier received separate compensation for its hauling; and neither Gull nor Dompier maintained any significant storage facilities.

2) Since D conceded that its sales were made in interstate commerce and that the gasoline sold to distributors was of the same grade and quality as that sold to Ps, to prevail on its price discrimination claim, Ps only had to show that D discriminated in terms of price between the distributors and Ps and that this discrimination had a prohibited effect on competition. Proof of the price difference establishes the requisite discrimination and, according to the Court's decision in *FTC v. Morton Salt Co.* (*supra*), entitles Ps to a presumption of injury to competition.

3) Both Gull and Dompier received the full discount on all their purchases even though most of their volume was resold directly to consumers. The extra margin on those sales obviously enabled them to price aggressively in their retail as well as their wholesale marketing. To the extent that Dompier and Gull competed with respondents in the retail market—and at least with respect to the commission stations, Gull's function as a gasoline retailer—the *Morton Salt* presumption becomes all the more appropriate. Their competitive advantage in that market also constitutes evidence tending to rebut any presumption of legality that would otherwise apply to their wholesale sales.

4) The fact that D's executives encouraged Dompier to expand its retail business and recognized that the magnitude of the distributor discount and the hauling allowance had a dramatic impact on the market, while refusing two of the Ps permission to haul their own fuel makes it peculiarly difficult for D to claim that it is being held liable for the independent pricing decisions of Gull or Dompier.

d. **Concurrence** (White, J.). Under no definition of a legitimate functional discount do the discounts extended here qualify as a defense to the charge of price discrimination. I would stop there. The Court need not define what a legitimate functional discount is at this time.

E. **MORE REMOTE EFFECTS**

In *Perkins v. Standard Oil Co. of California,* 395 U.S. 642 (1969), Standard Oil Company sold gas at one price to a jobber and another to Signal Oil, which sold to its controlled corporation, Western, which sold to its controlled corporation, Regal, which competed with the jobber. The Supreme Court held that a violation of the Robinson-Patman Act could be found where the effect was in fourth-line competition.

F. DEFENSES TO ROBINSON-PATMAN ACT ACTIONS

1. **Cost Justification.**

   a. **Introduction.** The burden of proof is on the party claiming cost justification for the difference in prices charged.

   1) In some instances this justification might be easy to prove, as where a quantity discount is offered and direct costs of packaging and freight can be shown.

   2) However, in many other instances proof is very difficult—for example, with respect to discounts given for large total purchases over time. Delivery practices may vary with the individual customer; and alleged differences in manufacturing costs, advertising costs, and others will be difficult to prove. These issues present very difficult and complex accounting questions, even when such accounting data is available.

   3) The courts seem to have developed a rule of reason approach on this issue.

   b. **Inadequate evidence--United States v. Borden Co.,** 370 U.S. 460 (1962).

   1) **Facts.** Borden and Bowman (Ds) sold their milk products on a volume discount basis to independent grocers and at a flat discount to the large chains (which discount was larger than any volume discount given to the independents). A section 2(a) action was brought. Ds rely on the cost justification defense.

   2) **Issue.** Was evidence adequate to establish that price discrimination was in fact cost justified?

   3) **Held.** No. Judgment remanded for further findings.

   a) Borden put the large chains into one category; the independents were placed in four other categories by volume of purchases. Then cost data was considered, including direct personnel costs, truck expenses, and losses on bad debts and returned milk. Various formulas were used to make the allocations. Bowman used a study of driver time in various operations and costed these operations. It was not shown, however, that all independents used these extra operations and that the chains did not.

   b) It is not necessary to establish cost differences with respect to each customer. It is permissible to put customers into classes. But these classes must be divided by the relevant criteria that determine cost differences.

    c) Here the classes were not shown to have sufficient relevant homogeneity. With respect to Borden, some of the independents had higher volume than some of the chains; and all independents were assigned added cost factors that were not shown to have been possessed by all (such as cash collections). Bowman had similar defects in its classifications.

4) Comments.

    a) In *FTC v. Standard Motor Products, Inc.*, 371 F.2d 613 (2d Cir. 1967), there was adequate evidence of cost justification. In that case, the defendant sold auto replacement parts, giving percentage discounts that grew larger with the annual volume of purchases. The defendant classified buyers into several volume categories and attempted to justify the differences in discounts by cost differences from four classes of selling expenses—direct selling, catalog, branch warehouse, and administrative expenses. A significant number of those in each classification had costs that were different from the average costs of their classification and closer to the class above or below them. However, the FTC did not show that there was a better means of classifying customers, nor that it would accept any such classification. There was also evidence that taken over several years the costs of the customers in the classes averaged out to be very close to the stated average cost of the class. The court found that the FTC should also have shown whether any firm in any industry could meet the classification standards that it had set; otherwise there was a question whether the standards left room for the cost justification defense.

    b) As always, the desired economic results behind the passage of the antitrust laws are only partially accomplished by the law in actual practice. For example, the cost justification defense was designed to allow economic efficiency to prevail where it existed. But the cost of proving the defense is so extreme that in most cases it is not possible. Other efficiencies are denied by the Act (for example, charging discriminatory prices in some instances may enable a plant to operate at full capacity and at this optimum cost level reduce prices to all customers, which condition might not exist if the firm has to charge the same price to all customers).

2. Good Faith Meeting of Competition.

a. **Introduction.** The defendant may also defend a section 2 action by proving that the lower price offered to some purchasers was simply a good faith attempt to meet the competition offered by another seller.

b. **Good faith attempt to meet competition.** In *FTC v. A.E. Staley Manufacturing Co.*, 324 U.S. 746 (1945), the FTC found that the defendants had not sustained the burden of rebutting the prima facie case of price discriminations involved in their booking practices, since they had failed to show that their lower prices were "made in good faith to meet an equally low price of a competitor." The discriminations were made in response to verbal information received from salesmen or intending purchasers, without supporting evidence. The defendants believed such reports but made no efforts to verify them. In some instances, the defendants made sales upon bookings that they suspected had been made without knowledge of the buyers. The United States Supreme Court agreed with the FTC that the statute at least requires the seller, who has knowingly discriminated in price, to show the existence of facts that would lead a reasonable and prudent person to believe that the granting of a lower price would in fact meet the equally low price of a competitor. The Court also found that the FTC was correct in holding that the defendants failed to meet this burden.

c. **Interseller price verification and reconciling the Sherman Act--*United States v. United States Gypsum Co.*,** 438 U.S. 422 (1978). *United States v. United States Gypsum Co.*

   1) **Facts.** Eight large manufacturers of gypsum board (Ds) with 94% of the market routinely phoned each other to determine at what price they were selling to particular customers. The United States (P) contends that this exchange violated the Sherman Act because it tended to stabilize prices. Ds assert that the exchange was to comply with section 2(b) of the Robinson-Patman Act and prevented fraud, and was thus a "controlling circumstance" exception to Sherman Act liability. The jury verdict was for P, and the court of appeals reversed. P appeals.

   2) **Issue.** Is interseller price verification a "controlling circumstance" so as to free it from Sherman Act liability?

   3) **Held.** No.

      a) In order to comply with *Staley*, *supra*, the defendant need only possess a good faith belief as to his competitor's prices; absolute certainty is not required. Therefore, price information exchange among competitors will not be tolerated.

   4) **Comment.** The Court apparently considered that a "one-shot" exchange would serve no useful Robinson-Patman Act purpose and that an ongoing exchange ran such a high risk of encouraging undesirable behavior as not to warrant its utilization for purchases of interseller price verification.

d. **No duty of affirmative disclosure by buyer.** (*See Great Atlantic and Pacific Tea Co. v. FTC, infra.*)

e. **Meeting competition on area-wide basis--Falls City Industries, Inc. v. Vanco Beverage, Inc.,** 460 U.S. 428 (1983).

   1) **Facts.** Vanco (P) was the sole distributor of Falls City's (D's) beer in Evansville, Indiana. P charged D with selling at a lower price to distributors in Kentucky, and consumers from Indiana would travel to Kentucky to purchase beer. P sued D under section 2 and D raised the meeting competition defense. At trial P won a judgment for $1.7 million. The court of appeals affirmed as to liability but remanded on damages. Both courts rejected the meeting competition defense, stating that D's setting of a state-wide Kentucky price to meet a general range of competitors was inadequate.

   2) **Issue.** Does a lower price issued to a wide range of customers to meet a general range of competition satisfy the "meeting competition" defense?

   3) **Held.** Yes. The court of appeals majority opinion is vacated.

      a) The fact that the discrimination was created by an increase in P's price rather than a decrease in the Kentucky buyer's price is not relevant, nor is it relevant that D raised P's price to increase D's profits.

      b) A price discrimination to meet the competitor's price is just as lawful when used to get new business as when used to keep old business.

      c) A "customer by customer" response is not necessary to sustain the meeting competition defense, provided the seller is satisfied that the entire favored class is receiving the lower price from a competitor.

G. **BROKERAGE, AD ALLOWANCES, AND SERVICES**

   1. **Introduction.**

      a. **Section 2(c).** Section 2(c) makes it unlawful for a buyer of goods, or any agent or representative of the buyer, to receive from or to be paid by the supplier any brokerage or other commission "except from services rendered in connection with the sale or purchase of goods."

b. **Closed loophole.** This section closed a loophole that buyers used to set up affiliated agents or brokers who got the same advantage in effect as though the buyer received price discriminations.

c. **Per se rule.** No effect on competition need be shown; this is in effect a per se rule.

2. **Reduction in Brokerage Commissions.** The Supreme Court found a violation of section 2(c) in *FTC v. Henry Broch & Co.*, 363 U.S. 166 (1960). The defendant, Henry Broch & Co., was a broker handling Canada Foods on a 5% commission basis. Smucker wanted a larger order and asked for a lower price than Canada normally gave. Canada dropped its price and arranged with the defendant to reduce its commission to 3% (so that Canada and the defendant shared in the total reduction to Canada) and sold to Smucker. All other customers got the normal price and the defendant got the normal 5%. The Court found that Section 2(c) is aimed at all means by which brokerage can be used to effect price discrimination. It is unlawful for a buyer to have its own brokerage so that it can in effect get price reductions. It is also unlawful for a seller to sell direct to a large buyer at a lower price that reflects the commission savings that it must pay in other sales. It is unlawful for the seller and its broker to split the brokerage commission with the buyer (or to give part of the brokerage to the seller). Finally, only if the buyer renders some service to the seller, then a discriminatory price by a reduced brokerage commission may be permissible. Note that the seller does not have the defense of cost justification and good faith meeting of competition in a 2(c) action. Note also that there are many cases concerning the issue as to whether the recipient of the allowance is a "broker" or a "purchaser."

3. **Advertising Allowances, Services, and Facilities.**

   a. **Introduction.** Section 2(d) makes it unlawful for a supplier to make any payment to a buyer in consideration of services or facilities provided in promoting the sale of goods, unless similar payments are made available on "proportionally equal terms" to other buyers. Subsection 2(e) makes it unlawful for the supplier himself to provide promotional services and facilities to a buyer unless he accords facilities on "proportionally equal terms" to other buyers. These sections were aimed at discrimination where a large customer demands and sellers grant sale-promotional services or special advertising allowances, but other buyers do not get these allowances. Such an allowance is unjust when the service is not actually rendered, or even if rendered, when the payment is grossly in excess of its value, or when the customer is deriving as much benefit to his own business as the seller is. These are per se rules in the sense that no effect on competition need be shown.

   b. **FTC guidelines.** The law requires that customers be treated fairly and without discrimination and that allowances not be disguised discriminatory price discounts. It applies whenever the buyer furnishes services or facilities in connection with the distribution of the seller's products, or when the seller provides any such services. A "customer" is someone who buys for resale directly from the seller, the seller's agent, or its broker, or any buyer of the seller's product for resale who purchases from or through a wholesaler or other intermediate seller. Services or facilities involve such things as window and floor displays (where the seller pays the buyer for furnishing them), or catalogs, prizes, etc. (where the seller furnishes them to customers). When such services are provided, they should be furnished in accordance with a written plan. The services or payments should be available on some proportional basis to all competing customers (such as one determined by relative volume of sales). All customers should be informed of the plan. The seller should take reasonable steps to see that all services are actually performed and that it is not overpaying for them.

    c. **Definition of customers.** In *FTC v. Fred Meyer, Inc.*, 390 U.S. 341 (1968), the defendant, Fred Meyer, Inc., a large chain of stores in Portland, Oregon, had an annual promotion where it sold a book of coupons offering store products at about one-third off. The defendant sold each page in the book as advertising to the supplier of the product offered; suppliers also helped with the promotion with various ways of reimbursing the defendant. It was shown that two wholesalers that sold to retailers competing with the defendant did not get similar allowances. The Supreme Court found that the suppliers owed the same treatment to the defendant's competitors and thus there was a violation of section 2(d). The Court stated that customers competing with the defendant at the retail level, even though not dealing directly with the suppliers, must be given the same allowances, but there need not be proportional equality between the defendant and the two wholesalers. In his dissent, Justice Harlan noted that "customer" means a party dealing with the supplier directly.

H. BUYER'S LIABILITY FOR INDUCING OR RECEIVING DISCRIMINATIONS IN PRICE

1. **Introduction.** Section 2(f) makes it unlawful for any person knowingly to induce or receive a discrimination in price that is prohibited.

2. **Inducement by Buyer Where Seller Has Defense--Great Atlantic and Pacific Tea Co. v. FTC, 440 U.S. 69 (1979).**

    a. **Facts.** Borden Company had long supplied Great Atlantic and Pacific Tea Company (D) with Borden brand milk. When D decided to introduce its own private label milk, it asked Borden to submit an

Great Atlantic and Pacific Tea Co. v. FTC

offer to supply it. After negotiations and concessions on D's part concerning delivery, Borden offered a plan that would save D $410,000 per year. D sought offers from other suppliers, including Bowman Dairy Company, which submitted a proposal that would have saved D $737,000 per year. D's buyer contacted a Borden sales official and told him that Borden's offer was "not even in the ballpark" and that a $50,000 improvement "would not be a drop in the bucket," but he did not directly disclose the Bowman offer. Borden then submitted a new offer that would save D $820,000 per year, and D accepted this. Based on this series of events, the FTC (P) filed a complaint against D charging in count I that D violated section 5 of the FTC Act when it misled Borden by not informing that company that its second offer was better than Bowman's, and in count II that D had violated section 2(f) of the Robinson-Patman Act by knowingly inducing or receiving price discriminations from Borden. The ALJ found against D on both counts, but on review P reversed as to count I, finding no affirmative duty of disclosure. The court of appeals affirmed the FTC, finding that D had neither a meeting competition nor a cost justification defense.

b. **Issue.** Did D knowingly induce or receive price discrimination from Borden in violation of section 2(f) of the Robinson-Patman Act?

c. **Held.** No. Judgment of the court of appeals is reversed.

 1) Under the Act, a seller is liable if a prima facie case can be established against it, or if it does not have an affirmative defense.

 2) A buyer such as D may be derivatively liable for violating section 2(f) unless the lower prices it received are either within one of the seller's defenses or not known by the buyer not to be within one of those defenses. Thus, if Borden had a valid meeting competition defense, there is no prohibited price discrimination.

 3) To find that D had a duty of affirmative disclosure would foster anticompetitive cooperation among sellers; such an exchange of information violates antitrust laws. [*See* United States v. United States Gypsum Co., *supra*]

 4) P's position is logically inconsistent since it is seeking under section 2(f) to require the same duty of affirmative disclosure it found "contrary to the public interest" under section 5 of the FTC Act. Thus, we hold that a ***buyer*** does not violate section 2(f) when he does no more than accept the lower of two competitive bids.

 5) Borden, the seller, clearly had the defense of meeting competition. This is shown since Borden had a good faith belief that it was meeting competition when it made the second bid. Furthermore, Borden

could not have verified the terms of the Bowman bid without risking Sherman Act liability. Thus, it could only make a substantially lower bid.

d. **Concurrence and dissent** (White, J.). This Court should not decide here if Borden had an affirmative defense. The case should be remanded for that determination.

e. **Dissent** (Marshall, J.). I concur that P and the court of appeals applied the wrong legal standard in assessing D's liability under section 2(f). I disagree with this Court's holding that a buyer is precluded from liability under section 2(f) unless the seller is liable for price discrimination. The same elements of a prima facie case and the same affirmative defenses are available to buyer and seller alike. Thus, a buyer who in good faith induces a seller to lower a bid is not liable under section 2(f). This case should have been remanded to P to resolve its numerous ambiguities.

f. **Comment.** This case is the flip side of *United States v. United States Gypsum Co., supra*. Here, the Court was asked by the government to hold that there ***was*** a duty of interseller price verification. There, the Court was asked by the government to find that there was no such duty.

TABLE OF CASES
(Page numbers of briefed cases in bold)

A.H. Cox & Co. v. Star Machinery Co. - 105

Addyston Pipe & Steel Co., United States v. - **7**, 8, 23

Albrecht v. Herald - 80, 81

Allied Tube & Conduit Corp. v. Indian Head, Inc. - **50**

Allis-Chalmers Manufacturing Co. v. White Consolidated Industries - 136

Aluminum Co. of America, United States v. - **15,** 19, **157**

American Banana Co. v. United Fruit Co. - **157**

American Building Maintenance Industries, United States v. - 13

American Column and Lumber Co. v. United States - **74**, 75

American Linseed Oil Co., United States v. - 75

American Motor Inns, Inc. v. Holiday Inns, Inc. - 84

American Tobacco Co., United States v. - 9

Anderson v. United States - 7

Anheuser-Busch, Inc. v. FTC - **174**

Appalachian Coals, Inc. v. United States - **24**, 25

Arizona v. Maricopa County Medical Society - **25**

Arnold, Schwinn & Co., United States v. - 80, 81, 82, 83

Aspen Skiing Co. v. Aspen Highlands Skiing Corp. - **93**

Associated Press v. United States - **44**

Bates v. State Bar of Arizona - 57

Berkey Photo, Inc. v. Eastman Kodak Co. - 16

Blomkest Fertilizer, Inc. v. Potash Corp. of Saskatchewan, Inc. - **72**

BOC International Ltd. v. FTC - **148**

Boise Cascade Corp. v. FTC - **68**

Borden Co., United States v. - **179**

Broadcast Music, Inc. v. Columbia Broadcasting System, Inc. - **26**, 28, 34

Broadway Delivery Corp. v. United Parcel Service of America, Inc. - **90**

Brooke Group Ltd. v. Brown & Williamson Tobacco Corp. - **107,** 175

Brown Shoe Co. v. United States - 127, **151**

Brown University, United States v. - **29**

Brunswick Corp. v. Pueblo Bowl-O-Mat, Inc. - **134**

Business Electronics Corp. v. Sharp Electronics Corp. - 32, 83, **87,** 88

California v. American Stores Co. - 136

California Dental Association v. FTC - **30**

California Motor Transport Co. v. Trucking Unlimited - 50

California Retail Liquor Dealers Association v. Midcal Aluminum, Inc. - **57,** 58, 59, 61

Cantor v. Detroit Edison Co. - 57

Cargill, Inc. v. Monfort of Colorado, Inc. - **135**

Cascade Natural Gas Corp. v. El Paso Natural Gas Co. - 11

Cement Manufacturers' Protective Association v. United States - **75**

Chicago Board of Trade v. United States - **23**

Citizen Publishing Co. v. United States - **132**

Citizens & Southern National Bank, United States v. - 148

Colgate & Co., United States v. - **85**, 86, 87, 123

Columbia v. Omni Outdoor Advertising, Inc. - **62**

Columbia Steel Co., United States v. - 125

Consolidated Gold Fields PLC v. Minorco, S.A. - 135

Container Corporation of America, United States v. - **76**

Continental Can Co., United States v. - **128**

Continental Ore Co. v. Union Carbide and Carbon Corp. - **160**

Continental T.V., Inc. v. GTE Sylvania, Inc. - 80, **82,** 84, 87, 88, 119

Den Norske Stats Oljeselskap As v. HeereMac Vof - **165**

Dr. Miles Medical Co. v. John D. Park & Sons Co. - **79**, 81, 88

Antitrust - 187

Dyer's Case - **4**

E.C. Knight Co., United States v. - 8, 13
E.I. DuPont De Nemours & Co., *In re* - 16
E.I. DuPont de Nemours & Co., United States v. (1956) - **17**
E.I. duPont de Nemours & Co., United States v. (1957)- **149**
Eastern Railroad Presidents Conference v. Noerr Motor Freight, Co. - **48**, 49, 50, 51, 53, 54, 55, 56, 62, 63, 169
Eastern Scientific Co. v. Wild Heerbrugg Instruments, Inc. - 83
Eastman Kodak Co. v. Image Technical Services, Inc. - **117**
Eastman Kodak Co., United States v. - **91**
Eiberger v. Sony Corp. of America - 84
El Paso Natural Gas Co., United States v. - **142**
Empire Gas Corp., United States v. - 106
Ethyl Corp. v. FTC - **69**

FTC v. A.E. Staley Manufacturing Co. - 181
FTC v. Borden Co. - 171
FTC v. Brown Shoe Co. - 123
FTC v. Fred Meyer, Inc. - 184
FTC v. H.J. Heinz Co. - **141**
FTC v. Henry Broch & Co. - 183
FTC v. Indiana Federation of Dentists - 30, **40**
FTC v. Morton Salt Co. - **175,** 178
FTC v. Motion Picture Advertising Service Co. - 96, 121
FTC v. Procter and Gamble Co. - **144**
FTC v. Standard Motor Products, Inc. - 180
FTC v. Superior Court Trial Lawyers Association - **42**
FTC v. Ticor Title Insurance Co. - **60**
Falls City Industries, Inc. v. Vanco Beverage, Inc. - **182**
Falstaff Brewing Corp., United States v. - **146**, 148
Fashion Originators' Guild of America v. FTC - **36,** 38
Fisher v. City of Berkeley - **63**
Ford Motor Co. v. United States - **153**

Fruehauf Corp. v. FTC - **154**
General Dynamics Corp., United States v. - **130**, 133
General Leaseways Inc. v. National Truck Leasing Association - **34**
General Motors Corp., United States v. - 32, 88
Goldfarb v. Virginia State Bar - 29, 56, 57
Great Atlantic and Pacific Tea Co. v. FTC - 182, 184
Grinnell Corp., United States v. - **19**, 20, 21
Gulf Oil Corp. v. Copp Paving Co. Inc. - 13, 171

Hanover Shoe, Inc. v. United Shoe Machinery Corp. - 12, 13
Hartford Fire Insurance Co. v. California - **162**
Hopkins v. United States - 7
Hospital Corporation of America v. FTC - **133**

Illinois Brick Co. v. Illinois - 13
Image Technical Services, Inc. v. Eastman Kodak Co. - **102**
In re (*see* name of party)
In the Matter of (*see* name of party)
Independent Service Organizations Antitrust Litigation v. Xerox Corporation - **103**
International Association of Machinists v. Organization of Petroleum Exporting Countries - 167
International Distribution Centers, Inc. v. Walsh Trucking Co., Inc. - 106
International Salt Co. v. United States - **112**, 121,
International Shoe Co. v. FTC - 132
Interstate Circuit, Inc. v. United States - **65**

J. Truett Payne Co. v. Chrysler Motors Corp. - 172
Jefferson Parish Hospital District No. 2 v. Hyde - 115, 122
Jerrold Electronics Corp., United States v. - 114
Joint Traffic Association, United States v. - 7

Klor's, Inc. v. Broadway-Hale Stores, Inc. - **37,** 38, 88

Lessig v. Tidewater Oil Co. - 105, 106
Loew's, Inc., United States v. - 114
Lorain Journal Co. v. United States - **104**

Maple Flooring Manufacturers' Association v. United States - **75**
Marine Bancorporation, Inc., United States v. - 146, **147**, 148
Massachusetts School of Law at Andover, Inc. v. American Bar Association - **52**
McGahee v. Northern Propane Gas Co. - 111
Microsoft, United States v. - **96**
Mitchel v. Reynolds - **5**, 8
Monsanto Co. v. Spray-Rite Service Corp. - 32, 73, **86**
Monopolies, Case of - **5**
Montague & Co. v. Lowry - 36

NYNEX Corp. v. Discon, Inc. - **38**
National Association of Window Glass Manufacturers v. United States - **31**
National Collegiate Athletic Association v. Board of Regents of University of Oklahoma - **27**
National Society of Professional Engineers v. United States - 29, 30
New Motor Vehicle Board of California v. Fox - 57
Nippon Paper, United States v. - **164**
Northern Pacific Railway v. United States - **114**
Northern Securities Co. v. United States - **9**
Northwest Wholesale Stationers, Inc. v. Pacific Stationery & Printing Co. - **39**, 67

Occidental Petroleum Corp. v. Buttes Gas and Oil Co. - 167
Official Airline Guides, Inc. v. FTC - **94**
Olympia Equipment Leasing Co. v. Western Union Telegraph Co. - 16, 95
Otter Tail Power Co. v. United States - 93

Pabst Brewing Co., United States v. - **128**
Pace Electronics, Inc. v. Cannon Computer Systems, Inc. - **88**
Paddock Publications, Inc. v. Chicago Tribune Co. - **95**

Palmer v. BRG of Georgia, Inc. - **35**
Paramount Famous Lasky Corp. v. United States - 36
Paramount Pictures, Inc., United States v. - 66
Parke, Davis & Co., United States v. - **85**, 86
Parker v. Brown - **56**, 58, 62, 63, 64
Patrick v. Burget - **61**
Penn-Olin Chemical Co., United States v. - **142**, 143
Perkins v. Standard Oil Co. of California - 178
Perma Life Mufflers, Inc. v. International Parts Corp. - 12
Pfizer, Inc. v. Government of India - 160
Philadelphia National Bank, United States v. - **125**, 128, 130, 131, 133, 141, 142
Professional Real Estate Investors, Inc. v. Columbia Pictures Industries, Inc. - **54**

Radiant Burners, Inc. v. Peoples Gas Light & Coke Co. - **39**
Realty Multi-List, Inc., United States v. - **46**
Roland Machinery Co. v. Dresser Industries, Inc. - 123
Rothery Storage and Van Co. v. Atlas Van Lines - **42**

SCFC ILC, Inc. v. Visa USA, Inc. - **45**
The Schoolmaster Case - **5**
Sealy Inc., United States v. - 32, 34, 35
Silver v. New York Stock Exchange - 39, 40
Simpson v. Union Oil Co. - 81, 89
Socony-Vacuum Oil Co., United States v. - **24**
Southern Motor Carriers Rate Conference v. United States - **58**
Spectrum Sports, Inc. v. McQuillan - **105**
Standard Fashion Co. v. Magrane-Houston Co. - **120**, 122
Standard Oil Co. of California v. United States - **120**, 122
Standard Oil Co. of New Jersey v. United States - **9**, 10
State Oil Co. v. Khan - **80**
Structural Laminates, Inc. v. Douglas Fir Plywood Association - 39
Sugar Institute, Inc. v. United States - **76**
Swift & Co. v. United States - 8

Tampa Electric Co. v. Nashville Coal Co. - **121**, 122, 124

Terminal Railroad Association, United States v. - **44**

Texaco Inc. v. Hasbrouck - **176**

Theatre Enterprises v. Paramount Film Distributing Corp. - **66**

Timberlane Lumber Co. v. Bank of America, N.T. & S.A. - **166,** 167

Times-Picayune Publishing Co. v. United States - **113,** 114

Timken Roller Bearing Co. v. United States - **32**

Topco Associates, Inc., United States v. - **33**, 34, 35, 81, 84, 88

Todd v. Exxon Corp. - 71

Town of Hallie v. City of Eau Claire - **59**

Toys "R" Us, Inc. v. FTC - **67**

Trans-Missouri Freight Association, United States v. - **7**

Tysons Corner Regional Shopping Center, *In re* - 46

U.S. Healthcare, Inc. v. Healthsource, Inc. - **124**

United Shoe Machinery Corp. v. United States - **112**

United States v. ___ (*see* **opposing party**)

United States Gypsum Co., United States v. - 78, 181, 185, 186

Utah Pie Co. v. Continental Baking Co. - **172**

Valley Liquors, Inc. v. Renfield Importers, Ltd. - **118**

Von's Grocery Co., United States v. - **129**

W.S. Kirkpatrick & Co. v. Environmental Tectonics Corp. - 167

White Motor Co. v. United States - 81

Woods Exploration and Producing Co. v. Aluminum Co. of America - 50

Worthen Bank & Trust Co. v. National BankAmericard, Inc. - 37

Zenith Radio Corp. v. Hazeltine Research, Inc. - **160**

NOTES

NOTES

NOTES

NOTES

NOTES

NOTES

NOTES

NOTES

NOTES

NOTES

NOTES

NOTES

NOTES

NOTES